GHOSTS OF THE AIR

GHOSTS
OF THE AIR

True Stories of
Aerial Hauntings

Martin Caidin

Introduction by John Keel

2003
Galde Press, Inc.
Lakeville, Minnesota

FIRST GALDE PRESS EDITION
Second Printing, 2003

Previously published by Bantam Books, New York, 1991

"A Mighty Fortress" by Robert "Mutt" Osborne reprinted with permission from *Guideposts* magazine.
Copyright © 1989 by Guidepost Associates, Inc., Carmel, N.Y. 10512

Cover photo by H. M. Mason, Jr.: B–17G Flying Fortress being flown by Martin Caidin
Chapter heading photo of Martin Caidin's Ju-52 "Iron Annie" by George Shipler

Library of Congress Cataloging-in-Publication Data

Caidin, Martin, 1927–1997
    Ghosts of the air : true stories of aerial hauntings / Martin
Caidin. — 1st Galde Press ed.
      p.   cm.
    Originally published New York : Bantam Books, 1991.
    ISBN 1–880090–10–4 (softcover)
    1. Ghosts.   2. Air pilots—Miscellanea.   3. Airplanes-
-Miscellanea.   I. Title.
    BF1461.C25   1994
    133.1—dc20
                                                     94–23741
                                                    CIP

Galde Press, Inc.
PO Box 460
Lakeville, Minnesota 55044

For a friend …

DICK BIERY

Some Other Books by Martin Caidin

Contents

—=A Note From the Publisher

There has never been a book quite like *Ghosts of the Air*, the telling of strange and wonderful true events where the author, and the people involved in the events themselves, leave no argument as to where they stand, what they have seen and encountered, and what they know is real.

Books that cross the threshold of accepted natural events almost always provoke, even incite, an outcry of disbelief and rejection because they diverge from the "safety" of believing only in so-called normal, everyday events that do not rock either the boat of belief or the precarious balance of timidity in minds closed to what lies just beyond our immediate understanding.

Not to believe Martin Caidin is certainly the province of any and all readers, and we as the publisher share Mr. Caidin's position that skepticism is natural and healthy—and even welcomed. But together, author and publisher, we remind our faithful readers that to reject the events portrayed in these pages is to reject out of hand the dozens of pilots, engineers, scientists, skilled and veteran observers who have told their stories not to a writer, but to Martin Caidin—*fellow pilot* of decades of experience throughout the world.

That is the difference understood by few people. Pilots as a class unto themselves distrust the news media. What they tell reporters is more often than not twisted and distorted out of all proportion and reality to what they related to the newsperson. It requires only one or two such encounters to bring pilots and engineers, scientists and technicians to swear off *ever* talking again to the press. Pilots, as a prime example, especially pilots who captain jetliners, have been rebuked, criticized, placed on probation, and even fired by the airlines for which they work, if ever they relate an encounter with an aerial object they cannot identify or explain. Military pilots, much more under the thumb of authority, are *ordered* to clam up, to relate to no one other than officials of higher rank, their encounters with things and events that do not fit neatly into square boxes for pigeon-holing their extraordinary moments.

Because these pilots, and their crews, *know* Martin Caidin, or at least know of him and his reputation, they have come forth to share with all of you their most extraordinary moments. Banding together in these pages, they have in effect told the carpers and the naysayers just where they can get off this world and go hide in whatever corner they choose to grumble and complain in.

That is why we have been enabled to pass on these stories to you, the reader.

As publisher, we feel it incumbent upon us to reveal more of author Martin Caidin than might be otherwise be presented in a book of this nature. And we feel, as well, that the words should not be ours. The *International Biographical Centre* of Cambridge, England, issued a worldwide biography of leading science writers, including Martin Caidin. We have extracted from that report for the benefit of our readers. The report follows:

INTERNATIONAL BIOGRAPHICAL CENTRE

CAIDIN, Martin Karl von Strasser, born 14 Sept. 1927, New York, New York, USA. Author; Commercial and Professional Pilot; German heavy aircraft Federal Aviation Administration Examiner; Teacher; Lecturer; Telekinetics Researcher & Instructor; Bionics Researcher and Development; Radio & TV Broadcaster; Radio & TV Talk Show Host; War Correspondent; Stunt Pilot & Actor; married 1976 to Martha (Dee Dee) Autry Caidin. Education: Graduated High School & College, 1948; A-2 Advanced Course with U.S. Air Force; Atomic-Radiological-Biological-Chemical Warfare Advanced Course completed with U.S. Army & Air Force, and, Instructor in these and related subjects. U.S. Maritime Service training; combat zone active service with U.S.

Merchant Marine, and, U.S. Coast Guard 1945. Advanced Flight Training (heavy equipment) transports, bombers, aerobatic and experience with various fighter aircraft types. Astronautics OJT U.S. Air Force. Parapsychology lecturer at Santa Fe College; Lecturer at Institute of Advanced Studies, Nebraska.

Consultant to many publications, broadcast networks, and business firms in science, aviation, advanced technology. Former Consultant to the Flight Surgeon, FAA; Former Consultant to the Administrator, FAA. Former operative U.S. Air Commandos. Parachutist; military and civilian vehicle test driver. Pilot-qualified extensive variety military, civilian and foreign aircraft. Researcher for Office of Paranormal Research. Former special agent state and federal law agencies.

Nearly 200 published books (140 under the name Caidin), including internationally well-known works such as *Zero!*; *Samurai!*; *Saga of Iron Annie*; *The Tigers Are Burning*; *The Night Hamburg Died*; *The Messiah Stone*; *Hydrospace*; *Aquarius Mission*; *Marooned* (major best seller hardback and paperback, Oscar-winning motion picture, internationally recognized, feted by NASA for accuracy); *Cyborg* (became the two television series, *The Six Million Dollar Man* and *The Bionic Woman*). Books published in more than thirty languages. Major contributions to international publications of thousands of articles, short fiction, and newspaper stories and series.

Honors include (this is not a complete list) James J. Strebig Memorial Trophy of Aviation/Space Writers Association, and others from 1958 on; coveted Brewer Aerospace Education Trophy; *Master Aviator* and *Pioneer Aviator* awarded by Silver Wings, 1987; Best Warbird Reconstruction, Experimental Aircraft Association; many awards from Air Force, Army, Navy, NASA and other government agencies, etc.

Memberships (not inclusive) Aviation/Space Writers Association; Author's Guild; Writer's Guild of America; Screen Actors Guild; Stuntmen's Association; U.S.A.F. *Thunderbirds* permanent member; Knight of Mark Twain; Silver Wings; Honorary Member of Society of Experimental Test Pilots; Mach Buster Club; British Ten-Ton Club; League of New Worlds; American Rocket Society; Fellow of the British Interplanetary Society; one of founders of the American Astronautical Society; U.S. Aerospace Education Society; Charter Member U.S. Aviation Hall of Fame; Confederate Air Force; Valiant Air Command;

Warbirds of America; Missile, Range and Space Pioneers of Cape
Canaveral Missile Test Annex (since 1950); Experimental Aircraft
Association; Aircraft Owners and Pilots Association; National Aviation
Clinic; American Airlines Admirals Club; Delta Airlines Flying Colonel;
British Airways Executive Club; American Aviation Historical Society;
Canadian Warplane Heritage; Canaveral Press Club; Honorary Member
Hump Pilots Association; International Oceanographic Foundation;
National Geographic Society; The Smithsonian Associates; The
Wilderness Society; Wingwalk Record Holders International; many
more. List is only partial.

Address: Studio 222, 2023 N. Atlantic Avenue, Cocoa Beach, FL
32931.

═ INTRODUCTION

Some very peculiar things were buzzing our aircraft high above Europe during the 1940s. Allied pilots were seeing bobbing, colored lights, fluttering disks and ghostly aircraft that, they reasoned, could only be German secret weapons. The German pilots were seeing the same things and thought they were British or American secret weapons. A few newspapers mentioned them in befuddlement, calling them "foo fighters" after the popular American comic strip Smoky Stover, which used "foo" as a catch word. After the war ended, they were quickly forgotten and no one bothered to research them further. A whole generation passed before a young pilot/author dipped into the yellowing archives and studied the ancient reports and debriefing records with great interest. More years passed while he patiently located those wartime pilots and collected their stories firsthand. The results are in this book.

His name is Martin Caidin.

We first met in NBC's legendary "green room" over thirty years ago. I was then a writer for a Goodson & Todman TV show starring Merv Griffin. Martin Caidin was on a book tour promoting one of his seemingly endless stream of best-sellers. He was already a very prominent aviation historian and a member of that very exclusive club that included Ernest K.

Gann, Antoine de Saint-Exuprey and other pilots with pens. A very lofty crowd, indeed.

As the years passed, Martin melded into another lofty crowd. That of the astronauts and space pioneers. He was able to write knowledgeably about the space program because he was there at Cape Canaveral when everything was happening. His novel Marooned, about a team of astronauts stick in orbit, was made into a major motion picture, and if you watched closely during the press conference scenes you would have spotted Mr. Caidin playing the role of a newspaper reporter.

During the exciting 1960s, he also somehow found the time to join the U.S. Air Force's flying saucer-chasing Project Blue Book, too. He worked from the inside, investigating UFO sightings firsthand, learning what the Air Force learned, and participating in wild adventures pursuing mysterious lights in the sky. Later, he pit some of this knowledge into his saucer novel, *The Mendelov Conspiracy.*

So here is a very rare man, a "saucer expert" who actually knows what he's talking about. A man with real qualifications to study and interpret what has been going on in our skies for at least half a century. He's even been inside the notorious Bermuda Triangle! When he and his pilot-wife Dee Dee were flying their private plane over that peculiar section of the Atlantic a few years ago, they actually entered a zone where their instruments went amok and the sky and ocean turned murky. But they can claim many other mysterious encounters as they fly around this planet in their vintage World War II aircraft. When Mr. Caidin is not busy writing another book or screenplay, he is on the move, searching out new wonders and examining old ones.

Considered to be one of the world's leading aviation historians, he has spent a part of his life sorting through musty records in military archives, sifting out the facts of aerial battles fought long ago. His books *Black Thursday, The Night Hamburg Died* and *The Last Dogfight* have become classics. He has not only carefully recorded the horrors of aerial warfare, he has flown the bombers and fighters that participated in those terrifying struggles at thirty thousand feet.

This is a man who knows what he's talking about. A man who has earned the respect of pilots and aviation buffs everywhere. Now, in this book, he is venturing into an even riskier arena. An arena of saucers and alleged conspiracies that has long been dominated by cultists and crackpots who have generated endless myths and nonsense while they battled with each other and blundered about in total ignorance and confusion. He is bringing with him not only common sense, but his rare gift for turning complicated technical language into words and explanations that all non-pilots can understand. He carefully explains what pilots see and feel as they operate their high tech machines and blunder into the kind of Twilight Zone that he, himself, invaded over the Atlantic. When you finish this book you will know more about flying than you have ever known before. Perhaps even more important, you will know more about UFOs than you ever imagined and you will understand them better.

The testimonials in this book come not from Ozark farmers and little old ladies in tennis shoes, but from highly trained, intelligent, very experienced pilots who have often gone unexpectedly to places where the UFO buffs have never been. These are not dubious trips into the unconscious mind via hypnosis. These are trips through distortions of time and space by competent observers as recorded by one of the greatest aviation writers.

Our paths have crossed occasionally since those distant days at NBC, but Martin Caidin is usually way ahead of me and I am always running, trying to keep up. In this book he has scooped me again. Out there on the tarmac I hear his vigorous shout, "Clear!" and we're off and running again. Welcome aboard, ease those throttles forward and hunker down for a great reading adventure.

JOHN A. KEEL
New York City

T-2 Buckeye trainer

Martin Caidin Archives

Chapter 1

—=10 OCTOBER 1967

T he weather was severe clear. One of those absolutely perfect morn-
ings for flying. Seven-thirty in the morning and an altitude of
twenty-one thousand feet, a beautiful jet trainer under my control.
You could see just about forever. It doesn't get much better than that. You
know what it's like when CAVU becomes a reality—*ceiling and visibility
unlimited.* Everything was crystal clear, sharp and sparkling. The date was
10 October 1967, and I was flying in my assigned sector of the military
practice area of Naval Air Station Meridian, in Mississippi. I have all the
details of that date; of that moment. I flew as a military student pilot in a
North American T-2B jet trainer, a powerful, smooth, and very responsive
aircraft. Squadron VT-7 was my outfit.

"Now, what's important is that in this kind of training mode the student pilot pays attention to every little detail. I know I did. And I mean
every detail."

The naval aviation student pilot is James Don Cochrane, a solid citizen then and solid citizen today. He kept the explicit military logbooks not
simply expected, but demanded, of all student pilots flying jet trainers. On
the morning of 10 October 1967, Don Cochrane was on his third aerobatic

training flight with an instructor in the rear of the tandem-seating T-2B. Student instruction and practice in the area of Naval Air Station Meridian took place in defined sectors; aerobatic training limited each sector to one aircraft. On this morning four T-2A and T-2B jet trainers were aloft, and ground controllers and radar confirmed that each aircraft was in its assigned sector.

At the time, that October morning in 1967, Don Cochrane was twenty-three years old. He stood six feet tall and was a rangy 160 pounds (with flight gear, 180 pounds), in perfect health and perfect condition.

Until this moment Don Cochrane has never told anyone, including his wife and his children, about what happened that morning.

When we reviewed this incident, there wasn't any doubt that Don Cochrane was your solid, reputable, professional citizen with a great family. That's important; it's the pattern he's maintained through his life. Today he's a certified safety professional and a certified product safety manager specializing in product liability safety and worker compensation safety. His meticulous attention to detail has marked his entire professional career. He's also one of those businessmen who's not only an active pilot but who flies often on company business and so puts in a great deal of time at the controls.

You can't get much more granite solid than the Cochrane family. Don Cochrane and his wife Linda, at the time these words see print, will have been married more than twenty-four years. Their daughter is a triple major in college and carries a steady 3.85 average. Their son is a high school senior, a three-letter man in sports, plays lead trumpet in the school jazz bands, and sits first chair in the concert band. He also carries a steady 3.85 average.

The preceding may not seem of specific importance to what happened the early morning of 10 October 1967. It would be wrong to make that assumption. Persistent reliability is *always* important for believability.

Now, back to that flight at twenty-one thousand feet with Ensign Don Cochrane at the controls.

"I recall asking my instructor for permission to begin my assigned maneuver, a high loop. Preparatory to beginning the maneuver I was in a clearing turn to the right. You clear to the right, and you clear to the left, and you check above you and below you and in all directions, and you do this no matter if you're told that the area is clear.

"I had just finished my scan to the right, and for some reason—I still don't know why I wanted to look again in that direction—I looked over my left shoulder.

"Flying very close wing position, tucked in really tight, *was another T-2B* with a student in front and the instructor in the rear. This aircraft was in a shallow left bank with both pilots looking at us. Everything was absolutely crisp; the vision factor was perfect."

Don Cochrane froze as he looked through the canopy of his jet trainer. The nose numbers on the other T-2B were the same as the aircraft he was flying. There was no mistake about that. Cochrane thought it couldn't be; that was impossible. The navy didn't paint identical numbers on different aircraft.

Cochrane's instructor had no reason to turn and look at anything, and he kept his eyes straight ahead, anticipating Cochrane initiating the loop. That moment was delayed as—

"The student in front waved at me. *I was looking at myself.* I didn't know what to think as that other pilot waved to me and then banked hard left and rolled away. Startled, even shocked, I glanced away, and when I looked back, the aircraft was gone. I looked everywhere: *nothing.*

"I asked my instructor, as was my habit, if he'd seen anything during the clearing turn. He told me he hadn't. I didn't mention a thing to him at the time, because I was concentrating on the maneuver and the other aircraft was long gone, and I was nervous and this was an aerobatic hop and he was a real screamer, and I was unsure of what I was supposed to do, and hell, I was a *student!* So I flew that airplane..."

All the way back to landing, Cochrane considered what he'd seen. And the more he thought of the incredible moment, the more convinced he was that everything had happened precisely as he saw and remembered it. He had seen his own aircraft in tight formation with him, he had seen his own instructor at that instant in the rear seat of his trainer, *and he had seen himself in the front seat of the other plane, waving!*

Back again on the ground, Cochrane went to the operations control room. How many other planes had been up at the same time? "Only three other flights were out," Cochrane explained. "All three were confirmed in other and different areas. There was no one else anywhere near us; the closest other plane was miles away. So I did what any smart and enterprising ensign student pilot does under so incredible a situation: I kept my mouth shut.

gravitate toward Liberators, Bostons, Beaufighters; a litany of winged thunder coming slowly to life.

Everyone suffers from the morning fog squeezing into the barracks and hangars. The fog is a living creature: it pervades the nostrils and squeezes delicate chest membranes, it hangs in a tenacious and clammy grip to the curving walls and ceilings of the Nissen huts and slicks their floors with a greasy film. It is the bottom of a black ocean of dampness.

Nevertheless, Mission 115 will be flown. And it will be flown against Schweinfurt—merely the name of a city if you're studying a map of Germany. But if you're one of those men prepared to invade from the skies, Schweinfurt is a profanity, synonymous with savage and powerful defenses, the main center of ball-bearings production in the Third Reich, a vital cog in the heart of the Nazi war machine.

In writing the book *Black Thursday,* I researched Mission 115 for more than a year, pursuing strange reports that I had never encountered with any substance from any other mission. Word had it among the bomber veterans of October 14, 1943, that "something strange" had happened on that savage day over Germany; more to the point, it had also been documented in the official files, reports, and intelligence debriefings of the mission. I spent months with Colonel Budd J. Peaslee, USAF, Retired, who in recent times has departed this life. When we worked together, we flew together, pored over combat logbooks and stacks of other records. Budd Peaslee was the air commander of Mission 115 against Schweinfurt.

Beirne Lay, Jr., formerly Lieutenant Colonel, USAAF, a great combat pilot and gifted writer, "was there," and we went over the mission in detail. Lieutenant Colonel Keith M. Garrison, USAF, also flew the Schweinfurt raid. Keith Garrison and I have flown many types of aircraft, including various bombers, and we searched together for the "something strange." We didn't complete the joint effort. Seventeen years after the Schweinfurt raid, Keith was flying a huge B-52 jet bomber, a mission ending in a terrifying crash and a horrendous fireball that ended the lives of the men in that machine.

Still the search went on. Finally I was ensconced deep among the files of the Research Studies Institute, Air University, United States Air Force, and there was the Rosetta stone—the *original* combat reports and debriefings of the men of Mission 115. Here I went through literally thousands of sheets of paper as I examined the handwritten notes of returning crews. I

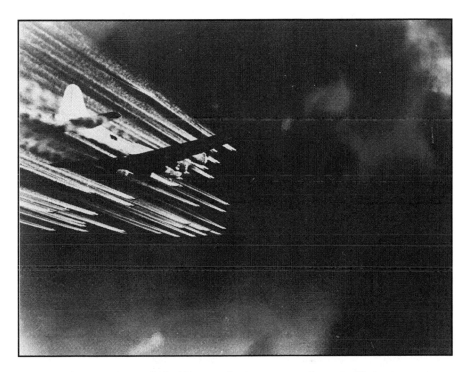

A formation of B-17s on their way to bomb Germany

USAAF

also went through the detailed reports of men who fought that day and who went down in dying B-17s; some escaped to return to England, some waited out the war in POW camps and then submitted their recollections to the official files.

I went through the final reports of the headquarters of the Eighth Air Force and the Eighth Bomber Command, the records of the United States Strategic Bombing Survey with its twenty-twenty hindsight review of the mission; I studied the reports of the German fighter command and its pilots. I've flown German fighters, transports, and bombers, and struck up free-association exchanges with German pilots.

When it was all done, I submitted my findings to the Historical Division and the Security Review Branch of the U.S. Air Force.

Out of that effort, narrowed down to the issues of *this* book, here is what we confirmed.

A B-17 pilot sat in an intelligence debriefing, his eyes hollow, and spoke calmly of hell four miles high. "The German fighter raked us the length of the Fortress's belly. It was like sitting in the boiler of a hot-water heater and being rolled down a steep hill. The right wing was shot to hell. There were holes everywhere. A lot of them were twenty-millimeter cannon holes, and those shells tear a hole so big you could shove a sheep through. The entire wing was just a goddamn bunch of holes."

Mission 115 put 257 Flying Fortress bombers over the German border on a massive run to Schweinfurt. "Company appeared" far below the bombers as swarms of German fighters rose to meet the invaders. Bedlam exploded through the interphone systems of each bomber, ten men to a plane. *Everyone* sees German fighters—because there are that many German fighters in an ascending cloud. In his own plane Budd Peaslee curses his crew with every bit of choice profanity he can jam into several seconds, admonishing them for their outbursts. Discipline, teamwork, concerted effort, necks on a swivel, words to a minimum—those are his commands.

"The opening play," Peaslee reports later, "is a line plunge through center. The fighters whip through our formations…six formations of Messerschmitt Me-109s charge us…. The shock of the first attack is over, and I start to get scared. Gunners call out the new attacks. I try to look simultaneously in all directions. I can see the fighters on my side. They've half turned and are diving toward us in a continuous string, their paths marked in the bright sunlight by fine lines of light-colored smoke as they fire short bursts. It is a coordinated attack, the finest I have ever seen. Their timing is perfect, their technique masterly…. A few hundred feet in front of us, a bomber has been hit by a rocket. I catch sight of it just as the right wing starts to fold upward. The fuselage opens like an eggshell, and a man dressed in a flying suit spins clear out in front. I see the pilots still at the controls, then the plane is swept with flame. The right wing breaks free, and with the two engines still spinning, it drifts to the rear, flaming at the ragged end. The shattered mess disappears under our left wing, and the sky is clear again…."

A gunner reports: "When a cannon shell smashes into a Fortress, the way it sounds depends on where you are. If you're not too close, it's a kind of metallic *whoof!* like a small bark from a big dog—and you feel a jar that shakes the whole ship. It is a tremor. It reaches and leaves you quickly. But if the shell explodes nearby, then there is nothing gentle or distant about what happens, and it sure as hell isn't a momentary tremor. It sounds like some giant smashing his cupped hand down on the surface of still water. A double sound, really—the first from the impact and the second when the shell explodes. *CRAA-AASH!* Like that. Like firing a shotgun into a bucket, so that the sound and the blast all come exploding back up into your face, shaking you up and stunning your mind. For the moment you're not scared, because your senses are knocked silly, and you don't know how to be scared or anything else. Your bowels seem weak and watery, and your stomach shrivels up until you know how much damage has been done...."

Schweinfurt grew closer. The trail to the German city was marked clearly by flaming metal, brown and dirty smoke, tumbling wreckage, fleets of parachutes. To many pilots and aircrew, a strange serenity seemed to settle as the German fighter force mangled the B-17s. "I had accepted the fact," said one hollow-eyed pilot in after-mission debriefing, "that I was not going to live through this mission. It was as simple as that. I was calm; it was a strange sort of resignation. I knew for certain that it was only a matter of seconds or minutes. It was impossible to survive...."

Another pilot on his way to Schweinfurt: "There is a terrible feeling when a bomber dies...as you watch, helpless, the flames streaming backward. These are the sights that tried our souls the most. To watch from your own bomber as a sister ship suffers the flame and begins to fall off in her opening death throes, to know that within her blazing heart the men are your friends and buddies, and maybe you know the pilot's wife well, and you know the kids, too. It involves more than the men. You don't fly a Fortress for months and years without coming to know that gallant lady in the most intimate respects. You know her, and you place in her sturdy construction, the manner in which she flies, in everything about her, not only your life, and those of the crew, but all the life to come—*if* we survive this stinking war, that is.

"But one thing I'll tell you. A queen dies hard. She doesn't want to go, no more than any man inside her. You may not believe this. If you don't, *it's only because you haven't been there,* and you haven't watched combat-hardened men cry as a ship goes down; cry as much for the machine as for the men. Because, you see, when ten men claimed her for their own, she was no longer just a machine. She was *their* bomber. That made her special, and made her come alive."

* * *

As the bomber force within full visual range of Colonel Peaslee approaches the final run into its target, so we in these pages approach the "impossible" of the Schweinfurt attack.

"We are right behind the leading formation as the bomb run starts," describes Peaslee. "They are in good order, but one of their groups of twenty-one bombers has been reduced to *two!* The unit has been devastated, and it's more than a little pathetic to see those two lonesome guys plugging along as though all were intact.

"The fighters come at us from all directions.... We begin to get a few bursts of flak.... It is past time now for the fighters to leave us, but they do not. They stay with us, fighting in their own flak. This is very strange.... The stakes in this game have been terrific for both sides, and the devil took the pot. Below us Schweinfurt is rapidly going to hell as the bomb strings ahead of ours walk through the city. Its dead will outnumber our own by fantastic figures.... *Primary bombed....* At our level I can see the rear formations approaching Schweinfurt. They look ragged and are under intense attack.... Our formations do not waver as they crawl across the sky. It is as though they were being pulled by an invisible chain into the thresher of flak over the city, and there they will disgorge their heads of grain, the thousand-pounders.... Far below them on the ground I see part of our ante to the devil's pot. Our course is plainly marked by rising columns of smoke. I know what those columns mean, and I count them—nine, ten, eleven. They represent eleven bombers, with one hundred ten men aboard, punctuating the line from the Initial Point to the target...."

Then, it *begins.*

More than four miles above Schweinfurt, a new element adds to the bombers, fighters, rockets, flak bursts, bombs, and swinging parachutes. Pilots and gunners scan the sky for incoming German fighters. They cast quick glances at burning planes and parachutes, but there's precious little time to follow a dying aircraft all the far way down to earth. The fighters; they had to keep looking for, calling out the positions of, and firing machine guns at the fighters.

These are experienced men, combat veterans, with life-and-death skills at observing objects moving through the air.

Something new appeared as boxes of bombers swung onto the Initial Point and began their runs to the target.

Not one or just a few bombers, but entire *groups* of B-17s encountered small formations in the air that should not have existed. They were not aircraft, or flak bursts, or falling bombs, or fighters, or spent ammunition cases, or debris of shattered planes, or falling bodies, or parachutes.

B-17s from the 8th Air Force, 16 November 1943

United States Air Force

It is recorded in the official histories of the Air Force, deep in the vaults of the historical files, "as one of the most baffling incidents of World War II, and an enigma that to this day defies all explanation."

As the bombers of the 384th Group swung into the final bomb run after passing the Initial Point, the fighters attacking this group swung away, leaving the bombers to the attention of the heavy flak batteries far below. This point is vital, and pilots were queried extensively, as were other crew members, as to the position at that time of the German fighter planes.

Every man interrogated was firm in his statement that "at the time there were no enemy aircraft above."[1]

At this moment the pilots and top-turret gunners, as well as several crewmen in the Plexiglas noses of the bombers (gunners and bombardiers),

1. Memorandum of 24 October 1943 from Major E.R.T. Holmes, F.L.O., 1st Bombardment Division, Reference FLO/1BW/REP/126, o M.I. 15, War Office, Whitehall, London, S.W. (copy to Colonel E. W. Thompson, A-2, Pinetree).

reported a *cluster of discs* in the path of the 384th's formation, and, *closing with the bombers.*

The startled exclamations focused attention on the phenomenon, and the crews called back and forth to one another on the interphones, discussing and confirming the astonishing sight before them.

The discs in the cluster were agreed upon as being silver-colored, about one inch thick and three inches in diameter.

They were seen easily, and repeatedly, by the B-17 crewmen. The discs appeared above the bombers, gliding down slowly in very uniform clusters.

And then the "impossible" happened.

Boeing B-17 Number 026 closed rapidly with a cluster of discs. The pilot jinked the aircraft violently, attempting to evade an imminent collision with the discs. The sudden and violent maneuvering of the B-17 proved the maneuver futile.

The pilot reported at the intelligence debriefing that "my right wing went directly through a cluster with absolutely no effect on engines or plane surface."

The intelligence officers pressed their questioning. The pilot stated further that one of the discs was heard to strike the tail assembly of the airplane.

Neither the pilot, nor any member of the crew that heard the disc striking the tail, felt or witnessed an explosion of any kind.

The pilot explained further that about twenty feet from the discs—a report confirmed by other pilots and crew members—they watched a mass of black debris of varying sizes, in clusters of three by four feet, floating past their aircraft.

The interrogation and debriefing was stamped SECRET. The SECRET REPORT also stated in part: "Also observed two other A/C [aircraft] flying through silver discs with no apparent damage. Observed discs and debris two other times but could not determine where it came from."

There has never been an explanation of this baffling incident. Dozens of experienced combat veterans, pilots and gunners and observers, confirmed the incredible sightings and encounters.

But there was another footnote. A search of combat records showed that similar discs, in formation, performing as described in Mission 115, were observed by other aircrews on bomber missions prior to, and after, Mission 115 of 14 October 1943.

Nothing in the records of the German air force, or interrogation of its pilots, provided any further information.

The silver discs remain in the SECRET files as "unexplained."

Mission 115 went into the official history of the U.S. Army Air Forces as *Black Thursday.* No mission ever received a more grueling examination than did this strike. It was one of the worst days in the history of our bomber fleets.

Two hundred and fifty-seven Fortresses penetrated German airspace. Only 197 returned. Five of these were abandoned or crashed. That leaves 192 bombers of the combat force. Of these, 142 were damaged. Only 50 bombers—in the wings that miraculously escaped with only negligible opposition—were not torn up by German defenses.

Nothing could change the numbers. Fifty-nine B-17s shot down over Europe, 590 airmen lost with them. One crippled B-17 ditched in the Channel. Three bombers, lost and low on fuel in the fog covering their fields, were abandoned; the crews bailed out. Two more attempted landings that failed; the planes crashed and were destroyed.

Sixty-five bombers gone forever. Seventeen more so badly damaged they never flew again. More than forty men badly wounded.

Every aspect of the mission was subjected to the most intense scrutiny.

A special intelligence team did everything possible to learn more about the incredible, inexplicable discs.

A mystery remains a mystery until it's solved.

This one is still a mystery.

Kenneth Bacon's Starduster II

Chapter 3

THE HANGOVER MINING COMPANY

ewsmen called it "a perfect setting for Rod Serling's 'Twilight Zone.' "[1]

A pilot at the controls of an open cockpit Starduster II sport plane had flown into an airfield that "shouldn't have been" and went through a series of incidents, including one that "couldn't happen, but did."

The pilot was unquestionably believable as a skilled observer of events. He was also beyond all question as to competence and reliability. His name is Kenneth D. Bacon, and his profession places him at the highest levels of judgment. Kenneth D. Bacon, who flew into what several lifetime flying veterans considered "being about as close to a bend or break in Time," was the presiding judge for the Oklahoma State Court of Appeals in Tulsa. He also has a reputation as an extremely competent and skilled pilot among his peers.

Judge Bacon's flight into and out of mystery took place "on a beautiful late summer day in 1976," he relates. "I planned a flight from Tulsa, Oklahoma, to Hays, Kansas. I planned to fly west of Wichita to avoid the

---

[1](*Tulsa World,* September 8, 1976.)

heavy air traffic in that area, and this would make my journey about a three-hour flight."

That's the impersonal record. On more of a personal level, Judge Bacon loves to fly, especially in machines that bring a man close to the elements so that he can feel, taste, and experience as many of the sensations of flight as there are. Even his choice of aircraft—lithe, fast, agile, extremely sensitive on the controls and demanding high skill—speaks for the man. Flying in a Starduster II is getting back to the elements.

Those of us who've flown these small ships, as well as the heavy iron, know the pleasures of "getting down among them, like in the old days." We'd slide back windows, jam swinging doors up under a wing, strip off our shirts, feel the wind against skin and face and hair. Some of us counted our flights by the cigars we smoked. I've done it in Cubs and Aeroncas and Stearmans and Wacos; the open-cockpit birds are the best. You've got that little curving windscreen between you and the hurricane-force wind, and you're one with your machine. This is the kind of flying Judge Bacon was doing on this day, even to the point of making wide circles to avoid areas where air traffic might be heavy, thus demanding more attention to watching for other planes than to experience the sheer pleasure that flying brings.

"Although it was early morning with not a cloud in the sky, I phoned Tulsa flight service for a weather briefing, as is my usual practice. Great news; I was told I'd have clear sailing all the way, and the sky would remain cloudless.

"I did preflight on my little Starduster II and had wheels up out of Tulsa about nine-thirty A.M. The temperature was already in the upper eighties and going higher when I took off. It was perfect for flying without a shirt on, and this kind of weather was an experience of great pleasure in my little open-cockpit airplane.

"I'd been flying for about an hour or so. It was marvelous. I hadn't seen even a wisp of a cloud or another airplane. The whole world was mine. I cruised at an altitude of sixty-five hundred feet, and the Starduster ran like a fine Swiss watch. The variable-pitch propeller I'd installed on the ship was doing its job as intended; higher speed and less vibration. It was pure flying at its best. The little bird trimmed out well, and all I had to do was sit there and enjoy the flight."

And then—

"I had my head down in the cockpit looking at a flight chart. It apparently had been some time since I glanced up or looked at the sky, because suddenly I felt what appeared to be cold air on my bare back and shoulders. *That* didn't make any sense. What I saw as I looked around...well, let me explain the temperature. It had dropped *instantly* at least fifteen or twenty degrees.

"That kind of temperature change, where I was flying, and the weather forecast I'd had from flight service, simply does not compute. I looked around in disbelief. A short time before I'd been in a cloudless sky. It was that old 'you could see forever' drill. Now I was surrounded by black clouds that seemed to be churning with great energy and mixing with off-white colors. I was actually shocked at how the weather had changed so quickly, so drastically. I looked down at the ground, and my disbelief mounted, because I saw strong winds hurling up clouds of dust across the fields below and all about me.

"Even faster than I can relate what was happening, the clouds were closing around me as swiftly as they had formed, seemingly out of nowhere. No question but that this was more than 'just clouds.' I was in the midst of a huge thunderstorm, perhaps an entire line or area of such storms, and I didn't cherish the idea at all of finding myself in a hailstorm in my little fabric-covered bird. That can really mess up the airplane, me, and my whole day, and I didn't waste another second in searching for someplace to land, to get on the ground safely.

"The clouds came at me from all sides. They were enormous and becoming more violent with every passing minute; I could feel the Starduster taking strong blows from sudden turbulence. Landing as quickly as I could now became my entire world. I looked to the left of the cowling. Talk about a break! I saw a clear, bright opening in the wall of blackness rushing closer and closer against me. And in the center of that hole, like a miracle, was one of the largest airports and, I might add, one of the most welcome airports I had *ever* seen. There were very long runways and no obstacles. I was already in my descent, one eye on the boiling clouds and the other on my flight chart, circling down in that hole and at the same time trying to locate that airport on the chart.

"Finally, I found *something*. On the chart I saw an airport layout that resembled the long runways toward which I was flying, still coming down in that tight hole, always keeping the ground in sight. Getting wrapped in boiling clouds was something I could well do without.

"The chart read *Habit Field*. I'd never heard of it, and I was even more surprised to discover the chart didn't indicate any listed radio frequencies for the field. The place was *huge*. Still circling, I came around in the descending turn and caught sight of a control tower looming high above other buildings. I thought, for Christ's sake, I've got a chart and they've forgotten to print the radio frequencies. Okay; if there isn't a primary freq, I'll go to Unicom. I called to the tower on one twenty-two point eight megahertz. Nothing. I went through the frequencies we use for oddball airports and out-of-the-way places. Still nothing.

"The storm—and it was a full-fledged boomer by now—kept getting worse; the clouds were darker and thicker and the winds really gusting. I went down low and buzzed the tower, flying directly alongside so they couldn't possibly miss me. Well, I guess they *did* miss me the first time so I came around—by now I should have had half that field hopping with my low pass—and buzzed the tower again. Still nothing! I scanned the field for any planes that might be taxiing or on the runways. More nothing. I couldn't see anyone in the tower, I failed to get any light signals, and this was getting pretty stupid with that storm dropping on me, so I decided to land, no matter what, and argue with the FAA later.

"I didn't bother checking the wind sock. I didn't need to. The winds were so strong now that dust and tumbleweeds scoured the ground. All I had to do was fly *into* that mess, and the Starduster settled easily.

"When I sat the little bird down, holding the stick full back and taxiing slowly because of the increasing winds, I noticed immediately tall weeds growing out of cracks in the runway. That was tough to understand; I wondered why the people who ran this place were so neglectful in maintaining such a large airport. As I rolled to a stop, I pointed the nose of my bird directly toward the tower, making every exaggerated movement of control surfaces the wind allowed. Still no light! This was really crazy.

"I added power to taxi up to the front of the tower and killed the switches. I'd nosed the plane into the wind, and as soon as the propeller stopped turning, I scrambled out, bringing my own chocks with me, and secured the plane. Now I could find out what was going on and get the Starduster tied down.

"I looked up at the huge tower again, and the sense of 'something wrong' really hit me. One large pane of glass in the tower was broken out. The place had to be filled with dust and debris. Then I saw a door, banging open and shut in the wind, slamming back and forth with a great racket.

"Not a soul stirred. I began to wonder if all this was *real*. Nothing was right and everything was *wrong*. And the feeling became stronger and stronger. Not because of any imagination, but because of what I kept running into.

"I noticed a riding lawn mower sitting up on some blocks. Alongside the mower was an *open* box of tools where someone had obviously been working on that mower. Alongside the toolbox was a thermos bottle and a cup half-filled with dust-covered coffee.

"Everything looked as if the entire place had been busy and then, suddenly, absolutely abruptly, *everything stopped* right in the middle of whatever was going on at the field.

"I kept walking, looking about me. I whistled shrilly several times, and all I got back was the wind gusting and roaring. So I shouted. I did this for several minutes as I walked along. No answer, and still I couldn't see a soul moving. Or not moving, for that matter. I walked by several large hangars. I remember shaking my head in wonder; the hangar doors were either fully or partly open.

"Everything was covered with dirt as if this field had been abandoned—as close to instantly as you can get—several years ago.

"I continued to yell and whistle as I approached each building. Still nothing! I couldn't find a human being, a dog, a cat; *nothing*. Ever get the feeling you're somewhere between Here and There? A sort of limbo. Well, I sure had it now. The hair on the back of my neck felt as if it were standing straight up, and the sense of wrongness kept increasing steadily.

"I walked along a row of airplanes and vehicles, everything covered heavily with dust. I looked everywhere for signs, something that would identify this place out of nowhere. Nothing. I went back to my airplane and started the other way, and finally I saw an abandoned pickup truck with the name 'Hangover Mining Company' painted on the side. The windows were down in the truck. I walked up to a row of other vehicles, all with windows down, and all filled with dust. I heard a banging sound; it was the open door of an airplane slamming back and forth. The sense of eeriness grew stronger as I went along.

"Although now, when I look back on it and review the feelings I was going through, it seems kind of funny. You can laugh at yourself *when it's all over.* But it certainly wasn't funny at that time. Everything I was used to in an airport was foreign. It was *alien.* A strange airport, strange weather, strange feelings, and the large tumbleweeds bouncing and rolling along didn't help any. I remember thinking of a movie I'd seen as a child. In that film a pilot was flying cross-country and for some reason was forced onto a strange airport where no one could be found. Dishes were still on tables and windows were open. The movie ended when an atomic bomb was dropped on the town immediately nearby, which had actually been set up to test the effects of a nuclear explosion on an average town.

"By now I was headed back to the Starduster, and I recall I was wondering, 'Surely, I haven't landed in some place, in Kansas, where they're going to drop a damn bomb!' Sure, it's humorous now, but at the time it was mighty heavy on my mind.

"And then, just as crazy as was this crazy storm that came boiling into this area, it never did rain! The clouds rushed low overhead, and the wind howled, and it *should* have been pouring, but everything remained bone dry.

"That was it. I didn't want to stay any longer at that airport. No way! Every instinct I had was telling me to leave and to leave *immediately*. I looked up, and the weather was just as crazy as it was before. That rolling sky wasn't getting any worse, and if I judged my weather correctly, it also wasn't getting any better. It was if the weather situation was "locked in." To the devil with this place; I pulled the chocks, stowed them in the airplane, and fired up. As I taxied out, I went through strong emotions about taking off. No matter how weird this place was, I *was* on the ground. If I took off, it could be into some pretty nasty weather. I weighed both choices; the alternative to flight was to remain here in this airfield of incredible improbabilities.

"I took off.

"I stayed beneath the thick cloud cover; the storm above me remained constant, clouds swirling and boiling about as though from a heavy oil fire. It was a short flight to the town of Lyons, Kansas, and I wasted no time in getting down to the airport runway. As I blew in from the terrible-looking sky, an attendant ran out from the operations shack to chock and secure my plane.

"He had a look of complete astonishment on his face. A little Starduster II doesn't often come whizzing in through boiling clouds and a terrible sky, 'Where'd *you* come from?' he asked, disbelief still showing on his face.

"I told him what I'd been through, and that I'd landed at this crazy airport that showed on my chart as Habit Field.

"The man actually *recoiled*. I mean, physically recoiled. 'You really didn't land there, did you?' he asked, his mouth agape.

**Ken Bacon—"Impossible or not,
you're holding it right in your hand."**

photo by Richard Pulliam

"I told him that was exactly what I'd done. 'But so what?' I finished, and again I thought, Christ, I've broken some terrible federal rule.

"He looked at me, shaking his head. 'Mister,' he said slowly, his face reflecting all sorts of terrible inner thoughts, '*no one lands there*. There are some mighty strange goings-on there.'

"This was getting downright ridiculous. 'You're not making much sense,' I said to him, as easily as I could, because the man was acting real spooked. 'Why doesn't anyone land there?' He stared at me and then just started walking away. Never asked if I needed fuel or anything. Just started walking. *'No one* lands there,' he repeated, and he was gone.

"I waited in the local operator's office for several hours. Slowly but steadily the sky cleared. Other pilots showed up at the office, and I refueled the Starduster to continue my trip. As I usually do, I walked around my airplane for a thorough preflight check. Everything appeared normal. That was to be expected. The little ship hadn't really been out of my sight for more than a few minutes at a time. But the appearance of normal didn't set right with me. I had a strong feeling, an eerie sensation, that something was *not* right. I completed the preflight, and then started it all over again. This time I went by the book, giving the Starduster every detail of the strict military preflight I had been taught.

"I stopped when I got to the tail wheel. I stared at it in complete disbelief. I noticed immediately, on this second go-round, a wire sticking all the way through the tire. Bear in mind that the six-inch tire of the Starduster is two inches thick and made of solid, very hard rubber. I doubt that you could drive a nail through it, or even shoot a bullet all the way through. It's that hard and tough.

"But somehow a very thin piece of *soft,* flexible wire had been driven completely through the tire. And it was driven through the tire *sideways.*

"Now I checked out this thing from every possible angle and with the people most experienced with this type of equipment. They brought in a tire expert, a top mechanic and aircraft inspector, to examine the tire. He turned it this way and that, examined it as closely as he could, held up the tire to me and said, 'This, sir, is flatly impossible.'

"Impossible or not, I told him, there it is. 'You're holding it right in your hand. You're looking at it. It's happened. Now what?'

"He shook his head. 'I don't care what I'm seeing or you're seeing, and I'm touching it, and I've examined it from every angle possible, and I tell you again, sir, *it is impossible.*'

"A number of other mechanics and pilots examined the tire, shaking their heads in disbelief. They took pictures of the tire and that soft wire driven completely through the hard rubber. To this day, years later, following every lead I could to discover how it happened, everyone agrees on only one thing. It's a physical impossibility. But the photographs speak for themselves.

"Anyway, impossible or not, I was stranded in Lyons, Kansas, overnight. The next morning someone flew in a replacement tail wheel, and I went on my way without any further problems.

"I could have let the entire affair go, but curiosity's a powerful thing, and I don't like loose ends lying around. I called a pilot friend who worked at the Tulsa newspaper, the *World*, and discovered he already knew, generally, that something strange had happened regarding my flight. He sent some reporters to my office to take photographs of the tail wheel and get down the details of that airport-that-shouldn't-be. When they completed their interview, they got hot on the story. After a lot of futile attempts, they finally got a telephone call through to Habit Field.

The reporter called me back to relate his conversation with the person to whom he'd spoken. The reporter had asked what Habit Field *was*.

" 'Wal, I'm sort of a tumbleweed,' was the answer.

" 'What's that? What do you mean by tumbleweed?'

" 'Tumbleweeds,' was the strange reply. 'This here's an old military base.'

" 'But—' "

" 'It's in private hands. That's all you needs to know' and the 'tumbleweed' hung up, and they never could get him back on the phone.

"Several times I started to return to that field, to that Hangover Mining Company, or whatever it was on an 'old military base,' and I was going to take cameras and friends with me. But each time, for various reasons, something stopped me, and we never did get to go back there.

"From what I understand now it's as if that place I visited never existed. I've heard it's called Sunflower Field. Everything I saw there is supposed to be gone. Some say it wasn't ever there! But now according to what other pilots have told me, Sunflower Field is used as a glider airport and for parachute instruction and skydiving. That is one very big damn airport for gliding and jumping! But it's a bit comforting to hear the airport is functional and being used, *if*—and this is still a very big *if*—it was the same airport where I landed.

"However, no matter what happens at that field, or doesn't happen, I guess I'll never know when and how that flexible wire was driven through that solid tail wheel of my airplane. I guess I'll never know. The hair on the back of my neck still rises when I think about that day and how the impossible *did* happen.

"How—*and why.*"

Heinkel He–111 German bomber

Martin Caidin Archives

Chapter 4

=The Phantoms
of Montrose

The British pilots posted to the airfield at Montrose, Scotland, in the winter of 1940 found the military installation a bit of heaven. No matter that the weather was foul, the cold biting, the fog heavy and oppressive. These fighter pilots, who had flown Hurricanes for months in almost-constant air battles with German fighters and bombers, were worn to the bone. Many of their fellow pilots were dead; lesser numbers who survived combat and crashes were either badly burned or otherwise severely wounded. To the young pilots still sound of body and mind, Montrose meant regaining health in body and spirit.

Not that the German Luftwaffe had been banished from English skies. The Germans disrupted entire squadrons and airfields on every occasion they could manage—as happened on this wintry night. The squadron pilots were fast asleep, the long nights especially welcome to them.

But not for long on this particular evening. Montrose had been selected for night harassment, and a twin-engined Heinkel bomber crossed over the field, engines thundering, disappearing into the darkness and then roaring back for what promised to be a long-delayed bomb run. Alarms sounded in the sleeping quarters. Fighter pilots slipped into their flying gear and rushed to operations; at the same time, mechanics were already preparing fighters for immediate takeoff.

Operations ordered several Hurricanes prepared for flight but to be held on the ground ready for immediate takeoff. A single pilot, an experienced flight sergeant, got the nod to get into the air immediately to find and shoot down the Heinkel. The eight-gun fighter was soon racing down the darkened runway; it lifted from the ground and disappeared into the murk, visible only by the glowing exhausts of an engine under full power.

For the next thirty minutes the sergeant-pilot, sent aloft because of his experience in night flying, as well as his reputation for being not only unimaginative and single-minded in his duty, but also one of the most able combat veterans in the squadron, searched for the enemy aircraft. The night was dark, and he had no help from the moon as he did his best to find the telltale exhaust glow from the Heinkel's twin engines.

Thirty minutes after takeoff, operations decided the Germans had departed the area. For whatever reason, either low on fuel, or perhaps having caught sight of the Hurricane taking off, they were gone. The radio signal went out: "Return to base and land." The Hurricane pilot acknowledged. They heard the roar of his engine diminish as he throttled back and descended.

In those days no one ever knew when the Germans played a double game. They'd send over one bomber to entice British fighters into the night sky. By the time the fighter climbed to altitude, the bomber was gone. Landing a Hurricane at night on a dark field wasn't the simplest of tasks. It called for experience and skill. If the British turned on enough lights to ease the problems of landing, then the field became a beacon for a *second* bomber just waiting for this chance.

Stung more than once, the British turned on two rows of what they called *glim-lights*. They were so dim that only a pilot knowing where to look could find them in darkness. This pilot knew what to do, and every man on the ground could tell when the fighter's gear came down and the Hurricane was turned properly to land on the grass strip between the glim-lights.

Moments later a man called out: "There he is!" They didn't yet see an airplane, but the throttled-back exhausts cast their unmistakable glow in the night. The Hurricane came in smoothly, beginning its landing flare as the pilot skimmed over the trees at the airfield perimeter. As they expected, the engine sounds died away to a rumble as the Merlin was brought back to idle, and the fighter settled smoothly to the grassy surface.

Hawker Hurricane fighter plane

Unexpectedly, with a thundering roar and a flash of bright exhausts, the pilot rammed his throttle forward to full power and raced into the air again. For the moment, the operations staff was convinced the sergeant-pilot had caught sight of a German bomber, or perhaps had seen some obstruction on the runway. Neither bomber nor obstruction were seen. They heard the Hurricane circling the field and again setting up his approach.

This time the pilot, convinced no German bomber was about, but still catching everyone on the ground by surprise, turned on his navigation lights. Had there been an enemy aircraft in the area, the Hurricane would have made a splendid target. Something else was happening, but no one watching could figure out what it was.

The Hurricane began its flare to land; this time the pilot went to full power before his wheels touched, and again the fighter thundered away into darkness. They caught a glimpse of the navigation lights showing the direction of flight, toward and then over open sea.

Operations signaled the ground crews. To hell with whatever bomber might be upstairs. "Give him a way in," they ordered. Ground crews switched on the Chance beacon, a powerful searchlight mounted in a horizontal position, and set up to illuminate the entire grass airstrip's runway in a huge glow of yellow white light. The Hurricane came about again, crossed the perimeter, and this time the fighter touched down smoothly, power full back. Immediately the Chance light was shut down to darken the field. The Hurricane pilot taxied back using only the glim-lights, swung the fighter about, and killed his engine.

Pilots and ground crewmen crowded to the Hurricane. The sergeant-pilot slid back his canopy and stood high in the cockpit. With an angry gesture he yanked off his leather flight helmet. His voice boomed across the field.

"The fool!" he shouted, his face contorted with anger. "Who's the bloody fool who cut me out!" He climbed down and dropped from the wing. "Bloody stupid bastard! He could have wrapped up the lot of us with his stupidity!"

The other pilots looked at one another and shrugged. One stepped forward. "Look, Sergeant, no one cut you out. We were watching you the whole time. You were the only machine working the airstrip."

"That's a bloody pile," came the heated retort. "What's with you blokes? Have you all gone blind? Of course someone cut me out!" He renewed his shouting, stabbing his hand at the runway. "Why do you think I went round again? And *twice* at that!"

An officer moved closer. "Sergeant-Pilot, what type of machine?"

"Why, sir, it was some bloody madman in a biplane. Just as I was crossing the boundary and easing into the flare, that biplane balked me. Cut before me just as I was touching down. Looked like a Tiger Moth, it did."

Silence met his words. By now the flight commander stood before the thoroughly agitated pilot. "There's no one else flying," said the flight commander. "Besides, we don't have any biplanes on this station."

The sergeant-pilot set a famously stubborn jaw. "Sir, I knows what I saw, and I saw it not once, but twice, like I said, and that damned biplane *was right in front of me!"*

The group fell silent. Finally the flight commander gestured to his men. "That's enough for tonight. Pack it in, gentlemen."

The pilots and aircrews returned to their sleeping quarters. No one save the sergeant-pilot flying the Hurricane, and *he* was in the best position to see any other aircraft, had seen the mystery biplane. The story went round and round with the flight crews and mechanics and other ground crewmen, but in the press of combat and moving the Hurricane squadron to a new location, it was a report filed away and if not forgotten, at least relegated to an "odd story" category.

It didn't stay quiet too long.

*   *   *

Not quite two years later, in the summer of 1942, Montrose Airfield was a beehive of flying activity. Training went on seven days a week, in daylight and at night, as the Royal Air Force worked frantically to build up its force of competent pilots. Crashes were common in training, and the Scottish hills about Montrose were dotted with wreckage and wide burn scars where aircraft had plunged into the earth, exploded, and burned. The flying training schools were *always* dangerous, not only at Montrose, but at any such installation anywhere in the world.

But a particular crash early in the day in the summer of 1942 gained an unexpected and undesired reputation. One of the flight lieutenants stationed at Montrose was only too well-known to his squadron mates and especially the ground crews servicing his machines. The squadron histories make no bones about his sullen temper, his grim insistence on absolute discipline from all the ground staff, his lashing out at subordinates and using every opportunity to punish any infraction of the rules. In short, he was considered and apparently had earned his reputation as a thoroughly miserable son of a bitch.

One week before the crash of the airplane flown by this particular officer, there had been a nasty scene on the flight line between this flight lieutenant and a mechanic working on the airplane assigned to the pilot. For no reason anyone else within earshot could fathom, the pilot tore into the mechanic, shrieking with anger as if he'd lost his senses. He also put the mechanic on report for disciplinary action.

He might have selected a better subject for his vituperation. A week after the shouting incident, the same mechanic performed work on that same airplane—in which the same bellowing pilot took off. He didn't get very far. The airplane seemed to stagger as it left the ground and then whirled out of control, smashing back to the runway and instantly killing the pilot.

The hapless mechanic was again on report by a board of inquiry— which, however, failed to prove that the mechanic had rigged the airplane, in a desire for revenge, so that it would crash. Without even circumstantial evidence, the charges were dropped and the matter officially closed.

But it wasn't *quite* ended. There's no reliable record of a specific span of time involved; only the words "shortly thereafter" reports of a pilot's ghost began to sweep Montrose Aerodrome. Ghosts at British airfields aren't quite as common as stray dogs hanging about the garbage dumps, but they're not exactly unheard of, either. Yet the growing number of people who had reported seeing this ghost—an officer in flying suit and goggles, ready to take to the air—caused great consternation among the headquarters staff. A good many pilots and ground crew who knew the full extent of the circumstances surrounding the fatal crash of the bombastic flight lieutenant were convinced it was this same pilot, as vituperative in phantom form as in precrash days, who had returned to haunt and "drive wild" the mechanic still suspected of his death.

The stories sweeping the airfield's personnel didn't raise hackles at headquarters so much as the fact that replacements arriving at Montrose, who hadn't even had time to hear the ghostly gossip or murmurs of fear among the "regulars," *also* began to encounter this phantom figure in flying suit and goggles.

Suddenly the ghost was real in a completely unexpected manner. Seen along the flight line, emerging from fog and dimly lit areas at night by newcomers who had not an inkling of stories about his presence, he began to disturb the new flight cadets. Word passed swiftly, as such things are wont to expand with a rush, that the flight line itself was haunted and that taking up any airplane was now dangerous because of interference by the ghost.

Headquarters at Montrose then made it official policy to brief each new arrival with a full report on the Montrose ghost, as this figure had become known, so that the neophyte cadets would not be frightened into the kind of apprehension that would affect their flying.

That seemed to do it properly. The ghost appeared with decreasing frequency. He might still be found in odd buildings at night, but his presence appeared weaker and weaker, and at times he was but a ghostly remnant of his phantom self. And then the war ended, the station personnel rushed off to home or assignment to more permanent bases, and Montrose, while still active, eased into a much more comfortable routine...

Until the next year after the war, which was four years after the vituperative lieutenant had died in such dramatic fashion. By now the ghost was hardly even a memory. Those who knew of him best were gone. There seemed no one left to carry on the tradition of even talking about the ghost. That is, until 1946, when there arrived at Montrose for some "long awaited quiet duty" a battle-hardened veteran of heavy combat in Europe and through much of the Far East.

For some reason one of the station personnel saw fit to pass on to the newcomer the ghostly tales of the dead pilot and his murky appearances in the operational area of Montrose. The replacement laughed off the stories and lost no time in heaping ridicule on those who believed in such "errant foolishness." Then came the night when he was posted to aerodrome security patrol.

Security teams patrolled the aerodrome. Two men to each team, well armed, walked through the airfield perimeter, through the hangars and maintenance shops, and along the flight line or any other area where aircraft might be parked. The hangars were hardly a favorite of the security teams, especially if the men carried with them the unsettling stories of the Montrose ghost. This was hardly the friendliest thought nudging at a man as he moved through and past the great gloomy structures—because to get to the hangars from the flight line, the security patrols also were under orders to stop at and thoroughly check the security of the *morgue*. The fact of the matter was that even those guards who considered the Montrose ghost as so much spit and bosh hastened their steps in this area. All save the grizzled veteran recently arrived at the field.

The patrols' orders on this particular night in 1946 included a thorough security check of a new aircraft landed just that afternoon, parked near the control tower but coincidentally directly opposite the unpleasant morgue.

At approximately three o'clock in the morning the security team, including the new replacement, stood quietly by the parked aircraft. The field was quiet, no one moving about, most lights out except for the beacon and perimeter lights; the two men took the moment for a smoke, cigarettes cupped in their hands to conceal even this tiny spark of light. But not by an aircraft; that was a serious offense. They selected a deserted area well clear of any structures where fire might be a danger. The old-timer remained by the aircraft as his security mate slipped away.

Now the veteran stood alone in the shadows of the parked aircraft. He heard several strange sounds; weapon at the ready, he spun about to the source. The morgue, but—*They had just checked the morgue.* Tried every door and window, in fact. As the security man studied the morgue and the strange sounds, the front doors burst open as if hurled apart.

No question of what was happening with all that ruckus and the doors banging full open! The *locked* doors—

A figure rushed from the shadows, becoming clearer, more distinct to the eye with each second that it advanced. A pilot, fully clothed in his flight suit, wearing leather helmet and goggles standing out starkly against a face of dead white.

The new guard found his battle-experienced limbs failing to respond to a sudden overwhelming urge to flee. The pilot, solid as a rock before him, advanced steadily. The guard, knees locked in place and his arms frozen, stared with widening eyes and gaping mouth, then heard his own rifle thunk against the ground and tumble with a clatter as it left his unfeeling hand.

Trying desperately to speak, his wits a block of ice, the guard finally stumbled to his rifle and clutched it with desperate fingers. The figure still advanced! No question now—it was a pilot with a face of white chalk. The sentry stood erect—

A tremendous BANG! sounded from the morgue as the doors slammed shut. At the same moment the figure of the pilot vanished.

"What the 'ell was that?" The other sentry had returned to free the old veteran for his cigarette break. Slowly the sentry who'd seen and heard the doors, the sounds, and the white-faced pilot, shook his head. He shrugged. "The wind, lad. Must've been the wind."

He never told the other guard. He kept his silence on the incident. Perhaps the other men had played a hoax on him. But in the middle of the night? And no one mentioned anything.

Until some years later. Posted to another station, the veteran encountered a man who had also at one time been stationed at Montrose. Playing it as cool as he could, the older man leaned forward to his new friend. "You ever hear anything strange about Montrose?"

The other man smiled. "Almost everything's strange about Montrose. Especially that bloody morgue."

"Tell me."

"It was back in forty-two. Some lieutenant, a nasty bugger by his reputation, had a run-in with a fitter working on his machine. Put the poor fellow on report and all that. Well, the next morning this same lieutenant, he's ready for a flight, but first he has some business in the morgue, of all places to go before going aloft. Anyway, he's in the morgue, and he loses his temper at somebody and throws a fit, and then he kicks open the morgue doors and stomps his way in his flying gear out to his machine. Straight as an arrow it was, parked by the control tower."

The older man sat rock still. "And what happened then?"

"Well, he gets into his bird, fires her up, and takes off. But not for long. He was still over the runway when the ship rolled over and straight into the ground. Killed him soundly."

The older man still hadn't pieced it all together. "But why would he have gone to the morgue before his flight? Seems a nasty thing to do before—"

"Oh, it wasn't the morgue *then*. Um, back in 1942, right? It was the operations shack then. I've heard stories that his ghost shows up every now and then, you know, right from that old building to his plane on the line. You ever hear anything like that?"

But there's a third matter about Montrose. It is also the site of the most famous ghost story of the First World War—the only ghost story that received the official recognition of the British government. It has been investigated by government and scientific groups, and the name of the dead pilot has been kept alive on Montrose's official registry.

The story begins innocently enough—no, that's the wrong choice of words. There was nothing innocent about it. It began on the 27th of May, 1913. Lieutenant Desmond L. Arthur, a black-haired, intense Irishman from County Clare, was aloft over Montrose in a BE-2 biplane. Suddenly, without warning, his machine "folded up" in flight directly over the airfield to plunge Arthur to his death. It wasn't a typical training crash, for Desmond Arthur had been a certificated pilot since June of 1912, when he completed his trials flying a British monoplane at an airfield south of London, after which he was posted to Montrose.

The BE-2 collapse and crash were witnessed by dozens, perhaps hundreds, of people. Trainees watched as Desmond Arthur, flying at four thousand feet, initiated his descent to land. They heard the seventy-horsepower engine throttle back and saw the airplane begin a series of wide and gentle turns to come down. Then, at twenty-five hundred feet above the field, the upper right wing of the BE-2 snapped. Struts cracked free, the wing tore itself upward, destroying all lift and control, and in an instant what had been an airplane became a mass of disintegrating wreckage moving in tumbling, spasmodic jerks in its downward plunge. So wild were these gyrations that the seat belt securing Arthur to the airplane snapped in two. An instant later his body was hurled from the falling plane. Horrified witnesses watched the twitching form drop like a stone, arms and legs moving frantically but helplessly. Desmond Arthur died instantly, almost every bone in his body smashed when he struck the ground.

Training accidents were hardly unique in those days. But this pilot was experienced, and the machine was being flown in gentle turns. Immediately the Accidents Investigation Committee of the Royal Aero Club arrived at Montrose, soon issuing an official report that the wing had broken because of an incompetent repair. The mechanic—or fitter—was unknown, but a regrettable accident soon became considered grisly murder. Unauthorized repair work had been carried out. It had not only left uncorrected a broken spar; but the break was covered with new fabric, concealed from the pilot, and never reported in any maintenance log.

It was not to be the first investigation, but three years would pass before the issue of the collapsed BE-2 wing and the death of Desmond Arthur once again occupied the attention of British authorities.

Desmond L. Arthur was dead, he had died uselessly, and that was that. War raged in Europe, and Montrose buzzed with new students taking flight instruction. The instructors lived in the older mess, among many new buildings, which was the original home of the Number 2 Squadron of Desmond Arthur. The students, sneeringly referred to by the instructors as Huns because they broke airplanes faster than the Germans could shoot them down, lived in an expansive, new, and comfortable mess.

Now it was the fall of 1916. A senior staff officer, Major Cyril Foggin, was returning to the old mess. He noticed another officer in full flying gear walking just before him on the path. The pilot walked steadily before Major Foggin, who did not recognize him in the evening gloom and shadows. Foggin saw the pilot reach the mess door, *but he did not open it.* Moments later Foggin reached the door himself and touched the handle. *No one else was there.* The pilot had not opened the door, and he hadn't walked either left or right; he would have been in full view of Foggin the entire time. The major stopped; he was sharp, alert, and intelligent. He tried to accept the appearance of the pilot as nothing more than his own imagination, or a hallucination, then shook his head. He was solid, and he was pragmatic, and that was that. He accepted simply that he *had* witnessed somebody, or something; and that he, or it, had vanished in a manner impossible under those circumstances for any human being.

Several days went by without sign of anything unusual, and Major Foggin finally decided that he'd yield to the greater possibilities of imagination rather than believe in an apparition.

World War I fighter

Martin Caidin Archives

Then it happened again. Just as Foggin was about to reach the mess door, there was the other pilot, walking as before, right up to "that damned door and then vanishing." Foggin had a great wrestling match with himself, and in the end decided not to make any official report of what he had seen. It would not do for a responsible senior officer to see ghosts ambling about; such senior officers invariably are removed for extensive psychological probing and receive the boot from their post.

Major Cyril Foggin need not have worried. He kept his own counsel, but other officers began seeing the same phantom pilot! At first they also kept quiet. In the rarer instances when two men had both seen the ghost, they kept their murmurings to themselves.

But that which was kept subdued continued to spread. A senior flight instructor, sound asleep one night after a full day aloft, came awake with a start. Something woke him. He sat bolt upright and stared at a chair at the foot of the bed. There, visible in the light of the room's open stove, was a man in flight gear, seated comfortably in the chair. The instructor, as flight instructors are wont to do, asked in his own dulcet fashion: "And who the bloody hell are you, and what the hell are you doing here?"

No answer; the instructor moved from his bed, and the seated pilot vanished.

Other pilots were wakened. Some rooms had fireplaces, others stoves with open grates so that there was always some light in the rooms. The ghostly figure appeared only in the old Number 2 Mess, where Desmond Arthur had lived three years before.

Then the ghost, now known as the Irish Apparition, or simply as the Montrose ghost because word spread swiftly and far beyond Montrose Airfield, began to appear in other parts of the facility. By now most senior officers had seen the ghostly pilot, and this fact figures strongly in the events that followed.

During the long night hours, several men on guard duty had been frightened silly, had challenged a pilot appearing out of nowhere, and had watched the pilot flicker out of sight. The guards ran for their lives. In short, they abandoned their guard posts, which in any man's army is a criminal action with severe penalties.

When the reports were filed, and the reason for fleeing guard post was given as the sudden appearance of the ghost, all charges were dropped.

The stories spread swiftly through the entire Royal Flying Corps, not only in the home islands but throughout the world. As such stories are invariably subject to expansion, they became distorted, and the details often grossly twisted. Those embellishments do not concern us here, but what is important is that several senior officers and highly trained investigators threw themselves into the now-turbulent waters. The issue of men facing guard post desertion charges was not a light matter, nor did the senior staff find it easy to ignore several pilots who virtually demanded transfer from Montrose because of the now-persistent and frightening ghost.

Certain meaningful facts began to emerge. At this juncture no one had connected the ghostly pilot with any pilot *by name.* It was…just a ghostly pilot, if one may forgive the easy slap of the word "just" in this case. But the question became an issue. What had brought the ghost to appear *now?*

Then someone put two and two together. The editor of a British flying magazine who had known most of the people in the RFC, which was in 1913 still something more of a country club than a war machine, pointed out the link they were all seeking. The name of Lieutenant Desmond L. Arthur leapt to prominence. He had been killed in 1913, he had received a funeral with full military honors, and that had been that. But in the summer of 1916 an official investigation concluded that Lieutenant Arthur had died from his own incompetence rather than due to the negligence of a mechanic. This report had in effect smeared the honor of Lieutenant Arthur and tainted his name.

The story of the ghost began to fall together. Lieutenant Arthur had been killed in 1913. Then, in mid-1916, his name was sullied, and he was, even in death, accused of incompetent flying and of causing his own death. *It was then that the Montrose ghost appeared*—as if the slur of the investigation compelled him to make some defense of his honor.

Investigative teams now lashed out at the review boards that apparently had so unfairly castigated the memory of Lieutenant Arthur. A final report once and for all confirmed the damaged wing and vindicated the memory of Flight Lieutenant Desmond L. Arthur. On 17 January 1917 the Irish Apparition made his final appearance, and for the remainder of the war, through November 1918, the only bodies seen moving at Montrose were satisfyingly corporeal.

That seemed the end of it, all the pieces of the puzzle tidily arranged in their final resting places. The Royal Air Force (formerly the Royal Flying Corps) retained Montrose as a training facility, and officially the case was closed.

No one to this day knows for sure *who* had continued to haunt Montrose. For many years afterward, for decades, nothing was heard about the departed soul of Lieutenant Arthur. Then came the incident of 1940, when the Hurricane pilot searching at night for a Heinkel bomber made frantic gorounds because of a mysterious biplane that "cut him off on final landing approach" several times, a biplane that no one other than the pilot saw or heard. *That* incident seemed to fade away with time.

Came the crash on takeoff in 1942 of a flight officer, and the appearance soon afterward of the "new" ghost in World War II flight gear; bursting through the doors of what had been a morgue, and stalking out to where his aircraft had been parked. The similarities were a bit throat tightening. Both Lieutenant Arthur and the pilot killed in 1942 (whose name has yet to be found in released records) died because of their aircraft being rigged, either accidentally or deliberately, by ground crews.

Now it is 1949, and Montrose continues as a permanent training duty station. Among the newcomers assigned to Montrose in 1949 is Eric Simpson. He and the other new arrivals are stunned by their official greeting. "On arrival," he reported later; "along with our 'arrival chits,' we received a printed document welcoming us to the station and telling us the camp was haunted by the youngest ghost in the Royal Air Force, an officer named Flight Lieutenant Arthur."

The ghost was back. This time dozens of people saw the apparition, among them a Scottish clerk on early-morning duty hours "scared out of my wits" when he woke up to find himself staring at an officer in white flight suit and an officer's hat. "He was standing by a desk and quite immersed in rifling through some papers," he was later to explain.

He also explained why he was so terrified. He couldn't see any feet on the phantom figure, as though from the knees up the ghost was floating in air.

And then, at last, peace and quiet, at least in ghostly affairs. Until the 27th of May, 1963, *after Montrose had been closed for several years.*

His name was Sir Peter Masefield, one of the best-known figures of aviation in the United Kingdom. On May 27th of 1963, taking advantage of unexpectedly beautiful spring weather, Masefield was flying his personal Chipmunk, a single-engine, low-winged monoplane generally accepted as one of the finest types of its class in the world. His route from Dalcross to Shoreham brought him close to the now-abandoned airfield of Montrose. Masefield knew Montrose well, and he warmed to the thought of seeing the field from which he had once flown. He eased into a gentle turn and was soon flying along the seashore, cruising at twenty-five hundred feet. Well ahead of him, the old runways took form. He thought of the tens of thousands of takeoffs and landings of the past, and how swiftly an abandoned field becomes lifeless.

Ahead of Masefield there appeared another plane. He judged it to be at his own altitude and was surprised to see an unusually shaped biplane. Not that biplanes were rare in England; many of the flying clubs banged about in the old de Havillands and other machines. But this was no ordinary biplane. He looked with great surprise and some disbelief, for he was closing rapidly on a truly ancient machine—a seventy-horsepower BE-2 trainer that the Royal Flying Corps had placed in use *before World War I.*

Sir Masefield flew close enough to the other machine to see that the pilot was wearing a leather helmet and goggles, and the flying scarf so popular in ancient flying days. For a few moments he wondered if the BE-2 had been a rebuild project; flying enthusiasts were rebuilding all sorts of machines these days from past wars, but Masefield had never heard of anyone getting one of these rattletraps back into the air.

And then there was no more thinking about the origin of the clattering old biplane. In a scene that appeared so unreal it moved as if in slow motion, the outer part of the upper right wing appeared to break within the structure. The outer wing section lifted like a loosely flapping rag. The entire right upper wing followed in the same manner, wrenching free of its strut supports. Immediately the ancient BE-2 whirled crazily, out of control, the wind hurling about the tangling mass of structure and fabric. The aircraft staggered suddenly and, out of control, fell, twisting and spinning, almost straight down to crash on the abandoned Montrose aerodrome.

Shaken by what he'd seen, helpless to offer any aid from aloft, Sir Peter Masefield dove earthward and set up a frantic short landing on a long golf-course green that paralleled the old airfield. He shut down his engine and dashed from the Chipmunk, shouting to several players on the green to come to his aid. For several moments they stared at Sir Peter. No one had seen the plane crash, but, urged on by Sir Peter's sharp insistence, they hurried across the field to the crash site.

There was no wreckage. There was neither a BE-2 nor the crushed remains of any airplane.

As Sir Peter Masefield related the specific details of what he had seen from the air; and what he had failed to find on the ground, he repeated that he *had* seen the airplane collapse in flight, *had* seen it crash, *had* seen the dust thrown up by the impact. Later he did some checking. And perhaps there is an explanation for what happened that day.

What Masefield witnessed was precisely what is to be read in the findings of the Accidents Investigation Committee of the Royal Aero Club, dated 2 and 10 June 1913. Almost fifty years to the day before Masefield's flight—on 27 May 1913—the BE-2 biplane of Lieutenant Desmond L. Arthur folded its upper right wing and plummeted to the ground.

Montrose Aerodrome remains closed.

Piper Aztec

Chapter 5

=MOMENTS OUT OF TIME AND PLACE

ome of the best flying ever done takes place when the weather is for garbage. Either thunderstorms are pounding the countryside, or the clouds are so low the ducks are walking, or the world's a sheet of ice. Whatever the cause, it's that time when the experienced pilots recall the adage that *It's far better to be down here, wishing you were up there, than to be up there and wishing you were down here.*

There's just no fun in flying down a dark tunnel of vicious turbulence so wild you can't control your airplane, and your instruments have gone haywire, and you know your ship is on the edge of structural breakup, and you're gathering ice on the wings and about your engine intakes, and the controls keep getting stiffer and heavier. That's the time you keep in mind your friends who have their own private plot of ground and a granite headstone, because they were flying in weather that sends birds spinning and tumbling out of control, and too many of them didn't make it. Some of them don't even have headstones—there wasn't enough left of them to bury. Sometimes we never found *anything* to bury.

Just memories.

41

This, then, is the time for hangar flying. The old pros gather in the hangar or in the "war room," sprawled on the old couches and easy chairs, and it's time for beer and some hard stuff, and the room fills with cigar smoke and with stories that keep the newer and younger pilots hanging on every word. Hangar flying is also one of the best means of learning right from wrong in flying, how to get out of killer situations; doing the things that only hard experience can teach. It's been a bedrock of flying from Day One.

Now there's an important point to make here. When pilots get together for hangar flying or an all-night riproarer session, and the good scotch flows, and the smoke is so thick you could cut it with a rusty beer-can opener, they do *not,* as most nonpilots believe, spend their time reliving past amorous conquests. That's for the birds and the ground lovers.

And if there is one thing pilots do *not* do, the real pilots, anyway, is to relate to the group just how good or great they are, or how skilled they are. That's the *last* thing they'd ever get into. In fact, real life is just the opposite. What pilots talk about is how they screwed up. How they did everything *wrong* and somehow still survived. If there's any kind of contest, it's really about who's been the greatest screwup of all.

The first time someone gets up to play the fool and announce his skills and ability, the room rumbles down to a deadly silence, and the only place left for that idiot is through the door and *out*. That's the way it is.

In a sense, it's probably a good thing very few nonpilots are admitted to these sessions. If those of you who aren't pilots heard what went on so often up front in the cockpit or in the flight deck, your blood would run cold, and you'd never fly again!

But something else happens. Something very special. After a while the hoorahs die away, and the hysterical stories of these guys nearly killing themselves are ended, and a strange soberness comes into the room and affects these men (and women) in a quiet and respectful mood.

They begin to relate to one another past events, former flights, and "strange" moments and incidents that defy explanation. It takes a lot for these pilots to let down their hair (what's left of it, anyway) and admit to frailties they would never admit to anyone save other pilots. Sometimes there's proof of what they say; the events speak for themselves in photographs or witnesses or wreckage. Oftentimes proof is only in the speaking, but the people listening are pros with tremendous experience in flight, and they can pick out the bushwah instantly. When you're talking about what's happened to you in flight, or about a flight, or on the ground at an airport, any teller of tall tales doesn't stand a chance. He might as well be wearing a neon sign on his forehead that shrieks, LIAR!

There's the old saw that it's pretty dumb to try to con a con man. The only dumber thing I know of is someone trying to hand an experienced pilot a line of crap. It just doesn't cut it.

Not all such moments earn the position of a long story. Not all of them can fill a chapter. Some of these moments cover periods of days or even years, and they deserve space commensurate with the story itself. Others are quiet, contemplative, and they'll ice your spine.

And they do. Oh, my, sometimes that ice is damned cold.

Because sometimes they talk about ghosts. Phantoms and apparitions. Things that cannot possibly happen, but *do* happen, and to hell with those who won't believe.

The rule I've discovered in a long lifetime of driving fabric and iron through the skies is that the term *ghost* means different things to different people. To most people a ghost is a visitation by an ethereal figure, sometimes opaque, more often than not transparent, or sometimes never seen, and the reference is to someone who's died and inexplicably is "still here" to haunt a place, a structure, a person, or a group of people.

So it's time to corner the badger. *What is a ghost?*

Hell, I don't know.

I don't have to know. Nor do I have to understand that the term *ghost* doesn't fit certain moments and events that have happened not only to my friends, but to me as well. A "ghost voice," for example, is far more common to the world of flight than a literal visitation by an icy presence, visible or not.

Not too many people will admit to having experienced a ghost voice, or a supernatural event, or having heard a bodiless voice. Okay; my name's on this book as author. Do I stand up to be counted and say some of these things have happened to me?

You're damned right they have.

So before I get into a bit more explanatory material, which I'm itching to place before the reader, let me admit to one such event. I must preface this incident by saying that, mixed in with the stories of ghosts, who won't let certain scenarios end, that defy all "rational explanation," are mysteries so profound and astounding they appear to have no reasonable, rational, or other explanation other than *they happened*. Here we enter a

category of related events that mix in with so-called "ghost stories," with
the spirits and phantoms of the worlds that exist in sidereal fashion with
ours. The only way to tell these stories, to relate the events and incidents
of so many pilots, is to tell them as they are, with as much foundation as
to time, place, numbers, dates, and other such information.

And remember this: when it comes to tales that chill a man's blood, a
pilot will rarely, if ever, relate that event to anyone else who's not a pilot.

We have a basic rule by which we live. No matter what we *say* to
other people, no matter what we tell or relate or expound to anyone else,
that counts only when you're on the ground. You can tell tall tales all day
long on the ground, but you can't do it in the air, most especially when
you're at the controls.

We can entertain anyone on the ground, *but if a man lies to his airplane, it will kill him.*

Deader than hell.

THE VOICE

The years 1963 and 1964 were "good flying times." My logbooks showed
a bunch of spamcans including the Colt, Tri-Pacer, a bunch of Cherokees,
the Comanche and Twin Comanche, the Apache and the Aztec, some wild
flying in Pawnees, and a lot of banging around in the venerable J-3 Cub
and its bigger cousin, the PA-18. Then there were the Beech machines;
Debonair, Bonanza, Twin Bonanza, Musketeer, and the squirrely C-45G.
I ran up a lot of cross-country work in a string of Cessnas: 172, 175, 182,
180, the twin 310, and its Riley Rocket conversion, which was a real goer.

In between I got some great time in the Moraine-Saulnier MS-760 twin
jet, bounced around in a Luscombe 8-A on floats, did some good cross-
country work in a B-17G Flying Fortress, got in some heavy here-to-there
in an air force C-47 and a C-54G. Some of the best flying was a C-130B
Hercules to Europe and tooling around the continent in that bird. Then turning back the clock and flying a North American B-25N Mitchell over to
England, where I flew that airplane in the film *633 Squadron*, got in some
great movie flying in a couple of Messerschmitts, flew a Helio U-10 with
the air commandos back in the states, and, well, a bunch of great flying.

With a few moments of everything going to hell in a hand basket, like
deadsticking a Messerschmitt into a pig field in Virginia. And having a
Skylane engine blow up and start to burn over Highway U.S. 1 in Rock-
ledge, Florida, and landing on that highway in the evening rush hour, skid-

ding over gravel into the front lawn of the Garden Court Motel. We left behind us a trail of cars and trucks in ditches and elsewhere. Having an airplane with a flaming engine race through all that traffic in the dark is wont to panic drivers; so is rolling a tire off a car roof before touching down with a trail of fire and smoke behind us. To say nothing of the motel manager who looked outside his window to see an airplane's wingtip inches from his bathroom.

Strangely enough, the names of people involved in this little fracas carry over to the event that calls for our interest. When I put that Skylane down amidst all the hustle and bustle of the highway, the man riding the backseat of the airplane was Zack Strickland of the National Aeronautics and Space Administration (NASA). In the front right seat was an IBM missile engineer. We were all part of a group that banged about the airways local to Cape Canaveral. And after the uproar and the appearance of the state police and assorted other officials, a station wagon drove up with Eddie Keyes behind the wheel.

Eddie Keyes and I were longtime flying buddies. He had been flying forever. He flew C-47 transports in Burma in World War II, and he flew the civilian edition of the DC-3 after the Big Deuce was over. He flew fighters, transports, bombers, liaison and training ships. He was a flight instructor and a crop duster and a mechanic. Hydraulic fluid ran in his veins, and engine oil lubed his joints. He could fix anything with a few pieces of wire and some tin cans and masking tape. He was flying personified.

I'm going to delay getting to the all-important date of 13 September 1964 for a moment's digression. Eddie Keyes was also that kind of man to whom you'd never pay a moment's attention. He stood five feet eight, weighed about 160 pounds, and unless you studied his eyes very carefully, you saw nothing unusual. But if you knew how to look into the deep pools behind his eyes, you felt you were looking somewhere forever.

Eddie at one time was a civilian contract flight instructor for the air force, working out of Spence field in Georgia. Part of our gang at one time or another had flown at Spence, and I used to punch up there every now and then to spend time with world-renowned aerobatic pilot, Bevo Howard.

Even the other pilots found the quiet and affable Eddie "just a bit more special" than anyone else. And there *was* something special, something different, about Eddie Keyes. It's difficult if not impossible to put it into words; he was just—well, special. He made you feel that way when you were with him.

Came a night when Eddie was instructing a student in T-28 cross-country work. The students liked Eddie for night instruction. They knew he'd spent a couple years in Tibet, high in the far mountains, after the war and before returning to the states. Eddie considered himself just quiet; the others considered it contemplation.

On this night the stars seemed to hang lower in the clear, dark sky. One of those nights when you can see just as many stars, and just as clearly, from a cockpit as you can through the viewport of a spaceship in earth orbit. (You don't believe that? Ask the astronauts and cosmonauts who've done both; you'll be surprised at their agreement with what I just said.)

The student, quiet for an hour as he flew his course, notched his intercom. "Sir, what was that?"

Eddie had been in one of his "contemplations," as close to sleep as you can get, but just short of zombie time. He hadn't said anything, but he had *heard* a voice.

"I didn't say anything," he called to his student. "Why did you say for us to land?"

The student was puzzled. "I heard you say it, sir."

"What did I say?" Eddie asked, absolutely alert now.

"Why, you said just one word, sir. Land."

"The hell I did. I thought you said it."

"No, sir."

Eddie had heard the voice. It said, "Land." That was all.

The student had heard the voice saying, "Land." That was all he heard. Neither man had spoken.

For Eddie Keyes that was the fire bell, the tornado siren, and the earthquake warning all rolled up into one.

"I've got it!" he called over his intercom. In that time he'd already picked out the alternating white-green-white-green flashing beacon of an airport, and he hauled that T-28 over on one wing and chopped power and shoved the stick forward, diving hellbent for leather for that field. Nothing happened save their crazy dive. Eddie didn't care; he knew better. He leveled out, dropped the gear and flaps, and flashed over the runway boundary, and perhaps a few inches off the runway, just as the wheels were about to touch, the engine of that T-28 *exploded*. I don't mean it started to burn; it exploded in a huge gout of spewing wreckage and flames.

Eddie stood on the brakes, and as they ground to a stop, he had his parachute harness off and his shoulder and seat belts free and the canopy

T-28

Fred L. Wolff Archives

coming back, and he'd told his student to do the same, and Eddie shouted, "Out! Run like hell!"

They hit the wing and dropped to the ground and they both ran like hell, and behind them the T-28 tanks let go, and a huge fireball mushroomed into the sky, and Eddie and his student, flat on the grass beyond the edge of the runway, stared at one another, and Eddie smiled.

Now it's a good many years later, and we're at thirteen thousand feet on another one of those "you can see clear to the next galaxy" nights. Just plain, wonderful, magnificent. I'm flying from the left seat, and our bird is a red-and-white Piper Aztec, N5196Y. Eddie's in the right seat, and Zack Strickland once again is in the back, only this time he's sound asleep.

It is 13 September 1964, and we took the Aztec from Merritt Island, Florida, to Las Vegas, Nevada, spent a couple of days having a great spree of shows and dinners on the Strip, and we're coming home with a few bucks more than when we landed at McCarran Field in Vegas. We flew from Vegas to Grand Junction, and now we were on our leg from Grand Junction to Wichita to meet up with Jim Yarnell and Jim Greenwood of Beech Aircraft.

It was just past eleven P.M., the best I remember the time, but I do remember clearly that we were passing over Dodge City. It sparkled and flashed as power lines and trees interrupted lights, and we could see the tiny white and red dots of traffic on Highway 50, and Dodge City passed beneath us and slipped behind.

Eddie rustled a flight chart looking for the tower frequency at Wichita. The cabin light was red, and he had trouble finding the numbers. "What's tower at Wichita?" he asked.

"How the hell do I know? I live in Florida."

"Jeez, a real helper. Give me some light."

I reached above and behind me for the ceiling-mounted cabin light. I never had a chance to move the switch.

"What?" Eddie asked.

"What what?" I shot back.

"You just said something."

"Didn't say a thing. You said give me some light, and then you said turn right."

"No, I didn't."

"You asked for the cabin light?"

"Yep. But that's all. *You* said to turn right."

"I didn't say *anything*," I told him.

We looked at one another, we both glanced back at Strickland, who snored away blissfully, we looked again at one another, and Eddie said, very quietly, "Holy shit."

Everything else seemed the result of long practice; we both did the same thing at the same moment and with perfect timing. Neither one of us had said to turn right. *Someone said it,* and it wasn't us, and sure as hell it wasn't Zack, so—

We both tramped right rudder and banged the yokes over to the right and hauled the yokes back in our stomachs and as Eddie hit the props for flat pitch, I shoved the throttles forward, and the Aztec sounded like she screamed, and we hauled around in a wicked right turn under full bore. Zack was bounced about in the back and came awake with the side of his face mashed against a window, and it took him several seconds to realize the horizon was a vertical line, and then it rolled back to an even keel and seemed to raise up a bit as Eddie and I dropped the nose a bit for some extra speed, for what, we didn't know. But we were doing it.

That voice said to turn right, and we by God turned right.

Piper Aztec

Fred L. Wolff Archives

Then a glow appeared about the airplane. A golden glow that spread to the interior of the cabin through the windows. A gorgeous pure golden light in a huge bowl about us. And the light stretched from the southern horizon to the north as, right where we would have been had we continued on our course, a huge flaming object hurtled down from the sky and plugged into the earth far below.

Right where we would have been...

Eddie and I didn't need a guidebook to tell us what was coming next. We chopped power and raised the nose to bleed off our speed, and the shock wave hit us like a truck, and the airplane calmed down and trembled a bit like a dog shaking off water, and we looked down, and that golden light was gone, and we came in with power and turned back on course.

"You see it good?" Eddie asked.

"Yeah," I said.

"What the hell's going on? Why'd we turn? What the hell was that thing?" The questions poured from Zack like nickels from a slot-machine jackpot. We ignored him.

"You thinking what I'm thinking?" Eddie asked.

"Uh-huh. That was no meteorite."

"You got it. Meteorites don't burn with a yellow orange carbon flame," Eddie said.

"You see that solid flat surface?" I asked. "Looked like burning metal."

"It was," Eddie replied.

Something had come out of space. Most likely it was something very big that had been boosted into orbit either by us or the Russians, and we were right there at reentry.

I called Dodge City radio, identified ourselves, and announced a pilot report. "Go ahead," Dodge told me.

"We were pretty close to a flaming object a few minutes ago. We're just east of Dodge at thirteen thousand. Shook us up a bit with the shock wave."

"You guys just pass directly over the city?"

"That's affirmative."

"We're sure glad to talk to you. The way your course looked, it was coming down straight through you."

"Yeah," I said. "You get any other pilot reports?"

"Mister, that thing was seen in fourteen states, from Canada all the way down to Mexico. We got a call from NORAD flashed to all stations in this area. Meteorite.

"Thanks. We're going on to Wichita, landing there."

"Have a good flight. And watch out for rocks. Dodge out."

"Meteorite, hell," Eddie said.

"I know," I answered.

"Who the hell told you guys to turn before that thing came down?" Zack shouted from behind us.

Eddie never could pass up an opportunity. Not to tweak is to Eddie an unpardonable sin.

"I think it was Mrs. God," he said.

By the time I landed at Wichita, Zack had already wiped out half a bottle of scotch he yanked from his luggage. He was creamed. We couldn't blame him.

Postscript, I suppose, is called for.

What was that voice? Where did it come from? Who said to turn right? Three people in the Aztec; none of us said it. The radios were turned down, so that source was eliminated. That left only a voice from somewhere. Neither Eddie nor I could swear whether we heard the instruction, *"Turn right,"* as a spoken signal, or if we'd heard the words within our heads. We just don't know.

But we do know that if we hadn't made that turn, that was the end of the trip for all of us. *Forever.*

Second postscript. Zack Strickland is no longer with us. He moved from his NASA position at Cape Canaveral to take up new duties at NASA's center in Houston. Cancer nailed him, hard and dirty, and he came apart physically. No man should have to die like that. Eddie and I talked about that. Anybody with Zack Strickland's infectious grin and laugh should have gone swift and clean.

Same postscript winding up. Eddie Keyes is no longer with us. Some years back he figured it was time for him to get his own farm up north in New York State or maybe New England. I heard from him every now and then, standing in snow up to his ass and grinning out of his photo. He loved the farm and he kept an old airplane in a cow pasture behind his house and his barn, and he flew as easily as you or I walk across a room.

Then I received a phone call from his wife. "Eddie's dead," she told me. "He asked I call you before anybody else."

"How, Lil?"

"He had a heart attack. Oh, he survived it fine, just like he's survived everything else. But the doctor told him he'd damaged a heart muscle. Also told Eddie he'd live at least another twenty or thirty years, but—" I knew the "but" before she said another word.

"But he couldn't smoke or drink or fly anymore," she finished. "Eddie looked at the doctor. 'You call that living?' he asked him. The doctor just shook his head and left the room."

The rest of it came out a bit tougher. But I knew it before Lil told me. Eddie called his wife to his bedside. "Kiss me good-bye, Lil," he told her. Then he folded his arms across his chest, closed his eyes, and stopped his heart. He died. The emergency team came bursting into the room.

"Don't bother," Lil told them. "He's on a trip." She paused. No flight plan, I guess.

Like Eddie said about Zack: "No man should have to die like that."

Swift and clean. He did.

On the 27th of March, 1989, I received a letter from Headquarters, United States Air Force. It had been sent to me by Major General H. N. Campbell, USAF, Assistant DCS/Log and Engineering.

In part, General Campbell was responding to a request I'd made for input for this book. He stressed: "While I don't have any personal involvement, here's a story you may find of some value."

Before I quote that letter exactly, without changing a word, I recommend you consider the source and especially the people to whom the general refers in his letter. It speaks so well for itself, it requires no further comment from me.

The general wrote:

At Korat, in 1970, several of us got involved with discussing the Edgar Cayce concepts of "many lives..." which, as I'm sure you know, Dick Bach has written about extremely effectively both in short stories and with *Jonathan Livingston Seagull, The Bridge Across Forever,* and other works. In any event, one of the discussions we had was whether or not past lives lead in any way to present lives, with the concept being that if you didn't learn all you were supposed to in the past life, then you would have to come back on earth in some future incarnation and do it all over again.

One of the young officers who was working for me at the time was Captain Robert F. Tyler. He told me this story. "I was stationed in F-100s in the United Kingdom right out of pilot training, and like all good fighter pilots liked to make the rounds of English pubs. One night, shortly before closing, I had an uncontrollable urge to go outside and into a local English cemetery. To this day I don't know why, because I don't like cemeteries, and especially wouldn't normally go to one at night. In any event, I was drawn outside and found myself looking at headstones in the moonlight. In fact, I was unerringly drawn to one particular headstone...which read...*Flt. Lt. Robert F. Tyler, RAF, downed flying Spitfires during the Battle of Britain, 15 Sept 1940."* At this point Bob looked me in the eye and said, "Sir, I don't know about this 'many lives' stuff, but I was born 15 September 1940."

Flight Lieutenant Robert F. Tyler, RAF, died 15 September 1940.

Captain Robert F. Tyler, USAF, "unerringly drawn to one particular headstone." Of Robert F. Tyler.

As General Campbell concluded: "Kinda grips you a little bit."

"As a civilian pilot I had a haunting experience in June of 1979…"

So begins a report sent directly to me by G. T. McDowall of Decatur, Illinois. A story straight and to the point, with the conclusion being a perplexed, puzzled, and frustrated pilot—who was alive only because of an experience he could not explain.

McDowall spent part of the summer of 1979 helping his daughter move into a newly purchased home in West Palm Beach, Florida. "It was an older house, and I worked sixteen hours a day painting, hanging windows, doing fix-it work; whatever I could do to put the place in shape. After a period of some pretty intense work, I needed to return to my home in Illinois.

"I departed West Palm Beach—Palm Beach International was the airport—at six o'clock in the morning. Despite the heavy work load of the previous days, I got started with only about five hours of sleep.

"I managed to fly as far north as Ocala and then ran straight into a cold front complete with thunderstorms—a sky full of high winds, some really bad turbulence, and lightning on all quadrants. No place for me; I put down at Ocala Airport. There I waited until the front passed. I took off again, this time heading more westerly than I had originally intended, since Nashville, on my original route, was reporting severe weather. I always play it as safe as I can. Or I did until this day. I was fighting twenty-mile-per-hour head winds, and by nightfall I was in southern Kentucky dead tired and hungry. I landed at a small airport to refuel and get something to eat. Well, I got the fuel, but as for food, all I could find were some potato chips. I was so hungry, I devoured them."

McDowall was flying a Cessna 177 Cardinal; he owned the aircraft. His total flight time logged was just over seven hundred hours, of which three hundred were in the Cardinal, which had brought him to high proficiency in that particular model. The aircraft registration was N2911X, the Cardinal was manufactured in December of 1967.

McDowall had been flying a lot longer than his aircraft. His seven-hundred-plus hours as pilot in command had been gathered slowly, "flying on and off," since 1936. The Cardinal at the time of this flight had a total time for aircraft and engine each of twelve hundred hours.

Back in 1940 McDowall had undergone a mastoidectomy; to compensate for a hearing problem, he always wore a headset when flying. In 1979 he was fifty-six years of age.

"My radios in the Cardinal were an ARC 360-channel transceiver, and a Narco Escort 110 transceiver. I usually alternated VOR [navigation homing] between the two sets."

In Kentucky, with plenty of fuel for his airplane but precious little for himself, McDowall took off for Illinois.

"After I took off, I realized I wasn't really capable of riding a bicycle, to say nothing of flying an airplane!" He found himself flying erratically, drifting off course, unable to maintain his altitude. In short, he was so dangerously low on body energy, he had become an accident looking for a place to happen, and he knew he was in deep trouble. Then—

"Voices. There were voices. They talked to me. I don't know where they came from, but I heard them, and they gave me instructions and no nonsense about it. 'Get the left wing up…your heading is off five degrees; correct your heading…you are climbing; ease the yoke forward, ease it forward, settle down at your cruise altitude…change tanks; change tanks! that's it, go to the fullest tank…you're drifting out of radio range; tune in the next omni…' It went on like that for several hours.

"What do you say about such a thing? Of course I considered what I was hearing might be implanted thoughts following me, coming to the mental surface, so to speak, as I needed them. But that's the least realistic of all the scenarios I considered. So I considered the different possibilities. The voices that came out of nowhere. My own thoughts, but I don't think much of *that*. Or perhaps it was mere comedy that guided me all the way to a landing at Decatur, my original destination. What I do know is that it was like something was instructing my mind to tell my body what to do. I can't say with positive or absolute assurance I actually 'heard' those voices, but those commands were there, and they saved my life.

"I recalled, later, the same sort of thing in Charles Lindbergh's book, *The Spirit of Saint Louis*. He went through a similar experience.

"In all the years I've been flying since 1936 I have never had such an experience, before or since. I was so baffled by what had happened, I talked to dozens of experienced pilots, trying to find someone with whom I could share the same experience. No such luck. I was pretty much alone with this thing.

"I even went so far as to try to duplicate the situation, and I went on several long cross-country flights at night, hoping that what had happened to me so clearly might happen again.

"It never did.

"But I'm here, and I'm alive, because of those voices. That's good enough for me."

"Mr. Caidin, this isn't a ghost story, with wraiths floating about or rattling chains in the night, but a ghost tale might be more realistic and easier to accept. I suppose you can spell the word *accept* as *believe.* I've been putting off getting these details to you. Two steps forward and three steps back; that sort of hesitancy. And, as I say, this isn't your typical ghost story, if there is such a thing, but I've *got* to recount something so unusual that happened to me

I went through a long self-argument as to its reality. It is. I have no explanation of what happened, and until now I've told only one other person of the incident, the owner of the Cessna 152 I was flying at the time. He had purchased this aircraft new and had always kept it in first-class condition.

"Now, I've identified myself to you by name and address and my signature, as you requested, to the material sent to you. But I must request that you please do not identify me by name. I have no desire to be dragged off kicking and screaming against my will to the funny farm."

Okay. I've verified the person, his home address, his business, his pilot's certificate, the aircraft registration, the airport from which this man flies; everything I required to accept an incident when the individual involved requests anonymity. Here goes—

"On the evening of 26 September 1981, about 7:15 P.M., I took off from Butter Valley Airport at Bally, Pennsylvania, made a left turn to stay in the pattern, and followed Pennsylvania Route 100 to Bechtelsville. There I made a right turn of ninety degrees to take up my heading for Fleetwood. It was a Saturday night, and as usual in this area, I found the sky to be deserted; I did not see any other aircraft, either directly or through lights of strobes. Great flying. I loafed along, the engine turning at its usual twenty-three hundred RPM, when all hell broke loose.

"Without any warning of any kind, the aircraft began to vibrate like a giant tuning fork. The noise was so wildly high-pitched and the pain in my ears so intense, I clapped my hands against my ears and found myself screaming from the pain.

"I fought like crazy to keep my senses about me. My ears felt as if ice picks were jammed into them, and I had to struggle to see. I gave it everything I had, especially trying to *think.* My first impression, or conclusion, or belief—anything coherent—was that the engine was about to seize up, that it was on the edge of tearing itself to pieces. Immediately I went through a scan of all the instruments. I checked RPMs, oil pressure, engine temperature, fuel, mixture, carburetor heat—*anything* and everything.

"It wasn't until I fought hard to *think* about what was happening that I realized I was barely able to read the instruments. I wasn't just hearing that terrible noise, I was feeling it; and then I realized that not only was the Cessna vibrating like a giant tuning fork—*but so was I!*

"The instruments read in the green, everything where it was supposed to be. Some time had passed, the pain was still driving me mad, but I realized that now I could hear the engine. Another reality coming home. Sitting in a 152 isn't exactly quiet; that engine sound occupies much of your senses, and I'd never heard it through the vibrations and the pain.

"I was still afraid this thing was about to disintegrate in midair. What the hell; I'd never *been* a tuning fork before, had never been in an airplane vibrating like one, I hurt like crazy, and I felt anything could happen. I throttled back to twenty-one hundred RPM and started a *very* sedate 180-degree turn, meanwhile doing my best to keep up a good sky scan. No other aircraft anywhere. I flew back to the airport at reduced power and speed, made the most tender and precise approach I've ever flown, and put that bird down as gently and carefully as I could. When those tires squealed beneath me, I almost shouted with relief.

"Now I could start some real thinking. I taxied down to the parking area, shut down the airplane, climbed out, and tied her securely. I took a couple of deep breaths, got a powerful flashlight, and began a meticulous inspection of that bird from prop hub to tail. I was certain I'd find a hell of a lot of popped rivets in the wings. Wrong! The wings were perfect to this inspection. No missing rivets, no skin wrinkles, no deformation that could be seen. The same was true for the rest of the airplane. I began to wonder just how real had been that experience in flight, but I didn't wonder long. It was the first time I'd ever done a ground inspection in almost complete silence. I didn't regain my hearing for another hour.

"I got to the 152's owner as soon as I could. I left a note in the airplane that it was absolutely not to be flown until the owner checked it out and certified it as airworthy. The owner wasn't any once-around-the-pattern pilot. He had been a B-17 pilot in Europe during the Second World War. He was discharged but returned to combat flying when he was recalled to fight in the Korean War. After that stretch he flew as a four-striper, a captain, for Eastern Airlines until he retired. He was a magnificent pilot, but he was also more than that. He had his ratings as an airframe and power-plant mechanic and as an inspector. He was big-time *all* the way.

"When we got together, I related my tale of terror. I didn't leave out anything but told it just like it had happened, including my incredible pain and that wild tuning-fork vibration. The owner considered everything I told him, asked me a long series of questions. The only answer he could come up with was the possibility of some clown in a jet helicopter coming down on top of me, and his powerful downwash blasting the Cessna. Well, we had to discard that nifty theory. The air had been absolutely still. I'd lost no altitude during the incident. Since I was cruising at a steady course and altitude, a chopper whacking me with his downwash would have produced a change in my altitude—like, *down,* man—and I would have experienced turbulence and an indication of such downwash and altitude change from my instruments.

"Anything else? Well, there weren't any other aircraft I could see anywhere. That goes for flying saucers, too.

"We came up with—nothing. No answers, no explanations, no parallels—*zippo*.

"The amazing thing, to me at least, was that despite the fact that I was in terrible pain, and actually screamed, the scream was a reflex action, and it was gone quickly. An outburst, and that was all from me. Otherwise, as I reviewed everything that had happened, what amazed me was that I had otherwise been monumentally cool. I was calm and collected throughout. I imagine that I had immediately, perhaps automatically, accepted the fact that the plane was going to come apart in midair, that there wasn't diddly I could do about it, so why go ape? I sat there *detached* from imminent death and quite literally just waited for it to happen. I was so cool, you could have used me for a skating rink.

"Oh, we've thought of different possibilities, but from the outset, once we eliminated other planes, or a helicopter or even something so bizarre as a flying saucer, we were left strictly with what happened. We still haven't found, after years of searching, any other experience like it.

"Being at a complete loss to explain something so violent, so painful, and so far out of the norm, well, it's a damned *helpless* feeling."

Author's note: File under Unique, Bizarre, *Unexplained.*

World War I Spad fighters

World War I Fokker aircraft

Chapter 6

=THE GHOST THAT COULD NOT BE

S eptember of 1927 settled comfortably, like a blanket of late-afternoon sun and early mists, over the beautiful medieval walled city of Toruń. A city on the right bank of the river Vistula, nearly midway between Poland's capital, Warsaw, to the southeast, and the great port of Gdansk, standing to the north. Despite the devastation of a terrible war ended only eight years before, for a youngster of fourteen the world was rosy and really quite beautiful.

"Past destruction, terrible numbers of dead and wounded notwithstanding, the past was past. In the air you could almost feel a spirit of optimism. It was like the sun, rising so sparkling and clear, growing stronger as it lifted above, heating up a fervent drive to the future. Everywhere you went, you encountered young and old rebuilding a country *unified*. Everyone cherished, clasped to themselves, the independence gained after the end of the world war in 1918. For one hundred and fifty years, terrible devastation had been the lot of my country under the occupying boots of Prussia, Austria, and Russia.

"But that, I always reminded myself in those days, was behind us. Now a new life burgeoned all about me. And outside the walled city, beyond the modem western suburb, was a great and marvelous magnet— our airfield!

"Aviation, like me, was very young…"

So began a very special report sent to me from a marvelously ageless veteran of a lifetime in flight, Captain Tad Galler of Beeton, Ontario, Canada. It is a wonderful telling of a tale, as true and venerable as the man whose story has remained undiminished and unchanged for well over fifty years.

At the time Tad Galler (member number 60771 of the Experimental Aircraft Association, as well as a multitude of other aviation organizations and groups) established contact with me, he was seventy-eight years of age, and he had "fifty-four years of flying under [his] belt." I call to the reader's attention, once again, the tremendous experience of the pilots, aircrew, and other members of the fraternity of flight who have contributed to this book. They are men who have paid their dues, who have survived incredible dangers in the air, who are with us today because of their incredible skills and experience. Remember the adage of flight: no matter what you say to anyone else, if you lie to your airplane, it will kill you. The element of truth, the unshakable strength of veracity, the hard line of pragmatism, define these people.

To those who stand back and harp and criticize, who know so very little themselves and are so dingily devoid of freedom of mind and thought, well, they have denied themselves much of the wonder of this fraternity that soars so high and so far above our world. We will meet Tad Galler again in these pages, but for now rejoin him in this unexpected and startling tale of the "ghost that could not be."

From what I felt and had read at this young age (continues Captain Tad Galler), I knew that for millennia man had dreamed of flying like a bird. Only recently, within just the last few decades, Lilienthal and the Wright brothers had realized the dream. Five months ago the great American pilot, Charles Lindbergh, had flown solo across the Atlantic from New York to Paris. These things I knew. As a fourteen-year old, what could *I* do? How could I participate in these dreams come true?

Well, I did what I believe many youngsters do who are so interested in flying. I built model airplanes. Whenever possible I sneaked away to the airfield. In those early days of aviation, in my part of the world, flying

World War I British fighter

Fred L. Wolff Archives

was a military affair. But surely not to despair; in six or maybe in five years I could be a fighter pilot, like my heroes, the fighter pilots of the squadron based at our airfield.

Today, reaching my seventy-eighth year, and with fifty-four years of flying under my belt, I still wonder from what source I draw the drive and my continuing admiration of everything to do with the flying of airplanes.

Back then I had a friend and fellow classmate, Stan Sidor, no less keen on flying than I was. His father had an administrative job at the base, and through him Stan and I learned the names of all the prominent "aces" based on the field. I must add that my admiration was silent. None of the pilots knew me nor the feelings I harbored.

The line fighter plane for the squadron was the Spad 61. In the training flights, however, we had an assortment of other fighters on hand. These were Nieuports, Caudrons, Morans, Henriots, and Balillas.

With the exception of the Morans, they were biplanes. All were tail draggers and powered with engines ranging from 150 to 450 horsepower. The Italian Balilla had the worst look of them all. Up front there protruded an ungainly mooselike nose. The wings, thin and seemingly too small, were almost frightening. Stan confided to me that the flying reputation of this machine wasn't much better than its looks. The pilots considered it to be a tricky plane to fly. Many of them secretly feared the aircraft; their reasoning was sound.

Toward the end of the First World War, not so different from today, actually, aerotechnologists were hard at work producing air superiority fighters. In the old days much of the design work was a result of trial and error. Today three-dimensional computer analysis is employed. One aerodynamic observation made by the Italians was that the lesser the angle of attack of the wing (and the airplane), the faster the plane flew. Another observation was that the thinner the wing, the less drag it generated, which translated into still more speed.

Putting these observations into a single package led them to create the Balilla fighter. It was a daring aeronautical experiment with thin wings bolted to the fuselage at a minus one-half of a degree angle of incidence. The resulting consequences of this arrangement were left for the pilot to savor. As it turned out, the Balilla was indeed a swift machine, and many European nations were buying the fighter to bolster their military power in the uneasy postwar world.

Yet back then, just as today, there is no free lunch. The ruthless and clever design of the Balilla extolled a grim price. The Balilla was extremely unstable in the roll axis. I believe this instability was so bad that even a small pilot error in rudder action, or yaw, would produce a split-lift condition. This is a killer, because you suddenly have one wing with positive lift and the other with negative lift. Often the pilot who "slammed" into this condition had no time to counter the effect. Before he could react, the Balilla would roll violently and whirl into a fast and wicked spin. In calm air, or even moderate turbulence, it was possible, barely so, for the pilot to regain control through corrective action. But in anything even approaching severe turbulence, regaining control was flatly impossible.

That meant a machine that whirled wildly all the way down into the ground, and one very dead pilot. In those days parachutes were not standard issue. Ironically, the next year, 1928, parachutes were introduced to the squadrons. Quite literally as lifesavers.

My parents and I lived in the western suburbs of the city on the main thoroughfare. Two kilometers farther west lay the airfield. Our house itself was well secluded and some distance from the side of the road. On the ground floor lived the owner, an architect, and on the second floor were two apartments, one of them ours. In front of the house was a small garden, and in front of the garden, a larger yard in which youngsters gathered to play.

On one side was a large fence separating the yard from a lane leading to the street. On the other side of the lane stood a tall building that had once been a warehouse. The architect, over time, had transformed this warehouse into a building that was quite admired by the townspeople. It now housed a row of miniature storerooms, a laundry, a rest room, and on the far end a stable for the horses owned by the architect. In each door of this renovated building, just at eye level, was a little round window not unlike the portholes of a ship.

Now we come to Tuesday, 20 September 1927, a day with a slow and almost reluctant dawning beneath a thick, high overcast that obscured the sky. Clearly a blustery day was in the offing. A strong wind driving from the west whirled the still-green leaves in clusters. To me there was no doubt that the first major storm of the fall was brewing in the western approaches of Europe.

The night before I had a dream...

Usually in a dream the details are distorted and unclear. Even familiar surroundings are not quite the same. What I had dreamed, however, was very clear, and the surroundings were not in the least disturbed or distorted. In the dream I was leaving the house on my way to school. The day was like the morning, gray and blustery. As I was turning around after closing the door, my eyes caught the silhouette of a person crossing our yard. As I turned to get a better look, I was startled by the way the person moved. Dressed in a flying suit, unusually crumpled, he *floated* rather than walked.

My thoughts were racing furiously. What on earth was a pilot doing in our front yard! At that moment the pilot went right through the wooden door of our little storeroom. I felt a sensation of horror of horrors. The pilot had gone through the wooden door without opening it! That put my hair on end, and I stood terrified on the doorstep.

Through the little round windows in the doors of the storerooms, I could see that whatever or whoever it was, it turned right, and then moved through the inside walls of the other storerooms and the laundry, and before reaching the stable turned through the front wall right back into the yard. It hesitated a moment and then turned right at me.

It was Lieutenant Duchniewski. I stood there terrified, unable to move. I could see the face so clearly! A great chill engulfed me. I awoke with a jolt. My heart pounding, cold sweat on my back. With relief I saw my mother standing over me, alarmed, asking what was causing me so much pain.

I shook my head. "Nothing is hurting me, Mother," I said as quickly as I could after swallowing several times. "I saw a ghost."

Alarm grew on my mother's face. "What ghost? Tell me! Quickly!"

"The ghost of Lieutenant Duchniewski," I told her.

"Who is Lieutenant Duchniewski? Do you know him? Does he know you? When did he die?"

"Oh, no, Mother," I said quickly to stem the questions. "He isn't dead at all. He's very much *alive*."

She stared at me. "Where did you meet this man?"

"I haven't *met* him. You see," I explained, "last Friday, during the midmorning break at school, we heard the strains of music. It was Chopin's funeral march. Since it was still the beginning of the morning break, Stan and I ran to watch the passing of the cortege. It was very touching, and I remember thinking also how impressive it was. There was a large military band, and the drums up front were beating with a muffled sound. The coffin was mounted on the fuselage of a Moran fighter plane, with folded wings. All of it was covered in wreaths and flowers, and the carriage with the aircraft and the coffin was drawn by four pairs of horses.

"Behind the carriage walked the family members, relatives and friends, many of them crying. And behind them came officers and pilots of the air force. Stan told me the deceased was a very prominent navigator stationed at this base, who perished only last week in a terrible crash. It happened on takeoff when the engine suddenly failed. And only the navigator died. The pilot survived, and he's in the hospital now and will recover from his injuries. As we watched the funeral, Stan and I saw the familiar faces of the pilots who were passing. Every one of them *but one* was familiar to me. I asked Stan if he knew who this man was, and he told me that this was Lieutenant Duchniewski, who was posted to our base only two weeks ago."

My mother watched me in silence for several minutes. "So Lieutenant Duchniewski is alive," she said finally.

I nodded. "Yes, but then how could I have seen his ghost? A man who is alive can't have a ghost!" I was still obviously upset and absolutely convinced I had seen the ghost of this pilot.

"Listen to me, Tad," my mother said gently. "You did not see a ghost. I don't know what you saw. Now ghosts do exist, but they are of dead people, some of them dead only recently, some from centuries past, even millennia. That does not apply to what you saw. Put it out of your thoughts." With those words my mother left, wishing me a good rest for the remaining two hours of the night.

The rest of the night was untroubled, and in the morning I was off to school at my usual time. The school itself was in the crowded old city, but the gymnasium and the sports field, my destination that morning, were in my suburb. It didn't take me long to reach the gymnasium. Stan wasn't there because of a minor bicycle accident the previous night. He was off visiting the school nurse, a prerequisite to participating in the sports activities following any injury. After fifteen minutes of calisthenics, our instructor declared we would all practice the high jump.

While waiting for practice to start, I heard the faint drone of an aircraft engine; it was barely audible above the wind blowing through the trees bordering the sports field. The drone faded and strengthened as the wind gusted. Then the engine roar came in clear and strong. Under the high overcast I saw an aircraft approaching from the west

A Balilla; no mistaking that ugly thin-winged stump of a fighter. I estimated its height at about two thousand feet above ground. Then it was coming right over me. In spite of its altitude, I could see that the Balilla was bucking rolling, and pitching in the turbulent winds, likely much worse at altitude than on the ground.

The voice of our gym instructor brought me suddenly to earth. "Tad, don't stare into the sky! Can't you see the high-jump bar is missing? Go and bring it from the gym. On the double!"

I sprinted to the gym, grabbed the bar, and began running back. I was running but couldn't keep my eyes from looking upward where I had last seen the Balilla, and I looked ahead of its flight path to try to see it again.

My heart beat madly, just like last night in the dream. The Balilla was in a whirling, angry spin no more than twice the height of the spire of the nearby garrison church.

In seconds the Balilla disappeared from my sight. Several seconds passed before I heard a muffled thud.

I was screaming, *"Aircraft crash! Aircraft crash!"* as I ran madly back to my instructor and schoolmates. They looked at me first, then toward where I was pointing.

Nothing unusual could be seen, but at least our instructor had also been alert. "Tad, I also saw a plane fly overhead. Maybe a minute ago." He looked puzzled. "But no one saw or heard a crash."

"I saw it!" I yelled, my voice defiant. "I *saw* it and I *heard* it!" I kept shouting.

"Enough, Tad," my instructor warned. "Join the others."

Well, we went through the high-jump exercises, but my performance was very poor. I couldn't get my mind off that plane spinning down and what *had* to be a fatal impact.

A half hour went by, and Stan appeared, limping slightly and accompanied by another student. Our instructor showed his concern about Stan. "What took you so long at the infirmary?"

"I apologize, sir," Stan replied. "But there was no helping the delay."

"Tell us why."

"You don't know?" I stared at Stan. "There was a terrible airplane crash near the garrison church."

Now, everyone stared *at me*. How had I known? We had all been together, and I was the only one who knew anything about the crash.

I had the strangest feeling as I walked up to Stan. "Did you find out who was the pilot?"

He nodded. "Yes."

I knew the answer before I spoke the words myself. "It was Lieutenant Duchniewski," I said.

"But...but how could you know that?" Stan stammered.

I shrugged. What could I say? "I just knew," I said lamely, and turned away.

That night I discussed what had happened with my mother. "How could I have seen his ghost when he was still alive? How could I have known what would happen? And why did his ghost come *to me*?" I rattled questions one after the other to my mother.

Lile was simple in those days. Things happened. They didn't always have answers. My questions didn't.

My mother held my hand. "A prayer for the soul that's gone, Tad. A prayer for the lieutenant. Something strange, something even wonderful, happened to you. But now, you offer a prayer for his soul.

"That is all that anyone can do."

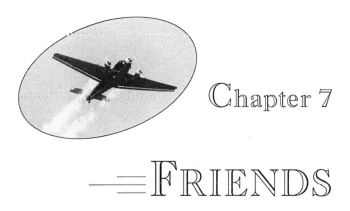

Chapter 7

═FRIENDS

oincidence is a marvelous stroke. Out of the midnight blue it brings together people of similar natures—often if they're in the same line of interest, with mutual friends. Then there are those times when you establish a new contact, but it turns out your paths have crossed years before, and in the most unique or peculiar ways.

For more than a year I had been hot on the trail of a "paranormal event in flying." That's how it was first described to me, and that's enough of an igniter to get a good blaze roaring. "There's this pilot down in the Miami area," friends told me. "He's about eighty years old, and he's still making commercial runs. You ought to find him."

There are only several tens of thousands of pilots "down in the Miami area." Finding one man who remained nameless ought to be a snap, right?

It was! In fact, Captain Robert J. Hanley, the man I was seeking, *found me*. If I was writing a book titled *Coincidences of the Air*, this would be one of the prime chapters.

I'd heard that in Bob Hanley's incredible, truly incredible, flying career, and its hundreds of great moments and unique events, there were two specific moments that would demand being captured for these pages.

I passed the word among my crowd in Miami, from Frank Quentin Ray at Page Aero (who was a lead figure in rebuilding my three-engined Junkers Ju-52/3m German bomber, and who knew *everybody*) to Phil Paxton out of Okeechobee, because Phil has flown (literally) hundreds, maybe thousands, of airplanes throughout the world on delivery and demonstration flights, and if Phil doesn't know someone, they sure as hell know him. Ray Martin raced around the ocean and island areas off the Miami coast and sometimes punched north and west in everything from luxury choppers to Lear jets, and since Ray and I had flown together in a couple of Messerschmitts and the Ju-52 (more affectionately known as Iron Annie), and Ray was in the charter business, he was a great bet to find one Robert J. Hanley.

After an enormous effort it all went to naught.

Bob Hanley found me without even knowing I was searching him out. Most of the aviation magazines and publications in the United States were kind enough to print notices and requests from me, explaining to their readers that *Ghosts of the Air* was in its research phase, and Hey! you guys and ladies out there, let's hear from you. Bob Hanley read one of those notices.

That started the roll of coincidence. Bob Hanley was and is a seaplane pilot, one of the grand masters of flying-boat skills and experience. I've done some water work in everything from jittery Luscombes on floats to Martin PBM Mariner boomers with everything from long-water takeoff runs to explosive leaps into the air, propelled by great banks of rockets on each side of the hull. More recently, in a venerable old Convair PBY-6A Catalina, a bird belonging to Connie Edwards of Big Spring, Texas, we'd done flying out of Oshkosh, Wisconsin, runways, off the waters of Lake Winnebago, and then on to Canada, the Azores, Portugal, Spain, England, and all the way back through Bermuda.

So the common thread was growing thicker between us, but I had no idea of just how marvelously far it would stretch. When I rebuilt my Ju-52 at Miami International Airport, I bought a bunch of engines and cowlings from Chalk Airways, right off the Grumman Mallard flying boats they used for commercial passengers flying out of Miami through the Bahamas and other points in Vacationland.

Then, before I even spoke to Bob Hanley, his first letter arrived.

"I've read a note about your forthcoming book that you plan to write—*Unusual Happenings*. And I've heard about what you're after, so I took the trouble to write down the details of two of those 'unusual happenings' that occurred in my flying career. I hope they will contribute to the work you're writing."

Martin Caidin and Iron Annie

photo by Cecil Stoughton

Bob Hanley, having been in the flying business forever and three days more, knew that a requirement of this book was verification. He didn't give me the opportunity to start that gristmill working, but wrote:

"I believe we have a mutual friend in Connie Edwards, who will attest to my honesty. In the eighteen years I owned and flew Catalina Channel Airlines, I landed in the open sea for some kind of record forty-four thousand seven hundred and fifty-four crossings to and from Catalina in flying boats...and that's without any accident of any kind."

Read that again. A total of 44,754 landings in the open sea in flying boats during a period of eighteen years with a perfect safety record! And that doesn't include another forty years and more of flying and landing in landplanes and other seaplanes throughout the world.

Bob Hanley has the knack of saying something quietly and leaving you short of breath. In his first letter he gave me a cut-to-the-bone capsule of some flying background.

"I soloed in 1926, and I've flown for Eastern Air Transport and Pan American Airways. I have extensive test pilot experience with Chance Vought, Seversky, Vultee, and Douglas."

If you hear a ringing in your ears, it's just the sound of the opening bell. When he first wrote me on 14 April 1989, Bob Hanley was one month short of his eightieth birthday. Right behind that word was the added note that not only was Hanley selling and flying amphibian aircraft for Amphibian Sales, Incorporated, in Miami, but he was also still flying Douglas DC-9 twin-jet airliners and the huge four-engine DC-8 jetliners.

He added a fillip at the end of his first letter: "I did have the pleasure of meeting you several times."

Well, that was nice. But when? Where? How? Hanley's next letter filled in the gaps:

"I promise you more stories in the future, especially along the lines of those eighteen years of flying to Catalina and doing all those landings in the open sea with no accidents, I might add, like yourself in the Ju-52. Speaking of your Ju-52 German bomber, and those engines you purchased from Chalk, I went with Jerry Dobby to Frakes to help select your engines. You, of course, may not remember, but you took me with you through the Ju-52 when you were based at Merritt Island, and we shared experiences, you on the Junkers, and I with my Ford Tri-Motor experiences."

Before getting into two separate "Friends" incidents of Captain Robert J. Hanley ("Friends" could just as aptly be titled "Voices"), share with me a brief look into that long and eventful life in flying. Consider his incredible flight record, his vast expanse of experience, and then, when someone questions what people like Bob Hanley say in absolute frankness and integrity, keep in mind that Hanley was there, and the others weren't anywhere but on their backsides, harping like chattering birds.

"My first solo flight," Hanley recalls, "was accidental. It was accidental because I was doing a fast taxi in an OX-5 Swallow when I guess I was taxiing just a bit too fast and maybe I hit a bump or something, but the next thing I knew that Swallow was going up, and the earth was falling away, and all I could do was *fly.* Very scary."

Soon after, notching hours steadily, Hanley was flying a Pitcairn Mail Wing biplane for an out-of-the-way airline and then transferred to Eastern Air Transport where the big thrill was flying Curtiss Kingbirds for eighteen months. Pan American Airways beckoned with an offer to get into

Bob Hanley

"different" flying, and Hanley was soon at the controls for Pan American flying boats.

This was the mid-1920s, and Hanley, a tall and ruggedly handsome man with piercing blue eyes, was approached by one of the best-known (if not most popular) businessmen in Florida. Hanley had gone to Saint Catherine

School in downtown Miami with another youngster; the two became fast school friends. With school behind them his friend, Frank, showed curiosity about Hanley's flying.

"You any good?" Frank asked.

"*Very* good," Hanley answered immediately. "You, ah, got lottsa time?"

Hanley's eyes locked on Frank. "Hundreds of hours. Maybe thousands," he boasted. He was fast and cocky, and he'd do whatever he needed to get into flying for a living, and he knew Frank's family was not only wealthy but powerful, and *that* spelled connections and flying. So he didn't add that he really had just about one hundred hours.

"My old man's having a pool party, you know, over at the Palm Island house? You come over tonight. My old man wants to talk to you."

Bob Hanley was there right on time. Frank's father took him aside. "So, you fly an airplane, right? Would you like to fly for us?"

Hanley looked Al Capone straight in the eye, just as he'd done with his son, Frank. "You bet," Hanley said.

"Okay. You set yourself up early by going by boat to the Bahamas. Then you go to West End, Freeport, *at night.* You can land and take off from the water in the dark? Good. We load up the airplane with the hard stuff, and you fly it right here to One Hundred Twenty-fifth Street in Biscayne Bay."

Hanley's career in seaplanes was launched. This was 1926, prohibition was the big brouhaha of the day, and "everyone, it seemed, was moving liquor and making a fortune," Hanley recalled. He had one slight problem; he was still only seventeen years old! Little matter; the next day he was "at work." He took the Bahamas ferry-type service from Miami for the five-hour run to West End. When night fell, he was in knee-length boots, leather helmet, scarf and goggles, and loading native whiskey, the bottles wrapped in straw and burlap, into the single-engine Commandaire biplane on floats. As soon as he checked to be sure no police were about, he fired up the airplane, took off on a long run in the dark, and one hour and ten minutes later he was tying up the Commandaire at 125th Street. He helped unload twenty-six cases of whiskey, his average load.

He was paid $26 per case or $676 for the delivery flight, and that is a whopping figure for a seventeen-year-old in 1926! Hanley was still attending high school, and to his friends he had all the heroic stature of an astronaut today. Soon he had several thousand dollars stuffed under his mattress at home—and then came that infamous cry of "Look out!"

He had just landed at 125th Street and sat comfortably on the top wing of the floatplane as servants unloaded the whiskey. Then a whistle blew shrilly, and someone yelled "Look out!" and another voice called to Hanley, "Get out! Get the hell outta here!"

Hanley dropped into the cockpit, the servants shoved the floatplane into the bay, Hanley fired up the engine and had just managed to get airborne when the coast guard blasted away at him. He skimmed inches above the coast guard ship. He had it made; he could easily have flown back to Freeport and obscurity on the island. But he was ticked off, and he banked tightly and with full power dived at the coast guard to buzz the boat. Big mistake; Hanley turned with the city's lights behind him silhouetting the plane, the gunners got a clear shot, and a heavy rifle slug tore into Hanley's leg. *Now,* his boot pooling his blood, he turned for Freeport.

He didn't make it. Shock and loss of blood worked quickly, and Hanley passed out in the air. By some incredible set of circumstances, whatever they were, and nobody knows, the airplane flew down to a landing in a mangrove swamp several miles from Freeport. When Capone's men got there, they found Hanley still unconscious and the Commandaire safely on floats—the engine still idling. They dragged Hanley from the cockpit and rushed him by speedboat to a secret Capone base in the Bahamas. No one suspected that the wrecked and "abandoned" cement boat lying off Bimini was a huge distillery, a packaging plant, a weapons cache, and a hospital. Hanley made it, stinking of blood and whiskey, and he came to with a doctor holding up the rifle slug for him to see.

As soon as he could walk, he was back in the air for Capone, this time flying Model 71-C Fairchilds with special loads out of the Bahamas and dropping in skillfully on short makeshift runways in the Everglades. He was making so much money now, he didn't have room to hide the cash under his mattress and instead buried it.

He was still going to high school five days a week during all this flying, getting top grades, and during evenings and weekends knocking off the delivery flights. Finally, after more than eighty trips for Capone (and some real derring-do sessions as well), he graduated from high school. It was time to bail out. He made his peace and parting from Capone, gathered up his earnings, now a sizable fortune, and used the rum-running money to finance his college education.

Bob Hanley prepared for me from his own records, logbooks, and other information he kept during his many years of flight, two separate "incidents," during which the reality we know in everyday life was put aside for the reality of the moment for him and the people who depended for their lives on Hanley's knowledge and skills. He titled each report; read it now as it came to me.

THE CATALINA VOICE

Pilots who have never related to the days when the only radio communications were the balky, intermittent, cranky, and often maddening low-frequency systems may regard this flight as something from the dinosaur age of flying. But it was the way the world went before superelectronics items came on the scene; it was the real and the *only* stuff of life, and flying under lousy weather conditions demanded knowledge and skills often missing in our bright young men of today.

Of course, some luck never hurt us then, just as it doesn't hurt today. But the past can and does teach. Often it teaches more than the mechanical acts of moving controls and judging your actions by what some gauges indicate to you. The point is, you can *always* learn something in almost everything you do.

A *long* time ago I flew as a lead pilot for the Amphibian Air Transport Company. Even the name seems antiquated, the sort of name you expect to see painted on a wooden board and swinging in the wind by the company office. But it was real enough. We were operating Grumman G-21 Goose aircraft, amphibians with two radial engines each, and the birds had bench seats that allowed you to stuff ten people in the cabin, or, if we were all a bit more candid than that, we carried whatever you could stuff through the door that we could get away with. Our route usually cut a line from Long Beach Airport to Catalina Island off the California coast. What a flight usually called for was an uneventful takeoff from Long Beach and then a most eventful landing in the water at Good Ole Avalon. It was always eventful because it was an open-sea landing that held—or concealed—the possibility of never being the same twice. You could always count on something unexpected that could snag you.

Yet we did it with persistence, safety, reliability that amazed even us, and the operation (against most predictions) earned money on a steady basis. The owners of the company must have been as much amazed as they were surprised when they found their coffers filling, so they decided to expand. They instituted another operation out of Burbank that offered close-in service to the Hollywood crowd that made Catalina Island a favorite for more damned hanky-panky than I believed was possible. But that was their game, and they played it to the hilt, and we were ready to wing them back and forth. The new operation went off with a bang—if you'll forgive the pun.

All this narrows down to a Sunday afternoon, in early autumn. The end of summer gave us a repetition of overcast skies and heavy cloud levels, but still retaining plenty of visibility. On this particular day we had a ceiling of eleven hundred feet. The cloud tops were reported to us as four thousand feet, but what counted was that we had eight miles visibility, and that's *great*. The kind of season's end with a peaceful Sunday.

Having operated out of Long Beach the entire day under the overcast, my last trip was from Long Beach for an "end of the day" pickup at Burbank. Going over the cloud deck wasn't usually a problem, but I was paying just a bit more attention to the weather because of clouds forming lower than usual, and in heavy concentration, in Cvenga Canyon; this was the canyon area between Hollywood and Burbank.

In short order our agent was loading ten eager passengers into the Goose. While we waited a bit for a ticket pickup, a young navy lieutenant came forward to me and asked if he could sit in the copilot seat. It's a privilege we usually provided for a guy who spent his own money on a ticket. I took stock of the man; young, small, junior lieutenant, and a pilot so new his wings were shiny enough to smart my eyes even through my sun shades! Damn, it made me feel *old*.

Well, everything got loaded, the cabin door was shut, and I got the signal to move out. We staggered off the ground from Burbank and shortly thereafter flew into the canyon. Everything normal, but damned sure not for long.

I noticed, with a bit of a start, that the cars along the highway were *higher* than the Goose. That's calculated to get your attention with a sharp snap. It dawned on me that these clouds had settled in a lot lower than I'd expected, and that something on the order of a "full instrument-flight climbout" had to be undertaken *real* soon.

At first I told myself, "Aw, hell, this is just a piece of cake for an old hand," and I was an old hand. The Goose had a good instrument panel, so for the few minutes it should take us to climb to the top of the cloud deck into clear air shouldn't present any problems. Just hold a steady climb of three hundred feet per minute, hold my course steady-on of 185 degrees to the island, contact Long Beach by radio, and the rest of it would be easy.

If things went the way they had in the past, Long Beach radio would approve a letdown through the overcast, and shortly thereafter I'd be able to see the island.

Then the old Murphy's Law went into effect. Whoever the hell Murphy was, he was also always right. *If anything bad could happen, it would happen.* And it damned well *did.* Climbing steadily and halfway up through that overcast, I noticed that the antenna wire that tied in to the insulator in front of the windshield was suddenly *loaded with ice.* The ice would shake violently and then burst away. That wasn't so bad, but then the entire windshield coated over with ice. I couldn't see a damn thing. I noticed my space cadet with the shiny new navy wings looking at me with a pale expression on his face, and it wasn't any reflection from the windshield.

We went upstairs a bit slower than I wanted, but that was to be expected, and we broke out into the clear with the altimeter pegged exactly at four thousand feet. That cloud layer, now below us, was absolutely flat as far as the eye could see. Not a lump anywhere; it looked as if it had been shaved by some giant razor blade. Now, I ask you to keep in mind these were the days of low-frequency radio, *and no radar* to get a dumb dude out of his stupid mistakes.

I realized suddenly I didn't have any radio. When that last chunk of ice tore away from the antenna, it took the antenna with it. I hadn't even seen it, I was paying so much attention to all the other ice forming on us. Now, how was I going to make radio contact with Long Beach? You need a working radio and antenna to do that. Mine had blown away with the wind from *Murphy's Law.*

So I told myself, aw, shucks, don't worry none. Fly your airplane, dude. Count just the minutes from Burbank to Long Beach. That's twenty minutes. Then from Long Beach to the island, it's only seventeen minutes more. Any air jock worth his salt could handle this one. Just figure the time from Burbank, that's twenty minutes, add another ten minutes, let down into the Catalina Channel, look for the island, and set up the landing. Nothing to it.

The thirty minutes went by. I began letting down, and we were swallowed up by the thick clouds. I played everything with absolutely tight attention. Another miserable five minutes in my descent, and the island would show. Piece of cake.

I was letting down on a bearing of 180 degrees when someone spoke to me. It took a moment to realize that was dumb. I still had on my earphones, *and they were dead.* Those phones blocked out all other voices.

But through the dead radio and the dead earphones, a voice spoke clearly to me: "Turn to nine zero degrees. *Turn now.*" That was crazy, but so was hearing the voice, and I don't know why I did what I was being told, but I rolled onto a heading of ninety degrees.

The shock hit me like ice water in my face when we broke through the clouds, the altimeter showing nine hundred feet. *Where the hell were we?*

Hills and mountains loomed all about, under and to the right of my wingtip. I was supposed to be over open water—that is, *if I'd followed my original course and flight plan.* Now, how the hell could hills and a mountain get under my right wing? Didn't I let down going to the *east?* According to my timing, if any hills were to show, they should have been the Palo Verde Hills on my *left.*

Well, the shock sort of settled in, and I kept flying, and I got another dose of figurative ice water in my face when I discovered Avalon *under the nose of the airplane.* Damn! Setting up the landing and taxiing to the dock was, frankly, pretty damned anticlimactic. The usual navy boy who greeted our flights waited on the dock for me. When I shut down the engines and the props quit, he dashed up to me and grabbed my hand and shook it wildly.

"Captain," he said with awe, "I'll never figure out how you knew when to descend and come into Catalina like you did. I've never seen such precision! And in this weather..." He shook his head and grinned. "It was like someone brought you in here right on the nose."

I stared at him and decided *not* to answer.

Now, want the epilogue to all this? Most pilots by now would be clamoring to know what went wrong. Well, you'll recall my saying how absolutely flat was that top of the cloud deck, right? It turned out later, when I researched every moment of my flight, that the tabletop flatness of the cloud layer had been caused by *a wind of seventy miles an hour from the north.*

And that wind had almost guaranteed that when I let down into the clouds, I would fly smack into Mount Arizaba, which reached to eighteen hundred feet.

I didn't hit the mountain because a voice in dead earphones, when I was flying absolutely blind, told me to *"Turn to nine zero degrees. Turn now."*

Where did that voice come from? That's where I run out of answers. The whole thing seemed impossible, but I'd heard the voice, *and I obeyed it.*

And whoever, whatever, spoke to me prevented the first air casualties on Catalina Island. If I hadn't turned, every one of us would have been dead.

Bob Hanley never found out any more about this flight than what you just read. But it wasn't the end of the "inexplicable." Hanley had friends that...well, that shouldn't have had any effect on what he was doing in his airplanes. But the fact of the matter is that he did have those friends, and there are few moments in the history of flight that are more compelling than what you're about to read in Bob Hanley's own words.

OLD FRIEND

Most pilots, especially the older guys with a great many hours behind them representing a hell of a lot of experience, have the wherewithal and the reality to weave tales intricate and fascinating, sometimes leaving their audience speechless.

Now, those of us who've been around the Horn a bunch of times usually select most carefully just what we'll tell to whom. It's one thing to relate mechanical details, or even harrowing moments of ice loading up a machine, or engine failure over the ocean, or being struck by lightning, or being on fire—that's the everyday working fare of the longtime pilot, and you really don't fuss much when it comes to whoever hears those stories.

But there are damned few pilots who will ever relate an ethereal happening, not just to the groundbound, but even to almost all other pilots, because of the reaction they might face. Odds are they won't be believed, except by other pilots who have faced these "impossible moments" themselves. Well, there come those times when to hell with disbelief and those who don't believe. They weren't there, they lack the knowledge or imagination to place themselves in other situations, so they don't count. And this particular telling, which either borders on the edge of unreality or steps far over its bounds *for the average person,* I must place in that category of "believe it or not." I was there, it happened to me, and *that* is what counts. I have no urge to deal with people whose blinders extend backwards from their eyes to squeeze their brains.

So, the memories of this event carry me back to the late 1940s when I earned my way through life as the captain in command of a four-engined Douglas DC-4 for a nonscheduled airline. The time of year is best described as *deep winter.* That means weather that not only concerns most pilots on regular or charter runs, but also means life-or-death situations. It spells ice on the wings, clouded and iced-up windshields, frigid cockpits, choking engines, metal becoming brittle, fuel lines clogging up, and being forced into wicked instrument approaches in high winds with blowing snow, in the dark, onto icy runways with absolutely *no* braking.

DC-4

Fun times.

Now to specifics. We flew out of Chicago with a solid load aboard the DC-4. Usually we made a "standard run" out of Chicago to Burbank, but the dispatcher gave us a destination change before we left. "It's Oakland, California, for you people," was his cheery departure. Hey, that was great. We delighted in the change because it broke an established ho-hum routine, and it also added additional pay for the extra stop on the way.

When I said we flew out of Chicago with a solid load aboard, I didn't mean crated cargo. I meant a solid load of *passengers*. The live kind, filling the seats. Our plane gave them a real sense of flight, for our DC-4 wasn't a new commercial model, but a surplus C-54 Skymaster converted to civilian passenger operations. She was a war-weary but tough old bird. We flew out of Chicago loaded right to the top numbers, and the DC-4 settled down to climb power and rose steadily to our cruising altitude of eleven thousand feet. There's something special about a plane that's been through the grind. This one had received a lot of super care and attention from her flight and ground crews. The engines were jewels. They *sounded* healthy, and that almost always means they are. Not a murmur or a kick or a miss all the way to our assigned altitude, and we eased back the power to long-range cruise and settled down for the route to Cheyenne, Fort Bridger, Salt Lake, Reno, and then into Oakland.

The DC-4 isn't anywhere near the size of the jetliners booming the flight lanes today, and like I say, we were a converted war-weary, but in addition to the crew, we had 120 passengers—live souls, as we say—aboard our bird. Being honest is a habit of mine, and I often thought about those passengers. Most of them felt a confidence in our trip that betrayed their anxiety to get to their destinations sooner than the old girl could carry them through the night.

Our present route took us along the airway known as Green Three, one of those invisible highways in the sky marked only by electronics and numbers. It also gave us, on this night, an "over the top" flight that put all the heavy snowstorms well beneath us. *That* was a lucky break for all concerned—airplane, crew, *and* passengers. Our view from the cockpit was its usual stunning night scene. It's strange to use that phrase, *usual stunning,* but that's just the way it really is. We didn't seem to be moving. We were suspended in night space, and the earth rolled slowly toward and beneath us, displaying its snowcapped mountains and a world of silver beneath a nearly full moon. It was incredible, the kind of sight you never really get accustomed to, but marvel at, and it's a sight not afforded to many mortals.

We settled down to the routine of eating up the miles, and the quiet set in. We drank a lot of coffee, called the flight-service stations along our route, and spoke to many invisible voices talking back to us by radio, and we also followed an erratic ADF—an automatic direction finger needle—to a destination ahead of us. The ADF was starting to be more erratic than it was automatic, and we all looked at the instrument readings with some automatic caution in our thinking.

This flight could hardly have been better. A machine purring like a contented big cat, the night, peaceful serenity, the weather well beneath us.

That's when Fate tosses in the cold dice.

One of the stewardesses rushed into the cockpit, her face showing alarm. Your first thought is that there's something wrong in the mechanical sense; not this time.

"Captain! One of our passengers has just passed out! It's a little Chinese girl. She's *very* pregnant and—"

"Where is she?" I broke in.

"In the middle of the cabin. On the floor. She's unconscious," came the staccato reply.

"You said very pregnant?"

"Yes, sir. And she looks terrible."

"You ask for a doctor?"

"Yes, sir." The stew showed her dismay. "None aboard, sir."

So I was suddenly smack in the middle of the emergency you read about that happens to someone else, but *never* to you. An unconscious, pregnant girl, passed out on the aisle floor, and no doctor aboard. *And* we were at eleven thousand feet—

"Take it down to nine thousand," I told my copilot.

"Got it," he confirmed. I was out of my seat like a shot and starting back into the cabin. As I ran down the aisle, I was wondering whether I had a dead girl on my hands or a young woman grievously ill. One could quickly lead to the other. But by starting down to our minimum safe altitude of nine thousand feet, we would at least increase both air pressure and oxygen content; that could be critical. I went back to the still form lying on the floor and found a tiny Chinese girl. I estimated her to be about twenty years old; unconscious and pale, she looked only half that age.

She was lying face up, and my stewardess was already applying oxygen from an emergency pressure bottle. One thing struck me that I remembered later. Her face coloring had the strangest even streaks, much like what I'd expect when looking at a multicolored venetian blind. I never did understand that. Anyway, what mattered at the moment was keeping her alive. The stewardess kept the oxygen under forced pressure to that tiny, helpless face, while I applied pressure to the sides of her chest, all the time exceedingly careful not to press against that mound that held her unborn child.

After that "eternity" of sweating it out, every bit of twenty minutes, she began to stir. Her eyes flickered. I call this sliding back to the edge of livability. And let me tell you, all of you, this is when a frightened pilot looks upward, and beyond, and unashamedly he says, *"Thanks."*

I returned to the cockpit. We were level at nine thousand; the copilot kept her right on the money. I eased back into my seat, and we established radio contact with the Fort Bridger flight station, telling them what had happened.

They asked us to stand by while they made an emergency call. "We recommend you divert for an emergency landing," Fort Bridger called back, "at Salt Lake. They've been notified, and they have confirmed a doctor and ambulance will be waiting for your passenger."

Until this moment I loved the weather for this flight. It was lousy down below, pure unadulterated rotten, but it was below us for the entire scheduled leg we were flying. Now, suddenly, rotten weather was reaching up to grab us.

From the ideal situation we enjoyed, we'd have to punch our way down to the airport at Salt Lake. Terrific. Five miles visibility, which wasn't bad, but the rest of it was going to hell in a handbasket. Blowing snow. Ceiling four hundred feet and liable to drop any moment. Poor or nonexistent braking on an icy runway. Oh, joy! Just what a pilot needs to round out a perfect emergency!

Then Salt Lake radio added to our joy. They warned us that the visibility in Diablo Canyon (damned well named, let me tell you), through which we had to fly, was *absolute zero*. We'd be flying blind in the true sense of the word, our existence depending upon instruments, an erratic navigation system, and just how well we performed.

Well, everything to this moment was part and parcel of a pilot's life. But here, now, hangs the absolutely serious, and the unbelievable—or call it miraculous—part of what happened. We cinched our straps, triple-checked all gauges and controls, and came smoothly to the Diablo Canyon marker, which signals the time to approach Salt Lake City. We contacted Salt Lake Tower and advised them we were leaving our altitude and initiating descent into the thick overcast.

In those days of flying, long before the marvelous "bells and whistles" of modern electronics, we flew by means of a low-frequency radio navigational approach reception, called "the beam." A pilot had to keep his aircraft in the center of the beam by coordinating the "null" of the merging signal letters constantly broadcast: an *A* and an *N* coded signal. When both of those transmissions came together, and you couldn't get the *A* or the *N,* you created the null, and you knew you were in the center of that beam that guided you straight to the transmitting station.

In the case of Salt Lake City, the transmitter was adjacent to the airport. It seems simple enough, but it wasn't. Unlike today's very high-frequency navigation systems that punch right through almost all weather situations, the old low-frequency beam could be and often was affected severely by static created from falling snow. I'll put it as simply as I can: falling snow turned a specific radio beam signal to hash. Screwed it up to useless noise.

The signal, when it did come through, wasn't steady or properly aligned any more. It could weave like a snake, and many an airplane followed that signal (because they had nothing else to use) and flew straight into a mountainside. You can count everybody dead in moments like that.

We had all that in mind as we rumbled down from the sky immersed in thick snow. By now we'd been on solid instruments for many minutes. We expected to be, we hoped we were, and we prayed we would be in, and would *stay* in, the center of Diablo Canyon. We were hanging on to that beam like a drowning man clutches a plank. The beam began to weave, and we didn't dare get far from the "null" part of the signal.

Suddenly someone spoke to me. Someone behind me, I guessed. "Bob, get over to the left." No question about it. I heard the man's voice. I *heard* it. Audible. Voice.

Now understand, with a sick girl in the cabin, descending through a real bitch of an instrument approach in horrible conditions, which I'd never tried before, keyed to explosive reaction by our emergency and any sudden change in our situation, I was *not* prepared for *anybody* ordering me to change my course of action!

Especially when the voice appeared to emanate from over my shoulder. The voice was interrupting my concentration of the flight instruments; I felt as if I'd been struck a physical blow. An old pilot friend stood by my side. A man I had spent many hours training to fly flying boats.

Harold Tucker. Unmistakable. We'd flown together too many hours not to notice every detail of his face.

Harold Tucker had been dead for many years.

Inside me I felt everything turning to ice. I gaped. He spoke again, this time his voice harsher, no-nonsense, and more commanding. *"Get over to the left!"* He almost snarled the words at me.

Then he was *gone.*

One instant there.

The next instant, not there.

My immediate reaction—and you cannot waste a second in a moment like this—was to react and to react properly. To me the only action was inevitable: fly to the *left* of the damned beam. I did, my heart pounding. My copilot thought I was mad. I stayed with it, grim, my lips pressed tightly together, and then we began to break out beneath the clouds.

We were at the bottom of Diablo Canyon.

My right wing was barely a few feet from the rocky wall of the canyon.

Salt Lake City Airport was already in view as we bumped downward into the clear, the canyon walls sliding away from us. Minutes later that grand old DC-4 slid her rollers down an ice-slicked runway, and we slowed gradually to a turnoff to the terminal. An ambulance and police cars waited with flashing lights. We went through the drill of parking, taking care of our patient, and then, with everything in the cockpit shut down, I took stock of myself.

I sat in a heated cockpit. I was also cold as hell. All through the shutdown checklist my voice had quavered. My copilot later told me I'd spoken the same way through the prelanding process of calling for gear, flaps, checklist items one after the other.

Was I being emotional? You're damned right I was. I could still feel the convulsive pulsations from my stomach.

Shouldn't this end, right here and now? No, my friends, because most such tellings should have an epilogue. We had ours. In more ways than one.

That little Chinese girl was rushed to the ambulance. Barely several minutes later she gave birth to a healthy baby boy. (Later I had one hell of a time explaining just what had happened to the Chinese girl, to about a hundred of her relatives who were waiting for her at Oakland! Those people did surprise me later with a gift and a notice that the mother had named her son after me.)

And the *real* epilogue?

Well, right behind us a cargo DC-3 also slid into that heavy snowstorm to land at Salt Lake City. They followed the beam right down into the storm, right down into Diablo Canyon. They flew their aircraft with absolute precision, following the beam.

And they smashed into the right side of the canyon. The ship tore apart, burned, and exploded.

They didn't have Harold Tucker as a friend.

Chapter 8

=WITHOUT ANSWERS
TOLLS THE BELL

No one is certain what took the bomber out of the sky. She was a North American B-25 Mitchell, a late model flying combat in the Philippines through part of 1944 and into the early days of 1945. Her name was *Sag Harbor Express*, and she flew missions hard and fast and low, the kind of combat for which the Mitchell was famed. *Sag Harbor Express* with her boxy shape, twin engines, and double tail, gained early fame as the bomber for the Doolittle Raiders that lifted from the USS *Hornet* on 18 April 1942, to conduct the first bombing strike ever on the Japanese home islands.

On 7 January 1945, *Sag Harbor Express* was on a combat mission near the area of Angeles City in the Philippines. The details are buried in the bomber's group history (not available to the writer at this time, and not that pertinent to this matter), so we don't know if the B-25 went down from Japanese antiaircraft fire or attack from Japanese fighters. Whatever the cause, *Sag Harbor Express* smashed into the ground fast enough and with an impact so great, it tore the bomber into wreckage and killed her crew.

End of story. For some years, anyway. A B-25, or any other bomber, or fighter, shot out of the sky in the opening days of 1945 was hardly an event demanding unique attention. We were ripping apart the Japanese, and they in turn were fighting fiercely to keep the Americans at bay as long as possible. It didn't take a strategic genius among the Japanese to understand that after the Philippines would come Okinawa, and after Okinawa, the sacred home islands themselves.

Sixteen years after *Sag Harbor Express* passed so violently with her crew into official combat records, the bomber emerged from the shadowy mists of the past to confront Filipinos living near that area where the bomber ripped apart.

Ged D. Dizon of Angeles City was then six years of age, in the summer of 1961, and playing in a deserted school yard one evening. The youngster froze, paralyzed with fear, as an apparition slowly materialized before him. Despite his young age he had learned enough of the war to recognize the flying clothes and features of an American pilot or aircrew member. The figure standing before young Dizon remained hazy and even transparent. Ged Dizon stared in disbelief. The youngster was sure he was seeing something real, but this was totally alien to him.

And then his brother, five years old, came running up to Ged Dizon—and stopped dead in his tracks, eyes wide, staring at the ghostly figure now facing the two boys. That was enough for them. This was no hallucination or game. The youngsters fled to tell the older people of their community what they had seen.

A supernatural experience; how wonderful! So they thought. But whoever heard the tale from the two youngsters, still both shocked and excited, laughed at what they heard and labeled the story pure nonsense or healthy imagination.

But for Ged Dizon there could be no simple dismissal. The young boy swore himself an oath that he would one day solve this mystery. As he entered young manhood, Dizon began to track down the details of what might have caused the appearance of the ghostly figure. He tracked down the squadron to which the B-25 had been attached; several survivors of the combat force wrote to Dizon to relate what had happened.

Then Ged Dizon, along with his brothers, Ivan and Daniel, Jr., began their own search for the actual wreckage. They passed the word to anyone and everyone who might have some word on the crash. To their surprise and delight, they located several Filipino witnesses to the crash of the B-25. They did more than that; they brought forth several parts of the shattered B-25 and presented these to the Dizon brothers.

B-25 Mitchell

Fred L. Wolff Archives

Ged Dizon planned to erect a historical marker in honor of the Americans who died fighting in the Philippines. But for several years the trail went cold. There had been only the ghostly airman, who had never again been seen. Yet Ged Dizon felt compelled to continue his original mission to create the historical marker.

The breakthrough came several years later, and it was a sobering find. It was finally confirmed that the playground where Ged and his younger brother had seen the B-25 crewman ghost was where the B-25 had crashed —and where the mass grave for all the crew had been dug! The remains of all the crew members were literally beneath Dizon's feet when he and his brother first saw the ghost.

The historical marker, the memorial, finally was in place. Ged Dizon felt enormous relief that his *own* spirit could finally end his years-long search. Ged Dizon wrote Ed Schnepf in the United States that, "I am sure most, if not all, of your readers will not believe the eerie part of this account, but I swear to God it actually happened to me, and up to now even my younger brother who saw it will attest to its truthfulness. He is now a soldier [sic] with the U.S. Marine Corps."

By now the local citizenry were less assured in their denunciation of the entire affair. The Dizon brothers met with their church officials, and a special solemn high mass was held to "free forever the departed souls" of the B-25 crew.

The marker was in place, the high mass was celebrated, and everyone involved with the effort shared, incredibly, an identical sensation that "all was at peace," and there would be no further appearances of ghosts or apparitions.

And there have been none.

IT IS ABSOLUTELY IMPOSSIBLE, BUT—

I found this reference, along with other incidents hopefully buried and forgotten, in official combat files. (Remember the silver discs in formation encountered over Europe by our B-17 bombers? Now recall how many episodes in this book concern details *that were seen by hundreds of combat crewmen.*)

As I did with the silver-disc combat reports logged forever in debriefings, I pass on to you this incredible tale. The details of this story are flatly impossible—but they were witnessed, and attested to, by several hundred officers and men of the U.S. Army, and Army Air Forces, *who were there.*

I have pursued this story since the late 1950s, and likely I have gone up more blind alleys than I ever believed could exist in reference to a single combat event of the Second World War. The frustration has been monumental because the incident deserves far more detail than I can bring to its issue. I've researched military combat files of many squadrons, groups, wings, and air forces. I was the official historian for the Fifth Air Force (among others) during my stint in A-2 (intelligence) in Japan. Even there, without reaching out for anything supernatural, I uncovered story after story that staggered the imagination and, had such events not been thoroughly documented and sworn to, would never have been believed. Yet there were no questions left unanswered, and history became a bit richer for the effort.

Not this one. This is one that baffles and infuriates and leaves you feeling sort of hollow. *But it happened.* No matter that it raises hackles on the back of your neck or leaves you with a twisted sensation in your gut when you try to accept what happened as true, and *then* do your damnedest to rationalize what happened!

The records at one time lay in my hands. When I searched through the official combat records of our air force operations in the Second World War in North Africa, *I read about this event.* In cold, hard, if not shocked, terms, it appeared as part of the official combat history of our military in World War II. At the time the historical records were still mostly classified. I could use them for research and take extensive notes, but I could not remove them from the vaults in their original form. What a bloody shame. In repeated visits to the historical vaults, this item has never again been found (at least by me).

Take it as it is, because that's what you re going to get.

The document I studied, wide-eyed and disbelieving, tells its tale in deliberately cold and official terms. Because the event that took place in North Africa that day was so impossible, the field commanding officer ordered that all enlisted and commissioned personnel sign their name, rank, and serial number to a document attesting to what they witnessed.

It began with a normal day, as normal as combat operations in the Mediterranean Sea and the islands and coastal areas can be when every flight is a potential life-or-death journey. Hundreds of fighter planes, large forces of bombers, and reconnaissance aircraft moved out against the German and Italian forces arrayed in North Africa and the Mediterranean. Pitched battles were fought, transport planes lumbered through hostile skies; it was another day of fly, fight, live, die.

Among the missions on this day was a long-range patrol assigned to a force of Lockheed P-38 Lightnings, big twin-engined, twin-boomed fighters. The formation of Lightnings worked northward of the North African coast into "German air" over the Mediterranean. No easy patrol this time. The Germans were out for trouble, and the Lightnings offered the same. A pitched battle raged high over the sea; like most such engagements, it was fast and furious, a surging melee of planes climbing, diving, twisting, tearing at one another. And then it was over, as if a switch had been thrown to disengage the combatants. When the Americans reformed into a group, they counted one P-38 fighter missing. The pilots radioed one another, for the pilot might have ditched or could have bailed out; in either case a rescue flying boat or a torpedo boat could be on its way for a rescue.

No luck; in the wild mix-up no one remembered a P-38 in distress that didn't emerge from its combat safely The P-38s spread out in a wide formation to search for any sign of the plane or pilot in the sea below. Nothing. The clock ticks on without concern for such problems, and fuel gushes through its lines into thirsty engines, making their demands on the Lightning fighters to start back to their home base.

One by one they landed, taxied to their revetments, and parked. All engines shut down, and the pilots climbed from their airplanes. They compared their notes and debriefed with intelligence. The one pilot missing from the group was listed as "missing in action." No death warrant yet. More than one pilot had returned long after his formation was safely on the ground.

But that clock kept ticking. Finally, even figuring the most conservative fuel burn, there couldn't be a drop of gasoline left in that P-38, not even if the pilot had shut down one engine and cruised at his slowest possible safe speed.

They gave him another two hours, "just in case." "Just in case" goes in the same box as crossed fingers and amulets.

You don't really give it much substance. The two hours passed. Men scanned the skies. They hoped for word from some other base anywhere in North Africa where a damaged P-38 might have come in for an emergency landing.

Nothing.

Scratch one P-38 and consign the pilot to missing in action. To the men the odds were overwhelming he wasn't coming back. There'd be an empty bunk in the barracks and an empty seat in the mess that night.

It happens.

That's war.

Then the air-raid alert sounded. Immediately guns were armed, fighters in the ready area came to life with engines throbbing, pilots climbed into cockpits, awaiting the signal to race into the air. Radar had picked up a single aircraft, type and nationality unknown, coming in toward the field.

Its speed was very high, its altitude low, and that almost promised it to be a fighter.

Then they saw the intruder. One P-38, approaching the field in a high-speed shallow descent, engines thundering—the sound of the twin Allisons in a P-38 is unmistakable.

The defense system called on the usual P-38 frequency; no answer. The field stayed on full alert. The P-38 pilot had not activated his IFF signal (identification friend or foe); well, it *could* have been shot up. Flares whistled into the sky arcing brightly to signal the pilot to do *something* to indicate his intentions—rock his wings, drop his gear, flash his landing lights. There was no response.

By now hundreds of men had spilled out from tents and buildings to look up into the sky A strange approach, that flat and unwavering descent. Officers signaled to the gun crews to hold their fire. The P-38 never slowed; that, too, was more than unusual. Then the speeding fighter reached a position almost over direct center of the airfield.

Suddenly the fighter seemed to stagger, as if hitting an invisible wall of vertically moving air—the equivalent of a brick wall to some machines. The P-38 jerked about violently, and then to the horror of the watching men and cries of helplessness, the airplane began to come apart in the air, changing from a sleek fighter to disintegrating wreckage.

There had been no sudden burst of bright flame, no sheet of fire erupting from the machine. No explosion.

One moment the P-38 flew straight and true; the next it was twisting, tumbling wreckage falling from the sky The engine sounds ceased, to be replaced by the whistling noises of twisted metal and the cries of the watching men.

Dozens of men stabbed their hands upward. "Look!" was the cry that chorused across the airfield as a body fell free of the wreckage. Instinct takes over at such a moment. "The chute! Pull the ring, dammit! Open the chute!" Men shouted as if the falling body could hear and then heed their cries.

The parachute opened. First the small pilot chute, pulling back in the wind, jerking taut, hauling the main canopy free. The silk churned, opened wider, and an audible pop! sounded as the canopy filled, staying the death fall of the pilot.

Cheers and shouts ebbed. Raised fists in triumph wilted. The body of the man in the chute hung limply.

Then, close to the tumbled, piled wreckage of the P-38, the parachute lowered its human form to the ground. Crash trucks were already driving at high speed to the scene, lights flashing and sirens screaming. Men piled into jeeps and trucks to follow; others ran toward the wreckage. They all watched the pilot's body crumple to the ground. The form didn't move.

Soon the trucks were gathered by the wreckage. Doctors were huddled by the body. Men stood about, staring in disbelief, whispering to one another. The latecomers thought the others were crazy They saw the stunned expressions on the faces of those close to the body of the pilot, shaking their heads, disbelief and shock mirrored on their faces.

They talked about it through the night. Some men drank themselves to oblivion; no one blamed them. The doctors who filled out the reports stared blankly at their papers. How in God's name could they sign and attest to what they had encountered? The same problem reached out to all those who were required to file forms, fill in the details, relate what they found. Because it was all impossible. It just could not be.

The light of the following morning seemed to make it worse, because what had happened the evening before was still with them all.

You see, it *was* impossible. Even though hundreds of men saw it happen, right before their eyes.

The fuel tanks of the P-38, that same fighter that was hours beyond any possible remaining fuel, were bone dry.

Yet the airplane had approached the field *with both engines running.*

The pilot whose parachute opened and lowered him to his home field, back to his fellow pilots, had a bullet hole in his forehead. The bullet had gone in from the front, through the brain and out the back of the skull.

He had been dead for hours.

Impossible.

But it happened.

And no one knows how.

Wisely they sealed the files, stamped them SECRET, and did their best to forget about it.

One of my closest friends is Terry C. Treadwell of Bournemouth, England. Terry and I have found some charming pubs in southern England that have been maintained, seemingly unchanged, for hundreds of years.

Nothing too mysterious about that: despite telephones and electricity and motor cars wending their way to such oases of calm and soothing moments in today's modern world, they manage through unflagging diligence to retain what was best of yesteryear. Terry and I have caroused, not in pubs, but on airstrips. We've had thumping great moments at British air bases, and a few years past, when Connie Edwards and myself and a gang of modern thieves (if you can call some of the world's best and most experienced pilots by that title) rumbled about England in Connie's PBY-6A Catalina, Terry and I also got in some time doing a bit of our own rumbling in British skies.

More to the point, Terry Treadwell is a modern-day bloodhound for researching stories almost impossible to grasp or to squeeze details from, unless you are very good at what you do. Treadwell's one of the best.

When he came to my assistance in researching the material for this book, we took advantage of our need to spend quiet time together studying notes and reports by selecting an outstanding place to hide and work. None other than The MildMay Arms of Queen Camel, near Yeovil, Somerset. It was marvelous, a bubble of time within which we vanished for several memorable hours.

And where Terry Treadwell brought to me—

THE LINDHOLME GHOST

Lindholme, during the Second World War, was a Royal Air Force station that figured highly in operations against German-occupied Europe. It wasn't your average British base, if you can call *any* operational British airfield average (and I don't). Lindholme was different because of the makeup and complexity of the combat groups that based at this particular airfield. They weren't just British bombing outfits. Lindholme was over-run with British bombers, and those of several other nations, many of them staffed by pilots and crews whose homelands had been occupied by German forces.

"And among this mixed bag," Terry Treadwell said, tapping his notes as he related the details of his research, "there was one very special group. A Polish squadron, in fact. They were all maniacs. They had the most marvelous zest for killing Germans. They lived more for killing Germans than anything else in this life. They had all left families and friends and loved ones behind, and they knew that many of those same relatives and friends had been tortured and butchered by the Nazis. So these Poles never missed a chance to take on *any* bombing assignment. They'd fly combat missions until they were so tired, they could barely walk from their planes back to their quarters, to fall asleep with their clothes still on. And as soon as they awoke and had coffee and food, they were eager to get it on again and go kill some more Germans. They'd made a really incredible record in their bombing strikes over Germany, and it was at the end of one of these raids that a most mysterious pilot was to make his appearance from this group...."

Lindholme Airfield was well isolated from the average British bomber installation. "Mired" down in South Yorkshire, it was surrounded with the great, sprawling Yorkshire moors, and a number of bogs that made the area almost impassable on foot and a treacherous nightmare for vehicles. At the end of one particular runway stretched hell itself for any

bomber that overran the strip: the infamous and sucking grip of Lindholme Bog. "Dumping into the bog" was a guarantee of an airplane tearing itself to pieces, and it was this same bog that would one day become
the final resting place for a huge four-engined Halifax bomber struggling
back from a mission deep into Germany.

On the night that commands our attention, the Polish-crewed Halifax
escaped from German skies by raw courage and the touch of a miracle, the
kind that manages barely to return mauled and crippled planes to their
home fields. At the controls of the Halifax was a sergeant-pilot, badly
wounded, bleeding profusely, and struggling simply to remain conscious,
let alone fly a huge and battered heavy bomber. At *night*.

The struggle to reach Lindholme was a relentless race against time.
With every passing hour the airplane seemed more difficult to control, and
the pilot grew steadily weaker. Flak explosions and fighter attacks had not
only left the plane a sieve from nose to tail but had also damaged the controls; a pilot fully alert and unharmed might never have been able to control the machine. All this was more than obvious to the sergeant up in the
cockpit, and he was painfully aware that even if he returned to Lindholme,
maneuvering the lumbering beast, especially after lowering gear and flaps
and trying to make a precision approach and landing, would be more than
he could handle.

Finally he had Lindholme in sight. By now he was convinced a safe
landing was only a long shot. He kept the Halifax steady and ordered his
crew to bail out; everyone must take to their parachutes. He would remain
aboard alone to attempt the landing. But he never got the chance.

He was already losing control as his crew dropped away from the
crippled aircraft. The last man had barely cleared the Halifax when it
dropped into a steep descent, careening wildly out of control. A superhuman effort at the last moment brought the bomber level, but that was the
best the sergeant could manage. The Halifax thundered across Lindholme
Airfield and went on to smash into the bog. A tremendous sheet of soggy
bog and water sprayed high into the air. The Halifax bounced and then
smashed deep into the bog. Within a minute or two the huge airplane sank
into the sucking morass and then disappeared completely from sight.
When the water calmed, there was no sign that only minutes before a great
four-engined bomber had crashed there.

As always, operations continued. The war went on, the raids against
Germany mounted in numbers and frequency. The loss of this one Halifax

became a statistic. British heavy bombers were being torn to shreds over Germany, and the loss of aircraft began to number in the many hundreds.

Several weeks after this particular Halifax thundered into the Lindholme Bog, the airfield had an unexpected visitor. A bloodstained, badly wounded, and disheveled sergeant-pilot, in complete flight gear, appeared on the field one night. He approached the padre assigned to the field. The padre remembered clearly that the man spoke with a strong Polish accent. "Sir, can you direct me to the sergeants' mess?" was the question.

The padre, taken aback with the sight of a man badly wounded and covered with blood, and walking about the airfield, managed to point in the direction of the sergeants' mess. He also started to question the man about his wounds and to offer assistance to take the man to the infirmary, but before he could speak, the sergeant-pilot was already walking away to disappear into the darkness.

The padre was baffled. No one else on the field saw that bloodied pilot that night, or during the nights that followed. He appeared mysteriously and vanished in the same manner.

For several months normal operations resumed; the bombers went out, most returned, some did not, and the bomber groups kept pounding at Germany and taking their losses.

The sergeant-pilot seen several months before, who had spoken clearly to the station padre, appeared again. He looked exactly as he had been seen months before—in full flight gear, clothes torn, obviously wounded, and covered with blood. This time he approached a group captain. The question was exactly the same. "Sir, can you direct me to the sergeants' mess?" Then he was gone.

The group captain ordered a search for the wounded man. No one could find even a trace of him.

The war ended, but not the inexplicable reappearance, time and again, of that same sergeant-pilot. For the next *forty years* he would show up suddenly on dark nights, always to ask the same question, always to walk off in the direction of the mess—and to disappear. It rattled the people involved. Rumors of the man—or ghost—that would not die, brought people to avoid walking alone at night.

Then, not quite three years ago, local officials decided to reclaim Lindholme Bog for its valuable peat deposits. Heavy machinery moved into the area and the excavation began. During the process of digging deeply and extracting peat, the work crews clanged their machinery against metal deep within the bog. They had stumbled onto the long-buried wreckage of the Halifax bomber.

In the cockpit, still clothed in the tattered remains of the flight gear he wore the night he died, was the skeleton of the long-deceased Polish pilot.

Polish officials were notified. Medical personnel came to the scene, and with the greatest care and reverence, they removed the remains of the pilot. The Royal Air Force ordered a funeral with full military honors. Former crews who could be found came to Lindholme for the ceremonies. The missing pilot had finally been laid to rest.

The bloodied, wounded man who walked Lindholme Airfield at night, who had been seen by dozens of officers and men, was never to be seen again.

OUT OF THE MISTS

If many of the people involved in what I am about to describe, especially the pilots, were not known to historians by name, rank, and serial number; if these people were also not known and respected for their honesty and courage; if these same people had not had their descriptions corroborated fully by other people with whom they were not in touch, before, during, or after; *and* if most of them had not signed documents in debriefings and intelligence sessions—I'd never put down a word in this book on the phantom fighters and bombers that appeared in the battle skies of Europe during the Second World War.

We've already encountered this extraordinary phenomenon before in "The Phantoms of Montrose," when a fighter pilot trying to land his Hurricane at night had to abort several landings because an ancient biplane suddenly cut in ahead of the Hurricane, and a collision seemed imminent. That Hurricane pilot was the only person among the living, at that time and place, to see the old biplane. Obviously he saw *something;* you don't slam the power to a fighter that's slowed down for a landing and kick off for a wild goround in the darkness without damned good reason! And if you recall, many years after the war, that biplane appeared *again,* to another pilot in flight, who then saw the airplane break up in the air and whirl to the ground where it crashed—and then vanished.

But now we speak of circumstances in which more than one pilot is involved. Now we speak of dozens and even hundreds of pilots and their crewmen, and we become involved with the personnel of the British (including New Zealanders, Australians, Canadians, and others) and their combatants, the pilots and aircrews of the Luftwaffe, the German air force.

The sudden appearance of "aircraft that cannot be" stretches the concept many people hold of ghosts. In the nomenclature of our everyday lives, a ghost is some reappearance, in some as yet unexplained manner, of a person once alive but no longer so. We use the term *ghost, apparition, spirit, soul*—whatever seems best to fit the situation. But ghostly aircraft, or ships, or other objects?

On the one hand, who was the authority that restricted "ghosts" to once-living biological entities? Who established the rules that everything else must be excluded? Of course there are several schools of thought here. One school says flatly that "there ain't no such things as ghosts" and, in one fell swoop of incredible knowledge of all things in this universe, dismisses any possibility of ghostly forms whether they be animal, vegetable, or mineral. These people profess absolutely to *know,* even if the fount of their knowledge is somewhat dimmer than the most transparent of all phantoms. Then there are those people who restrict ghosts to former humans—*former* in this instance meaning once biologically alive. One of their contentions is that often a ghost may not be observable by a person, but its mere presence will send animals, particularly dogs, into a wild frenzy and totally hysterical fright and reaction. There are plenty of such instances in the files; since I cannot verify the authenticity or even the accuracy of such reports, I leave that problem to some other author, and I return to one that is even more bizarre.

In 1939 and the few years following, when the rulers of the European skies were still to be determined by the outcome of battles, the aerial struggles were fought fiercely and with terrible casualties sustained by both sides. As the great air battles continued, and history began to accumulate more and more diverse struggles, there began to emerge from the records stories that were considered at first to be not merely strange, but totally out of the question.

At first the stories remained confined to the pilots and their crewmen. They spoke to one another in the assured privacy of their quarters, on their own airfields. What they had to say was not for the ears of anyone outside this "inner group." But the stories were overheard. Not only pilots, but aircrews, passed on the tales, as did mechanics and operations staff.

It became evident that the stories being told were not of a single bizarre, "impossible" incident, but that the "impossible" had happened again and again.

London, England. The German Luftwaffe has been battered and
bloodied during the massive daylight assaults against England. The Battle
of Britain was history; the Germans had lost so heavily in aircraft and
pilots, they now sought the greater safety of night raids against British targets. The men flying the defense fighters included old veterans ("old"
meaning they'd survived several months of fierce aerial battles) and the
newcomers, the replacements always ready to move their gear onto the
suddenly emptied spaces in the Nissen huts.

One of those replacements was a neophyte to combat; his name was
Grayson. When first sent into operations, he was launched on a solo
fighter patrol at night close to Dover. This would permit Grayson to keep
his bearings as to where he was at any time. He would not be concerned
with the dangers of formation flight in darkness, and his slow cruise above
the coastline of southern England would build experience in night-fighter
duties. The night was excellent for a pilot well above the surface. At times
clear weather fouled with sudden haze; then, just as quickly it seemed, the
haze blew away and clarity returned. Sensible enough; blustery winds
blew along the cliffs and the channel far below.

There was sufficient light for Grayson to pick out anything unusual,
and few things catch the attention of a man faster at night than the dim
glow of engine exhausts. Grayson glued his eyes to the faint light and
opened his throttle. Quickly the Hurricane closed in on the faint exhausts,
and Grayson confirmed another aircraft. He could see the machine only in
silhouette outline, but he was convinced it was *not* a friendly. Any British
operation would have been given to him before takeoff. So this was it!
First contact with the enemy!

As Grayson closed the distance and checked his eight machine guns
ready for firing, the unidentified plane began a turn that set it on course
toward occupied Europe. As the intruder flew over the channel, Grayson
went to full power to get into position to attack. Inexplicably, the
unknown aircraft maintained its same distance from the pursuing Hurricane. Over the channel they ran into scattered clouds; the bogey flashed in
and out of mists.

Then, abruptly, they flew into open air and clear moonlight. Grayson
squinted; making out colors at night was almost impossible, but he was
soon convinced the other aircraft was of a rich, red color. And then any
doubts of the bogey's identity were gone; moonlight showed him clearly
small black crosses on the other plane.

Grayson frowned; he still hadn't closed any distance between his Hurricane fighter and the German plane. He had flashes of clear views as they flew in and out of clouds and moonlight, and then Grayson felt a cold chill run down his back.

No one had told him to expect an enemy aircraft, apparently quite small and in the same size category of a fighter, *with three wings*. At this point it's important to stress that young Grayson wasn't restricted to a single swift glance at the other plane; he'd pursued it for several minutes and had excellent opportunity in full moonlight to study its features. Now he saw that it had a strange, small round tail as well.

The truth dawned slowly, and with great resistance, upon Grayson. That machine out there…was a *World War I* fighter plane. A Fokker triplane, from everything he knew of the planes used in that previous World War. Three wings, red color, crosses, the small round tail…the kind of fighter flown by Baron Manfred von Richthofen, Germany's greatest ace of that earlier war, killed in battle after shooting down more than eighty enemy aircraft.

The impossibility of what was happening left Grayson dumfounded. His Hurricane was at least four times faster than any Fokker triplane of wood and fabric out of 1917 and 1918! Yet he could not close on the triplane; it flew as fast if not faster than the Hurricane.

Rain pounded against his windscreen; he'd flown into a heavy shower. It lasted but several seconds, and then he was again in the clear.

The triplane was gone. Grayson searched the area; nothing. He began to ridicule himself. He *had* to produce *some* kind of explanation! So he manufactured one. He reasoned he might have smashed an insect on his windscreen. Of course; that was it. A insect that was whisked away by the rain squall.

That was it. He'd tell that story, laugh at himself with all good nature when he related what had happened, to his fellow pilots. *Of course, how that insect had crosses and three wings and turned over the channel…*No way, Grayson told himself. I won't even *think* about it! Insect it is, and insect it will stay.

He returned to base, made an uneventful landing, reported to operations, and went off to the squadron pub to have a deserved drink with his fellow pilots. He'd also decided, before his mates asked him how his "night out" went, just what he would say. *Better to laugh at myself than to be laughed at…*

"Well, I chased this bloody insect halfway to Berlin, it seemed like," he began, and then went on with the rest of his story of that night's "engagement." He expected knee slapping, chuckling, even raucous laughter, and worst of all, tolerant smiles.

None of it happened. The room slowly lost its conversational hum, as though a switch were thrown and a dynamo was winding down. The drone of voices faded away until there was only complete silence. Grayson stared in bewilderment from one pilot to another.

"I don't understand," he said finally. "Something's wrong. I was stupid up there tonight, but what did I say to all of you that has you so upset?"

"You weren't stupid, lad," said a veteran pilot.

Another pilot raised himself higher at the bar until he stood stiffly "So it's happened, what?"

"What's happened?" Grayson demanded.

"Tonight. Tonight you met him."

"Who?" Grayson cried in exasperation.

"The Red Knight, that's who, lad."

"Who the devil is the Red Knight?"

He wasn't prepared for the answer. Another pilot gave it to him straight out. "The Red Knight," he said slowly, "is a ghost."

"He's the ghost of the baron," another pilot added. "Baron Manfred von Richthofen, the ace of aces in the last big war. He took at least eighty of our people down before he was nailed himself, and that was in 1918."

"He flew different fighters. Scouts, they called them in those days," another pilot offered. "But his favorite was an all-red triplane, with black crosses. *Exactly* what you described seeing in the air tonight."

"You've seen him?" Grayson asked in amazement.

"Just about every man in this room, lad, has seen him," the oldest veteran answered. "I've seen him. All of us, at one time or another, *have been escorted by that bloody triplane.*"

"But...it's impossible," Grayson said in slow defeat.

"Impossible, all right," he heard. "But it's true enough."

"Why would it happen to ^squadron?" Grayson demanded. "Or does it happen elsewhere also?"

"As best we know, only to this squadron."

"Why?"

Several pilots pointed to themselves. "Our fathers, we suppose. They all fought against Richthofen's bunch twenty-two years ago."

A pilot smiled. "Maybe this kind of fight will never be over," he offered.

Perhaps it won't. The all-red Fokker triplane that joined the Hurricane fighters of this one particular squadron wasn't the only machine that "couldn't be." This was one of the quiet episodes. When you examine the records of the Royal Air Force, you'll find that on more than one occasion the wood-and-fabric biplane fighters of a World War I Germany appeared in battle.

And so did British fighters from that long-ago war.

On one of several occasions, the bright red Fokker triplane was encountered in *daylight.* The records attesting to several of these appearances are found in German combat histories. One incident described a group of Messerschmitt Me-109E *Emil* fighters diving against the Spitfires far below their own formation. Suddenly there appeared in the midst of the diving German fighters the bright red Fokker, an ancient three-winged machine of an earlier war, that now pulled away and outsped the swift German fighters in steep dives! When last seen the Fokker was tearing into the midst of the Spitfires.

I find it difficult to imagine a more phlegmatic and pragmatic group of pilots than the Germans who flew the Messerschmitts early in the war against the British. Yet on the occasion just described, every pilot involved not only swore to the truth of the incident, but also signed and swore to documents testifying to what they had seen, and what had happened.

Now there was the other side of the coin as well, especially with the SE-5A British biplane fighter, one of the best in the First World War. There are a number of stories involving these ancient machines, but none so well confirmed as this one.

A mixed bag of Hurricanes and Spitfires was diving steeply against a massive German bomber formation. Abruptly in their midst, speeding through their formation and then pulling ahead, was a single SE-5A. Everyone who saw the old machine knew that what they were seeing absolutely could *not* be, that it was unquestionably impossible—*but there it was.* The SE-5A, in remarkably the same manner exhibited by the Fokker triplane, raced ahead of the modern British fighters.

Later the pilots of the Hurricanes and Spitfires, questioned separately, had almost perfect agreement as to the colors and markings of the biplane, right down to the color of the pilot's scarf snapping in the wind.

There was another difference. The Fokker would rush before its modern German descendants and then, as it plunged into the midst of the British aircraft, would begin to fade away and then disappear. Not so with the SE-5A. The fighter from another time and another war ripped into the German bombers, both of its machine guns firing, causing German pilots to swerve wildly to avoid a collision with the "impossible" British machine. Then the SE-5A dived away, down through the German formation, to disappear.

The British demanded of their pilots and officers precisely what the disbelieving German officials demanded of their men: that every man who saw and reported on the ancient fighters in their formations sign, on his oath as an officer and a pilot, the truth of what he had described.

This the pilots did, and left us with the legacy, many decades later, of choosing to believe what was or is real.

You choose what you wish. I know pilots. We're of the same breed.

I believe.

The tales of ghost aircraft and ghost pilots and aircrews that emerged from the Second World War are legion. Many—indeed, most of the stories—are impossible to prove or even document. In the fury of air battles and the surging of great military forces, accuracy of detail is often elusive. For these reasons, many "ghost stories" of aerial combat do not appear in this book. They have emerged from years of story telling that can do little to preserve what original accuracy there was, and in retelling any story, accuracy and even validity are bound to suffer. When men are under pressure, especially when they are being hounded and smashed from the skies, and every day is bone-numbing weariness, and your friends are dying about you one after the other, the mind will reach for some sanity, and above all hope, even if it's from supernatural sources.

One such instance concerns the phantom aircraft known as the White Angel of Warsaw. It was a byword among pilots in their ready rooms and personal quarters. The White Angel of Warsaw, so go the tales, was an airplane never identified as to type—bomber, fighter, transport, or what. Some sources went for bomber, others for fighter, and so on, but consistency in the telling is not one of the notable elements of this tale. As the legend went, the White Angel would appear in the skies near Warsaw just before German bomber formations arrived to devastate the city. The spectral aircraft, shining a brilliant white, casting a brilliant glow even in clear sunlight, raced about the perimeter of Warsaw and then faded from sight. Or, as some stories had it, returned to the west from where it had appeared. The White Angel never seemed to interfere with the German planes but showed up to warn the city of the impending bomber strike. Once Warsaw fell to the invading German army, the White Angel was no more. It never again was seen.

Fact or comforting fiction? A touch of reality or a legend that grew from some source we can never identify? I must yield to the latter. A German reconnaissance aircraft painted a bright white, or even of polished aluminum (though why the Germans would do this is also its own mystery) would account for an airplane preceding the main bomber formations. The American, British, and German raids in Europe were often preceded by such swift scout aircraft to report on weather, conditions over the target, enemy flak or fighter defenses, and other information radioed back to the bombers following the scout. Whatever the actual events, or the reasons behind them, the White Angel of Warsaw, as much as I would like to include its story here, must remain what it appears to be—as ethereal as any ghost that never was.

However.

Not so the tales of—

"OLD WILLIE" AND THE WHITLEY

"Old Willie" has a great deal more substance. As the stories made their rounds among British pilots and crews early in the Second World War, much conversation hung on the legend of a Canadian pilot, Henshaw, who flew and fought in the First World War. Was his full name William Henshaw? I was unable to confirm the full name, but there is no question of his being Canadian, or a pilot, with the last name of Henshaw. Nor is there any question that Henshaw was near mad to shoot down an enemy plane in battle—and that he failed to do so. Instead, on his first combat patrol, when he was very much "meat on the table" to experienced German pilots, Henshaw got the hell shot out of him. Badly wounded, his aircraft shot to ribbons, he managed barely to make a crash landing between the German and the British lines. No-man's-land is no place to be caught when that area is under the guns of both sides, with everyone trigger-happy and willing to lob high explosives in the direction of anything that moved.

Henshaw paid the full price. For more than two days he lay low in a deep shell crater, his wounds driving him mad and sapping his strength. It rained and he lay in cold water, unable to crawl back to the British lines, and a target for the Germans no matter which way he moved. Any attempts to rescue him would be suicidal; German machine guns had the area covered in a vicious cross fire.

Then the same rain that almost killed him became a blessing; it rained so hard, visibility went to near zero. Henshaw crawled and dragged his battered body back to friendly trenches and safety.

He never flew combat again. He spent months in a hospital and was finally sent home to Canada, where he waited out the end of the war, his dream of an air kill against a German plane unfulfilled. The story ends on a quiet note; Henshaw died in 1929.

Then came the next world war, the great early air battles between the British and the Germans, and Henshaw was somehow resurrected in memory and connected to the new area of combat. He became known as Old Willie, although the exact connection has never been satisfactorily explained.

But there was not a shred of doubt in the report of a young pilot of RAF Fighter Command:

"When the Blitz began, we really had our hands full. During one night patrol our squadron got quite a surprise. We were preparing to attack a large formation of Heinkels when we noticed another plane in our formation. It was British, all right. Our squadron leader saw the cockade insignia, but it wasn't the latest-type machine by any means. We tried to signal, but there was no response.

"Then our squadron leader recognized the other plane as an old Canadian biplane that was somehow managing to keep up with our fast pursuits.

"Suddenly it peeled off our formation and screamed straight for the two lead Heinkels. They saw it coming, too, and they swerved in their tight formation, collided, and went down in flames. The Canuck pilot veered over toward us, waved a snappy 'thumbs-up,' and simply disappeared into the mist.

"He's been seen at night many times by other RAF pilots. They say he always uses the same trick—diving straight for the enemy planes until they collide, or unnerving their pilots until they get careless and become an easy mark for our lads."

The reports of Old Willie leave much to be answered and asked. Dozens of British fighter pilots saw the ancient plane—they saw a *British* aircraft. And in the report you just read, the young RAF fighter pilot seems quite sure the man flying the World War I aircraft is a *Canadian* flier. A assumption unproven, obviously.

Yet even for years after the war, investigation of such reports repeatedly substantiated the eyewitness reports of the pilots. So many questions remain unanswered, and there are many gaps left in the explanations, especially how Old Willie came to select certain groups over others, and why this long-deceased fighter pilot would remain in ghost form with a phantom aircraft that fired very live rounds of ammunition, seen not only by the protected British pilots but by an obviously hated enemy.

Label this item as "mysterious" and perhaps add the word "perplexing."

A bit more solidity attends the legends of a British bomber given the name of *The Hot One*. This time the phantom machine derived not from a war several decades past, but from the ranks of modern bombers, specifically, a Handley-Page Whitley. Now we find some startling variations in the reports of such aircraft. First, the eyewitness accounts were absolutely legion. Second, the eyewitness reports were startlingly similar, following the same detailed events. Third, there seemed to be no particular moment when *The Hot One* finally faded (in its full sense) from the scene. Fourth, this was a ghost plane in every sense of the word—all the British bomber pilots and crews who described the apparition remained unshaken in their reports that no one was ever at the controls. Fifth, and I add this as a personal observation, the Whitley wasn't really that much of a crackerjack fighting machine. It was a large and ugly machine, its performance desultory, and its survival on raids deep into Germany always a matter of question. The Whitley flew more like a truck than it did a modern bomber. Indeed, if ever there was a bomber that needed all the help it could get, the Whitley was certainly that machine, either alone or in full formation.

The Phantom Whitley first began to appear on long-range missions from England directly to Berlin, in the midst of other aircraft of its own kind. This wartime eyewitness report is taken from an official debriefing of a Whitley bomber pilot who participated in just such a night raid against Berlin—

"This huge Handley-Page swooped down on us from above, traveling at a terrific rate of speed. It was brightly lighted, and I could see there was no one at the controls.

"It dived past and quickly outdistanced us. Suddenly the Huns let loose with a great barrage of flak from hidden antiaircraft batteries on the ground. The bomber was caught squarely in the middle of the bursting shrapnel. I saw it in time and turned away.

"The bomber must have been hit in a thousand places, but it pulled away ahead of us, climbed steeply into the clouds, and disappeared. If it hadn't attracted the fire from those concealed batteries, the German gunners would have caught us in a trap."

What is most disquieting in such a report of a pilotless Whitley is the number of bomber pilots who swore adamantly that every word of the above is true. And that the phantom Whitley appeared suddenly during many night missions into Germany, always seeming to rush ahead of the main bomber formations, often snared by brilliant searchlights, and subjected to a terrific blasting by heavy flak guns. But no matter how much damage the phantom Whitley sustained, it always flew on, climbed higher, and disappeared from sight. Until the next mission.

Unexplained.

Of all the chapters, long and short, in the folklore of our world of aviation, none appears to be more vexing than an incident that took place early in the air war over Europe shortly after England and Germany committed to all-out combat. Many years ago I reviewed the official papers of an incident reported from those early days of aerial combat. I would like nothing more than to print here the specific dates and names of all those involved, but I have never again been able to track down and take into my hands those incredible documents. Because of every attempt to provide as much detail as possible, I present the following solely in the interests of providing the reader with as much background data as is possible to gather for these pages. What you will now read has emerged from the official records of the Royal Air Force Bomber Command. It has been confirmed repeatedly, despite its absolutely startling nature, and I swear by the authenticity of the original papers I studied, from which I extracted the following.

The time was still early in the war, when the overwhelming weight of air power rested with the Luftwaffe. Germany's best had shattered all defenses through Europe and then hurled itself in a terrible bloodletting,

but without final success, at England. In the duels and charges fought high
and low above the Isles of Britain, the Spitfires went high on their graceful wings to take on the best of Germany in the form of Messerschmitt
Me-109E fighters; those engagements freed the Hurricanes to swoop into
the midst of the German bomber formations to decimate their ranks.

When the great onslaught was done, the Germans, in effect, withdrew
to lick their wounds and to regroup. But the British victory was, for the
moment, just that: a momentary victory that served the purpose of regaining strength, replenishing pilot ranks, and rushing new machines into
striking back at the Germans.

Among those machines was a group of aircraft known as the Douglas
DB-7 Boston. The slim, twin-engined Douglas bomber (known to the
army air corps then as the Havoc) had been part of a rush order for France.
But France fell much too quickly, and the Boston, fast and powerful with
more than three thousand horsepower, seemed the perfect weapon to
throw at some of the most heavily defended and critical targets of the Germans—the military installations along the occupied coasts of the eastern
side of the English Channel. What was needed was bomb load and above
all speed, and this the Boston supplied in superb fashion.

Twelve Bostons were ordered out for a strike at German coastal
defenses. It was a mission to be conducted with alacrity; go in low, hit the
targets, and get the hell out of there. At the British bomber base, an air
marshal of the Royal Air Force was present to oversee the raid and to
learn from the returning crews vital information on the enemy coastal
positions. He watched from a window of the office he occupied on the
base as twelve Bostons raced into the air. The drone of engines fell away
as speed and distance absorbed the sound. Then it was quiet and perhaps
the worst time of all: waiting. The minutes ticked by slowly. The air marshal judged in his own mind the speed of the planes, their route, the miles
to be covered, how long it would take for the Bostons to go in beneath the
heavy German flak, make their runs, race away, and drop to the water to
run for England. Nothing he could do might speed up that awful waiting.
The seconds dragged, the minutes groaned slowly along the dials.

Time. The distant hum of engines, seeming to labor. The air marshal checked his time against the calculations he had made a hundred
times by now. He listened to the sound; American radials, to be sure.
He tried to count individual pairs of engines. Three, maybe four, the
planes circling; in his mind's eye he saw the propeller knobs going for-

ward and throttles easing back, flaps lowering from wings, tricycle gear extending into the air, the Bostons rolling out on final and *chunking* back to ground.

"Have the crews report directly to me," was his order. Soon after the engine thunder died, vehicles drove up to the operations building. He heard doors opening and closing, the thump of booted footsteps. The men of three Bostons stood before the air marshal. He ordered them at ease, wasting no time. Their faces told him of the ferocity of flak, the unexpected nightmare of a sky swollen with bursting fire and cutting steel.

"Any more?" he asked finally.

The men shook their heads. Twelve Bostons out; three back. Nine gone. Horrible numbers, but nevertheless true. It was a slaughter.

The crews filled out debriefing intelligence reports. The air marshal made certain the men signed the papers. That was important. Their names, serial numbers, rank, time, and date.

"Gentlemen, I suggest you all have a drink. Or two. Thank you."

The crews left, the air marshal was left alone to ponder the loss of 75 per cent of his crews. It was more than a beating; it was indecent for men to be thrown into the meat grinder in such a fashion.

The aide to the air marshal entered his office, where he sat with his misery. "Sir."

The air marshal looked up and nodded.

"Sir, there's no easy way to say this."

"Get on with it."

"Sir, we took terrible losses tonight. We—"

"I know, *I know.*" Unbidden impatience. "Nine out of twelve down."

The aide showed a flash of puzzlement. "No, sir."

A flicker of hope. Had more crews landed elsewhere? "What then? What do you mean?"

The words came like ice. "Sir, we lost *all* the aircraft. All twelve were shot down."

Silence.

Then: "That is ridiculous."

"I'm sorry, sir."

"That is *not* what I meant. Three of those Bostons landed back here."

The aide stared at his superior. "Air Marshal, I don't know what you're talking about, but none of those aircraft have landed here. I

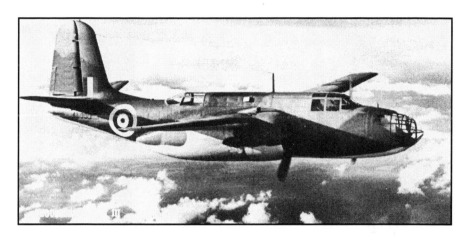

Douglas DB-7

Martin Caidin Archives

repeat, sir, and intelligence has confirmed this, *all twelve Bostons were shot dawn.*"

"Then look at this," the air marshal said icily. He pushed the signed, dated, and timed debriefing sheets at his aide.

The man whitened in disbelief. Every detail of the strike, as reported by intelligence, as determined from German reports, was exact. Everything that had happened on the mission was in those papers.

"How...how did you get these?" the aide asked.

"I debriefed those crews myself. Then sent them off for a well-earned drink."

"Sir, the...bar is, ah, empty. It has been."

"What do you mean?"

"No crews have been in there tonight. The crew quarters are also empty."

"Then how did I debrief these crews? How did they sign these reports? How in the name of God do I have the details of this mission? You're telling me I debriefed crews of three bombers that all this time have been dead?"

The aide didn't, couldn't answer. He still held the papers signed by the men who died as their planes were shot down over their targets across the channel.

*   *   *

Postscript: All twelve aircraft were lost, shot down by German defenses, over occupied Europe.

All the crews of those twelve bombers were killed. There were no prisoners, no survivors.

Three crews had signed the debriefing papers in the operations room. The men of three crews who had died more than an hour before told the air marshal of the raid, signed their names, left for the "well-deserved drink," and were never seen again.

Chapter 9

MORE MOMENTS OUT OF TIME AND PLACE

D ata from a pilot's logbook: *29 September 1961*. Make of aircraft: *Boeing B-17G Flying Fortress*. Registration number of aircraft: *N9563Z*. Type of aircraft: *Four-engine heavy bomber*. From: *Teterboro Airport, New Jersey*. To: *Logan Airport, Boston, Mass.*

This was one of the early legs of a wild and hysterical journey from Arizona to the northeast, then on up to Gander, Newfoundland, to lead a formation of three B-17G bombers across the Atlantic to England. The purpose was to get the planes across the ocean in the last formation flight of these great Queens from the United States to Gatwick, England, where the bombers would be used for the motion picture, *The War Lover*. A crazier bunch of Americans, Englishmen, one Australian, and one Apache Indian had never gathered together for *this* kind of flight. Before it ended, we'd have a rousing battle with a Russian crew in Newfoundland, a turbulent and frenetic ocean crossing, a few emergencies in the Azores, be tossed into a secret police prison in Portugal, play chicken with some Messerschmitts over Spain—well, it was a beaut. But that isn't *this* story. What concerns us is the run from Teterboro to Logan, one of the short hops of the flight.

Our bombers had been dragged from aircraft boneyards, where they'd been dumped as surplus, and were just about as worthless as pieces of machinery can get. They still wore their old markings, and beneath the scabby paint and sun-broiled exterior, you could just make out serial numbers and other military identification. Inside the Forts you were in the original machine. Everything was raw. Nothing was remotely close to pristine, and a hell of a lot didn't work. But we were flying them across the ocean.

We had two unexpected passengers on this run from Teterboro to Logan. A man named Bert Perlmutter and his teenage daughter. I knew Bert well. During the Big Deuce he'd been a B-17 crewman, flight engineer, and top-turret gunner, and he'd flown some very heavy and terrifying missions against the best fighters in the Luftwaffe who were trying to kill him and everyone else aboard his plane. Bert knew of our flight and made a request.

"Let me fly with you guys up to Boston. I want to bring my daughter, show her just what it was like in the Fortress, let her hear the sounds, feel the motions. Let her taste the kind of history her old man lived in. I want to share that with her."

We took them with us; there was no way to turn down that kind of request. Our Australian, a veteran of a hell of a lot of flying anything with wings, drove the Fort from the left seat. Greg Board went all the way back to flying with the Royal Australian Air Force out of Burma against the Japanese invasion through Asia. In those days he flew the export version of a stubby barrel-shaped American fighter called the Brewster Buffalo. It was a dog. Or the outcast cur from a pack of mongrels. A horrible machine to fly against the nimble Japanese Zero fighters, whose pilots laughed and snickered when they saw the Buffaloes trundling along like fat sows and then proceeded to shoot them to pieces. Greg survived all that.

We took off from Teterboro in a formation of two, leaving one B-17G behind for some mechanical work, to catch up with us later. It was a beautiful flight. Warm, about four-tenths cloud cover, and cruising up the countryside at seven thousand feet. The fuselage interior was jammed with spare parts and the huge B-17G tires. You either sprawled on that jumble or stretched out on one of two folding cots that swung down from the side of the airplane. Because there wasn't any need for machine-gun mounts or the waist guns themselves, the two waist-gunner positions had been sealed with Plexiglas.

Bert Perlmutter (left) and Martin Caidin

photo by Bill Mason

Well, it was warm, and the Fort bounced and rocked gently as we droned toward Logan, and before too long the motion and the sun's slanting rays worked like a sleeping potion for the young girl. She stretched out on one cot, and her father, on the other side of the fuselage, did the same. In moments they were fast asleep.

I had come back from the cockpit to talk with Bill Mason and Jim Nau, who were photographing and recording the salient points of the flight. We sat on crates and a tire, relaxing and smoking. Looking back from this position toward the tail turret, the interior of the Fortress had a misty quality, the result of dust bouncing from aircraft motion and the sun slanting in at an angle. You see the dust itself, and everything gains an ethereal quality because of it.

Then one man gaped as he looked back through the fuselage. "Holy …" The words failed to come. He stared wide-eyed at me and Bill Mason. "I can't believe…Am I really seeing what I think I'm seeing?"

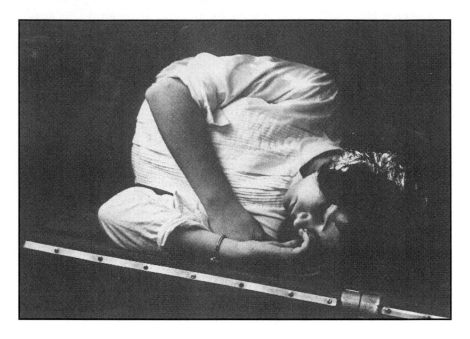

Perlmutter's daughter

photo by Bill Mason

I grasped Mason's arm. "Don't answer. Obviously we're all seeing something. Write it down, but don't discuss it with each other. I don't want anyone affecting the thoughts of anyone else." We did just that, and that night, on the ground, we compared notes.

First, everything written down by each man just about matched perfectly what the others had written—it is critical to emphasize that. Not until we compared our notes did we *know* what each of us had seen.

Bert Perlmutter, fast asleep, was obviously in the grip of a powerful, even violent, dream. Perspiration gleamed on his face; he was soaked through with perspiration. His face twitched; at moments his mouth opened, and in his dreams he was shouting or screaming. We couldn't tell which. At times he seemed to be struggling physically.

But that wasn't what had gripped us, almost hypnotized us. In that ethereal light, as if we were peering through waving gauze, we saw dim shadows moving. Two men in heavy flying suits, wearing oxygen masks, each with his hands on a fifty-caliber machine gun in the waist position.

B-17s

photo by Bill Mason

Calling out to one another, the guns visibly hammering, shell casings flying through the air. Not a sound. Absolutely soundless to us we watched the ghostly tableau of a battle raging in wartime skies. Phantom figures; we even saw the shell cases gleaming in the shafts of sunlight.

Then one man lurched and moved with great effort, coming toward us, unrecognizable because of his leather helmet and oxygen mask. He supported another figure, who seemed to be barely conscious. It was difficult to make out any detail, but then—and we all wrote it down—we saw that one hand of this second man had been blown away and at the wrist there was only a stump. The other was half dragging him to the open space of the navigator's upward gun position, where a single machine gun was mounted to fire upward. This was behind the power turret just aft of the cockpit. We watched the man in the mask heave the other upward and shove the blood-spurting arm into the screaming windblast. At four or five miles high, the temperature would have been forty or fifty degrees below zero: just what was needed to close off the ghastly wound and freeze the arm to stop the spurting blood. Then there was a gasp, and Bert Perlmutter awakened, sitting upright, exhausted, soaked with sweat. He looked like hell.

"What's the tie-in?" Mason asked in the hotel room that night.

"It's Bert," I said.

"But *how? What?*"

So I told them what only I knew at that time. "Bert Perlmutter was a flight engineer, like I told you, in a Fort, just like this one. He also operated the upper power turret. Bert flew a bunch of missions. On one of them, well, it was Black Thursday. The killer raid on Schweinfurt in October of 1943. On that raid one of his gunners had his hand blown off. Bert went back from his gun position to save the man's life. He dragged him back to the top fuselage opening, held him as high as he could, and stuck his severed arm into the wind stream."

Mason and the others stared at me. "But...*but that's exactly what we saw today in that plane!*"

"I know," I replied.

The next question came in a hoarse whisper. "But...but that would mean...*we were seeing his dream.*"

"Could be," I said. "You give me a better explanation. Give me *any* explanation. *We all saw the same thing.*"

"But...that's impossible! That's a materialization of a dream, for God's sake!"

"Okay. It's impossible," I agreed. "Tell me then how we saw what we did. And then explain to me that last little item."

No answer. Just before Bert Perlmutter moved across the fuselage to awaken his daughter so that she could be strapped in for approach and landing, something on the floor of the Fortress caught his eye. The three of us watched him lean down and pick up an object. He held it up, studying it in the bright shaft of sunlight. We all saw it clearly.

The casing of a fifty-caliber round. Shiny. Brand new. It wasn't in the Fortress when we took off from Teterboro. Bert turned it round and round; he shook his head slowly and placed the casing in a pocket and woke his daughter. They sat tightly together as we eased back to earth and landed.

BACK TO THE FUTURE

Ron Edwards is an ATP—an air transport pilot, referred to usually as an airliner captain, a pilot fully qualified to fly passengers on scheduled airline flights for hire. It's the top of the line for airplane drivers. And he's one of the best: experienced, careful, skilled, pragmatic. He doesn't talk about things unless he's convinced they're real. He told us about a fighter pilot of the Royal Air Force who quite obviously slipped into, for a brief time, anyway, one of those "breaks in time and space" that seem to be happening more and more. We'll be back on this subject of time jumps and twists in the fabric of space/time, but for the moment—

The British pilot flew a Hawker Hart biplane fighter, and he was in trouble. It was 1934, and the Royal Air Force pilot was caught in heavy thunderstorm buildups somewhere over Scotland. He was also on his own; 1934 was a time when flying about Scotland meant doing all your own navigation and attending to your own needs. A world of super-electronics and navigation aids was still far in the future. The pilot also knew all too well that getting caught in the belly of a giant thunderstorm would be asking to have his plane torn apart. He cut back of power and eased the Hawker into a glide, descending as carefully as he could, dodging and twisting about the blackest of the clouds as gave up his altitude. He knew generally where he was. Somewhere in this area was an abandoned airport known as Drem. If he could spot that field, he could whip down in a hurry and get safely onto the ground. The problem was, he had to fly more by intuition than by sighting known landmarks.

Intuition paid off. He eased beneath a boiling cloud base, squeezed between the still-lowering cloud deck and increasing turbulence, and the earth below Then he recognized landmarks; if he was right, Drem would be dead ahead of his position. He brought in power and barreled for the field that promised safety. And there it was, right in front of him. He'd made it!

He was still a quarter-mile distant from the abandoned airfield and closing rapidly to his goal when the thunderstorm seemed to split wide open. The booming clouds separated, opened wide in the form of a giant chasm in the sky. Brilliant sunlight burst through and cast a dazzling golden glow on the countryside below.

He brought the Hawker over in a tight bank so that he could fly directly over Drem and check the runway for his landing. The abandoned airfield *wasn't there.* He couldn't believe what he saw; he was over Drem, all right, but the ruined field had vanished.

He was circling an airport bustling with activity.

Victor Goddard was the pilot's name. This story is in the official registry of the Royal Air Force. Let's put that down for the record. He's real. What he saw beneath him was real—*even if it was impossible.*

Goddard kept his turn tight, staying within the boundaries of the beautifully laid out and maintained airfield. At a height of only fifty feet, he raced across the flight line, hangars, rows of airplanes, living quarters, vehicles, and hundreds of people—and no one even looked up at this fighter streaking by so low. Goddard stared at mechanics in blue coveralls working on rows of planes painted brightly yellow: *That* threw him for a loss. This was a training field, obviously, but the Royal Air Force trainers were all painted an unmistakable silver. And he didn't see a single silver-colored aircraft.

He made another pass—completely ignored from below. Goddard pushed aside his puzzlement; the clouds had lifted suddenly and strangely, he recognized the landmarks about Drem airfield, and he climbed back to altitude to take up a heading that would return him to his original destination.

Now for the kicker. In 1934 Drem airfield *was an abandoned relic.* Its buildings were partially collapsed, the runways broken and dangerous. Not a soul lived or worked there. It had been empty for years.

In 1938, with war with Germany fast becoming a reality, the Royal Air Force returned to Drem with a crash program to rebuild the airfield and transform it into a top-priority, top-quality training installation. Soon Drem was a major RAF training base—and when it opened for full operation, *the color scheme of all the RAF trainers was changed from silver to yellow.*

Somehow, fighting his way through the storm skies of 1934, RAF pilot Victor Goddard had slipped into a break in time/space; he descended through a storm that mysteriously split open with brilliant sunshine, and he flew over an airfield that would not exist until four years in the future.

EARLY TIMES

Joseph L. McKinstray is another one of those pilots who's solid, stolid, skillful—and about as down-to-earth as they come. He vaulted into the area of the unknown without doing a thing on his own part way back in 1938. Before we turn back the clock to something that happened years before it *could* happen, let me add, also, that Joe McKinstray is a highly experienced pilot. He's flown trainers and transports and bombers, everything from the ubiquitous DC-3/C-47 to favorites like the Lockheed A-29 Hudson and the swift Lockheed B-34 Ventura. Among other time logged in his book is more than fifteen hundred hours at the controls of the Boeing B-17 Flying Fortress. He's not only flown a wide variety of aircraft as a military pilot, he's also owned a few of his own, and he's *built* some of the airplanes he flies.

So we have about as experienced a man as we can find with aircraft, what they look like, feel like in flight, and what they sound like. That's important; keep it in mind.

In 1938, summertime, I was a typical seventeen-year-old accustomed to working long hours and seven days a week on our family farm (Joe McKinstray relates). On this particular day I was hoeing corn on a stumpy piece of "new ground" on our farm northeast of Indianapolis. The field was about a quarter of a mile long with woods on either side, and I was near the woods at the east end of the field.

The air was calm and humid on this particular day. I recall just about every detail. Overhead was a solid overcast that I estimated to be just about a thousand feet above the surface. Now, I make that statement with some solid reference to cloud heights. I'd been wild about flying, one of those true enthusiasts, ever since I could recall. I'd been flying since I was a little kid, with numerous flights in Wacos and Stinsons with my cousin, who was an aircraft dealer at the Indianapolis airport. So I'd been up and down enough times to know my cloud heights. Besides, I was also a budding pilot. I had a bunch of time as a student, and I'd already put in about four hours solo time in an old Piper Cub.

Now, in addition to my own flying, we were in an area of some heavy aviation activity. Once in a while a large machine would come over, but that was a rarity. However, I'd seen a few come by at different altitudes, and they weren't unknown to me. Our farm was on the opposite side of Indianapolis from the Municipal Airport and Stout Field. There was a military grass strip, this was Shoen Field, at Fort Benjamin Harrison, only five miles from the farm, and they operated a bunch of O-38, O-46, and O-47 observation planes from there. So I knew many different kinds of planes from the ground and quite a few from actually flying them.

I mentioned the cloud overcast this day at just about a thousand feet above the ground. I had no idea of how much higher the clouds extended; I was sure of only one thing, and that was the distance from the ground up to the clouds.

Well, there I was, whacking away at the corn in that stumpy field, and I heard an airplane far off in the distance. The sound brought my head straight up, and I recall I tensed, because I'd never heard a sound like this before. It wasn't just the sound of an airplane. This was a tremendous noise. I mean *tremendous;* it boomed and roared from the east, over the woods. It got louder swiftly until the roar seemed to pound against the earth. I couldn't understand what it was. Nothing like I'd ever heard, and the only thing I could compare it to was a freight train passing real close by. It was different; it had a cry like a monster acetylene torch.

I couldn't *see* the airplane. If it was an airplane, that is. The sound exploded on me, it came in so fast, and it tore directly over my head at a speed much, much faster than *any* airplane I'd ever seen or known about. As a pure guesstimate that thing was between two and three thousand feet above the ground. The whole world shook and rattled as it crashed above and beyond me, and it continued on a straight course due west. In a matter of seconds it had ghosted down to a thin, hollow cry, and then it was gone.

I was shaken, and I was mystified. Absolutely baffled. I couldn't account for either its speed or the nature or volume of that sound.

Some years later, with nothing to explain what I'd experienced, I read about the Italians flying their Caproni propellerless jet, a sort of bastardized ducted fan. But that was far away, in Italy, and it didn't fly very well or for very long. Then the British got into the act with the Whittle gas turbine, and of course the Germans were into jets. All this was on the other side of the ocean. Nothing with a jet engine was flying in this country for years after the 1938 incident, so *that's* out as an explanation.

And then it was 1945. I was an active pilot in the U.S. Army Air Forces, a captain, and walking along a flight line.

And I heard the same sound again that I hadn't heard since 1938. There was absolutely no mistake. *None.* I'll stand by my statement against what anybody says. This time I looked up, and a Lockheed P-80 Shooting Star jet fighter boomed across the airport, right over me, at just about a thousand feet.

The sound was identical.

Somehow, back in 1938, I'd heard a jet fighter, some kind of jet machine that I never saw that wouldn't be flying in this country for several more years.

THE NINTH OF JULY

Pick your year. Just so long as you're thinking of the beautiful and graceful Lockheed Constellation—and of the ninth of July.

Sometimes coincidence becomes more than bizarre. It happens against odds so great they challenge mathematical reality.

The Lockheed Constellation was a four-engined piston transport born in the Second World War as the C-69, which matured swiftly and beautifully into commercial models. Four pounding engines and propellers, the graceful body lines of a winged dolphin, and a high triple tail made the ship a standout anywhere it appeared throughout the world. The pilots loved the slim and graceful lines. She flew with as much sensitivity and grace as her physical appearance indicated, and "the Connie" spanned oceans and continents to shrink the world dramatically.

But there was one particular Constellation, carrying the foreign national registration of AHEM-4, from which fortune appeared to have fled. The AHEM-4 came off the production lines in the final months of World War II and went immediately into service.

On 9 July 1945 a mechanic working on the airliner stumbled into one of its whirling propellers and was instantly hacked to pieces, his body parts bloodily flung about the flight line.

One year later, on 9 July 1946, Constellation AHEM-4 was on a smooth flight crossing the Atlantic Ocean. It was, in fact, one of those dream flights when everything works beautifully. The passengers within the long cabin remained blissfully unaware of the stark drama in the cockpit. Captain Arthur Lewis, flying left seat, slumped over his controls. He was dead. The first officer (copilot) in the right seat took over the controls and continued the flight to a safe landing.

One year later, the 9th of July, 1947, AHEM-4 has put in a great deal of service. Several thousand hours flying time, in fact. The maintenance inspections follow a rigid guideline. Parts are replaced, others repaired, the sleek ship "kept up to snuff." AHEM-4, among other things, gets a new engine to replace one that's starting to lose its efficiency.

The Constellation makes its next takeoff beautifully, easing from the runway at Idlewild, gear coming up and—the new engine explodes into flames as the heavily laden aircraft is barely across the end of the airfield. Immediately Captain Robert Norman, pilot, punches in the engine fire-extinguisher system. Everything works; chemicals smother the blaze, and the fire is out. But now the Connie is a *three*-engine airplane, and it's at the heaviest in its flight, desperately needing power to clear buildings.

Norman looked at a huge apartment building directly before the laboring Constellation. *We're not going to clear that thing,* was his judgment. He rammed his throttles full forward to squeeze every ounce of power he could get from three engines, and the Constellation cleared the apartment building, many witnesses said, by inches.

Captain Norman and his flight crew sagged in their seats; they'd made it! As speed built up, Captain Norman started back on the throttles to high-climb power instead of maximum engine operation that could quickly overheat the engines.

The throttles were jammed into position. They wouldn't budge. Engine temperatures were climbing steadily. You need skill to fly an airplane, and rarely are you called upon to exercise brute force. This was that rare time. Norman and his copilot both grasped the throttles and by sheer force managed to ease them back to a safe position. Captain Norman had enough; he brought the big airliner around the field, declaring an emergency, and set AHEM-4 down safely.

One year later, on 9 July 1948, everyone waited nervously as the day passed. Nothing happened. The jinx was broken!

9 July 1949. The graceful Constellation fell from the sky to crash near Chicago, Illinois. Everyone aboard died in the carnage.

The pilot was Captain Robert Norman.

TIME FLICKER

Sometimes, no matter how much information you gather on a specific incident, no matter how much research you do, no matter how extensive the confirmation of details, the research and the investigation, you're left with a sense of emptiness, of inability to understand. *Something* has happened. So-called proof is absolutely out of the question because of the particular circumstances. Everyone involved is intelligent, capable, educated, in control of themselves and their lives. *But...*

On the morning of the 19th of March, 1917, a young woman, stationed with her husband in India, was busy dressing her baby. War was on the other side of the world. Her own world was comfortable and well protected.

She placed the infant on the bed, enjoying the obvious pleasure the child took in her attention. The mother glanced about the room and froze. At first her facial expression was disbelief; this yielded instantly to one of wild delight.

Standing at the end of the bed, where he had obviously slipped quietly into the room to surprise her, was her brother. He was a military flier on duty in Europe. There had been some promise that he would be posted to an airfield in India, and the entire family had looked forward to his arrival. He was also a bit of a trickster with his sister. She paused only a moment to check her infant son on the bed, then turned to rush into the arms of her brother.

He was gone.

For several minutes she searched the house, calling out his name. Finally, unable to find him, she implored her brother to end his charade. She never did find him in the house, and she returned at last, troubled and confused, to the bedroom and her child.

Later that day she learned that, at the exact moment she saw her brother in her bedroom, he was shot down and killed in aerial combat over Europe.

NO REASON

You've got a right to expect a ghost to have a history, a comprehensible purpose, *something* along those lines, for a haunting to exist. Especially a haunting (or an effect we'll describe as a haunting because we lack any other applicable term) that results in physical movements, phantoms, apparitions, and other effects that defy what those bigdomes, our scientists, call "normal reason."

But there's at least one large four-engined bomber, a Boeing B-29 Superfortress, that came out of the Second World War that appears not only to be haunted—but *shouldn't* be.

The B-29 was about the slickest heavy iron to appear during the Big Deuce. Faster, larger, heavier, and far more modern than anything else in that war, it was the machine that tore apart the cities of Japan. It unleashed a torrent of incendiaries and high explosives that shattered Japanese industry and economy, and it finished off the job by lobbing nuclear bombs into Hiroshima and Nagasaki.

That wasn't the end of its mission. During the more frigid years of the Cold War between the United States and the Soviet Union, the B-29 for many years was the mainstay of our aerial strike force against Russia or any other target. When we got embroiled in that "police action," as we politically misnamed the Korean War, the B-29 came back into the thick of action by striking at major North Korean targets. It also appeared in a special strike force operating out of Okinawa, prepared to dump a whole string of powerful nuclear bombs down the Inchon Valley to incinerate one or more Chinese armies; if Inchon's invasion turned into a defeat for Doug MacArthur, the nuclear fire would be unleashed. It's one of those episodes of near-full-war little known to the American public. It was well known to the MiG-15 pilots who climbed to the atomic strike force at thirty thousand and thirty-five thousand feet, circling off the Korean coast; the MiG pilots, most carefully briefed, studied the recognition symbols on the bombers packing nuclear stuff and dropped back down to twenty-five thousand feet to hammer at those B-29s carrying old-fashioned iron bombs.

The B-29 soldiered on in many fashions. It dropped a huge number of atomic bombs and hydrogen bombs in weapons tests. Try "many tens of millions of tons of high explosives effects" just for the notebook. When we needed more performance, Boeing used the basic B-29 to produce the much more powerful, more advanced B-50 Superfortress that was another leap forward in performance. Other B-29s were being used for weather reconnaissance, chasing hurricanes, and carrying scientists on special missions. Still others carried aloft strange-shaped, rocket-powered machines to sling those birds on their way to penetrate the sound barrier (way back in 1947) and reach new heights in the skies.

In sum, it was an air force, a national mainstay.

Come we now to the sprawling air force museum at Castle Air Force Base in Merced, California. In today's world, by virtue of its scarcity, the B-29 is almost truly a "ghost ship," so thin are its ranks. In the United States the Confederate Air Force was flying *Fifi,* a B-29 rescued from a junkyard and rebuilt at tremendous effort and expense. Elsewhere one or two more of these magnificent machines are being brought slowly back to life, but that is *it.* Except for the museum articles, the era of the B-29 may have reached the bottom of the resurrection barrel.

The B-29 at Castle Air Museum didn't fly into that airfield to be taxied to its museum stand. It came to the museum in trucks, delivered in bits and pieces from different junkyards, disposal fields, and metal-melting centers. In short, it was "saved" in a haphazard fashion.

The airplane stands proudly at Castle Air Museum, rebuilt as a combat machine, with its name painted proudly across the sides of its nose— "Old Raz'n Hell." It's also a B-29 that almost never saw rebuilding as a nonflying museum article, because for a while a number of mechanics working on this airplane slowly coming together refused to continue their work on the machine.

Old Raz'n Hell began to "come alive" during resurrection, enough to whiten the faces of many of the men creating a new machine out of the dumped and junked pieces of the old. The events didn't wait until the ship was pieced together. That's enough to bring almost anybody straight up to pay attention. Nothing official had yet been said about anything unusual. You had to be around when crew members of B-29s, and others working on the rebuild project, began to talk to one another. They spoke of things they wouldn't tell anyone else. As more than one pilot has said, they didn't want to "be carried off, kicking and screaming, because they admitted to seeing ghosts or saying this crazy machine was haunted."

At first the whole thing seemed so unbelievable that the people involved were convinced they were seeing things. Well, everybody sees things, of course, but these were air force crewmen and mechanics who were rubbing their eyes and starting to believe they were "seeing things that weren't there." That's a real neat trick: it simply isn't possible unless everyone involved started hallucinating the same thing at the same time. If you *see* something, then "something" is there. It doesn't have to be physical. It can be a reflection, a projected image, or even a holographic image projection, but the eye is responding to a physical/optical effect.

None of that fits *this* series of events with what would become *Old Raz'n Hell*.

It started with a mechanic shooting pictures inside various large pieces of wrecked B-29s in the "graveyard" at the China Lake Naval Weapons Center some two hundred miles southwest of Castle Air Force Base. China Lake receives airplanes and helicopters of all kinds that are no longer airworthy and places them in safe locations for pilots to shoot at or strike with machine guns, cannon, napalm, bombs, and other instruments of destruction. In fact, China Lake yielded one old B-29, battered and beaten but basically still in one giant piece, that became the Confederate Air Force *Fifi*. That group flew the airplane out of China Lake.

But no one was going to fly out *Old Raz'n Hell* because there wasn't any one plane left to fly. Bits and pieces, that's all. So the smart thing to do is to photograph everything that's available and then figure what you'll need to assemble a complete airplane. In the first batch of photographs printed, the mechanics stared at a photograph of a milky, round object that appeared to be hovering in midair. The men looked at one another, obviously sharing their first immediate thoughts, and one finally said, "Nah; no way, man," and they put aside the pictures they couldn't understand and didn't want to pursue any further.

Staff Sergeant Robert Kraus and another crewman went to China Lake to rummage through wreckage. Several times Kraus turned suddenly because he "felt someone" behind him. Not his companion, who was in sight in front of Kraus, but a third person. Kraus called it a "presence" that was "human." Neither Kraus nor his companion ever saw anyone during these times.

The parts started flowing north to Castle Air Museum. Part of a fuselage, a nearly complete tail section, and the larger part of a right wing began the assembly project. Other men went to China Lake, and the parts and element of three or four B-29s were shipped northward. With enough material gathered the mechanics started to put the puzzle together.

Apparently parts were being moved by people other than the mechanics. Sergeant Rickey Davidson and another mechanic stared open-mouthed, while in the yards at China Lake, when a *locked* door in a fuselage section opened. No one else was in the fuselage, but the door opened from a locked position, then closed and relocked itself. They felt it. *Locked.*

The door opened wide by itself and closed. The two airmen blinked their eyes, wondered, and then stared in awe as the door opened and closed once more and then remained in place. Davidson told others about what had happened, and in return they began to tell Davidson of the "strange things" they'd seen and that had happened to them.

"Something like this has never happened to me," explained Davidson. "I don't believe in ghosts, but I know there's something there.

"You know how you can tell when your back is turned, and someone comes up and looks over your shoulder. Well, I *always* feel that in the tail section."

Even if no one was ever there with him.

The first time Davidson experienced what he describes as "I know there's something there" was way back in 1980. Years later the strange events in the B-29 were still happening, and to people who never knew one another.

Major Ernest Wilde is the museum project director. The ghost stories started piling up on his desk. Finally the stories began to be heard off base as well, and the Associated Press dispatched reporters to track down what story might be worth telling. To their surprise Major Wilde told it straight from the shoulder.

"We're not saying there is a ghost," the major said firmly, "but there are many people who think there's something in there. Several crew members refuse to enter the plane alone, especially at night."

Hold it; *hold it!* We're talking about a museum piece assembled from different airplanes, standing in an air force base under solid security—*and airmen on active duty are refusing to enter?* What could they be frightened of so badly they would refuse to carry out their jobs?

Well, one night a mechanic walked beneath the nose of the bomber. It's a great rounded section of many windows; the visibility is fabulous from the B-29 cockpit. This particular mechanic, DeWitt, looked into the cockpit—and saw a person moving about.

No one was supposed to be in the airplane. DeWitt immediately called for the air police. While he was doing so, the figure in the cockpit vanished. The air police found an empty airplane.

Several times mechanics and crewmen working on the B-29 placed tools and aircraft parts on the pilot's seat in the cockpit. Every time they returned to that spot to pick up a part or a tool, it was missing—and later found somewhere else in the airplane. This happened even when only one man was in the B-29 at the time; no one else was present who *could* have moved a part fifty or sixty feet away.

Things went from strange to stranger. Doors kept opening and closing within the airplane when there wasn't enough wind to move a feather. Crewmen working in the plane began to carry walkie-talkie radios in an attempt "to nab right on the spot whatever's happening." There was some nabbing—the walkie-talkies sputtered, sparked, and went dead, repeatedly. The components were fine, but something was draining the energy from all the batteries.

Finally there occurred at Castle Air Force Base an event that certainly stands as one of the most unique in military history.

A group of airmen, mechanics, crewmen, and "other unnamed persons" gathered in a seance, the purpose of which was to confirm, discredit, or discover *anything* that might indicate supernatural forces were at work.

The conclusions? Well, very little was reported about the seance. The air force, obviously, wanted absolutely nothing to do with what had fast become a public-relations nightmare. And the people who gathered for the seance refused to talk about it afterwards.

But one piece of information, one name, did come to light. Long before *Old Raz'n Hell* began to come together from the parts of at least five planes, a gunner named Arthur Pryor had flown as a crew member on one of the B-29s that ended up in the junkyard at China Lake.

Arthur Pryor apparently died of natural causes sometime in the 1950s.

Absolutely nothing else was ever said. And if there *is* anything else, well, forget it. The air force doesn't admit to ghosts, and it would have far preferred that the seance had never taken place.

Mystery: *unsolved.*

Disposition of the case: *closed.*

Chapter 10

=PERPLEXITY WITH/ WITHOUT ANSWERS

The material for this book came from around the world. For every story, for every vignette, for every mystery, and for every explanation you read here, ten times that amount of material was studied, researched, scoured, and subjected to attempted explanation. In a surprising number of cases, investigation prevailed, and an answer, while perhaps not as neat and tidy as we might have chosen, emerged in story form within these pages.

In chapter 2, "Black Thursday," we saw the devastating losses of Flying Fortress bombers suffered in the strike against Schweinfurt, Germany; in that chapter we pointed out that several of the bombers that returned successfully to England were lost in crashes.

Recently, as we were putting this book "to bed," a letter arrived from Bedfordshire, England, from John T. Gell, with whom I shared research into other B-17 misadventures. Buried in Mr. Gell's letter was a notation that fairly leapt from the page, for it turns out that the five B-17s returning to England, of which two "crashed and were destroyed," had a bit more of a story than had surfaced earlier. John Gell takes us back now to that terrible October day in 1943...

On the eve of 14 October 1943, we had been watching the B-17s returning to the bases around us—the 303rd, 306th, 379th, and others—when
suddenly we heard a lone B-17 with her engines popping and stuttering.
That got our immediate attention, and we looked about to see this lone
bomber rushing almost directly at us. It approached our house at a dreadfully low altitude—we flinched as the mass of the airplane rushed low
overhead—and it smashed into the trees right in our back garden. It had
been even lower than I dared to think! Later we recalled, when we were
calm enough to discuss what happened, that we distinctly could hear the
wind whistling by from the aircraft's passage.

It was a terrible smashup, and we could hardly have been closer to the
disaster, a most distressing, and I will say even a terrifying, event. You can
feel the wind of the crash. Feel the impact as the earth shudders and even
shakes, and pieces of airplane go whirling about crazily. When we regained our senses, for we had gone through physical shock from that
impact, we saw that the Fortress had broken up into four large sections.
Not an instant had passed after the wreckage hit when my father was
dashing to the airplane to see if he could save any of the crew. He completely ignored the danger that the ship might burst into flames at any
moment, as crashed aircraft are so wont to do. But no flames appeared; we
sighed relief as the minutes went by. In the background there was the
steady roar and rise and fall of engines as more B-17s returned from their
raid, but we could hear the clang of moving metal as my father searched
for survivors.

Several minutes later he emerged from the wreckage with the most
perplexed look on his face. "You know," he said slowly, "there's no one
aboard this aircraft."

A chorus of startled, "What?" greeted his words.

"I said," he repeated slowly, "there is not a human soul aboard this
machine. I have found some soiled battle dressings. Pretty well bloodied
up, they are. This machine took a terrible beating. Blood everywhere, and
it's been holed by guns and cannon fire. That's evident even above the
damage from the crash."

Back in the house my father called in the exact location of the smashed
Fortress, supplying the serial number, and informing the people in American operations that there was no need for an ambulance, because there
wasn't a person aboard that airplane. There was a bit of fuss about that,
and they sent over the right people, anyway, but soon saw for themselves

B-17 exploding on ground

drawing by Fred L. Wolff

that an empty B-17, shot to pieces, had somehow returned to its home base, began a letdown for landing, and then crashed.

Now, for what came soon afterward! Some days after the wreckage had been removed by the Americans, my father noticed something lodged in the forked branches of one of the trees that absorbed the impact crash of the B-17. It was a propeller blade. We called the Americans again to tell them of what we had; they said they'd send over a crew to fetch it, but they never did. As the war began to wind down, we called them again about the blade, and they said we could keep it if we wished, as a memento. Well, we did just that, and I still have that blade. I'll tell you something else I doubt you expected. Without your knowing of the details I have just passed on to you, you describe that crash on page 232 of your book *Black Thursday.*

Some years later, interest in that propeller blade was renewed when some people came by to see us, explaining a strong interest in artifacts of the Eighth Air Force. I could not tell them much more than the date, the event, and the group to which the B-17 had been assigned. Then more pieces began to fall into place. This B-17 had been with the 303rd

Bomb Group, and then we confirmed that *the entire crew had bailed out over Belgium.*

Yet this Fortress, now entirely unmanned, had flown *in formation with the other B-17s,* turning and whatever was necessary to descend *and* turn, directly back to its home field before crashing in our backyard. The pilots with whom I have discussed this at first flatly refused to believe it, but the factuality of it all became ever more evident when we found that not only had the entire crew bailed out, but they had all escaped from German-occupied territory and ten days later were back in the air again aboard another B-17!

I simply could not let this affair go without further information. In 1984 I began to trace the crew, and over the last five years I have made contact and have corresponded with the regular crew of this airplane. It seems the crew assigned to this plane did not fly this day, and an entire replacement crew took her up, and when they bailed out, this machine was going to return home, no matter *what.*

So there were two complete crews involved, and fifteen of them are still with us today. Before the war ended, both of those crews were shot down, but deeper within German territory, and they spent the rest of the war in POW camps. So we do not have any ghosts, as such, attached to this story. Just an airplane that seemed to have a mind of her own and did everything she could to return to her own crew...

Postscript: For those with a bent toward numbers along with their personal accounts, the Flying Fortress in question was named *Cat o' 9 Tails,* had the official number on the tail of 25482, along with a large letter *C* in a triangle; beneath the serial number of 25482 was also a large *W* on each side of the vertical fin.

SOLVE A MYSTERY: CREATE A MYSTERY

23 November 1944.

A plowed field in Belgium, several miles southeast of Brussels. Thin haze filled the sky, normal enough for Europe in the early winter. In this area there wasn't much for three gunners of a British antiaircraft unit to do, unless a few German planes came over on the deck for ground-attack runs, an event that had become ever scarcer as the great air battles surged higher and deeper into Germany itself. But if nothing else, these men were treated to an incredible parade of fighters and bombers rumbling into and then out of German airspace. Today the routine differed. Distant engine thunder rolled over the gun position, the men took their places and charged their weapons. "Relax," one said, "it's the heavies, all right. Sounds like the world's coming to an end. They'll be high up."

A gunner pointed. "Not this time, mate. See that one? Just breaking through the haze layer? *He's* coming down. Right where we are."

The British gunners swung their weapons about, locked their sights on the four-engined bomber still descending toward them. "It's one of them Forts," called out one man.

"Yank Fort or not," the leader said sharply, "keep your sights on him. We don't know if there's a Jerry crew aboard. It's happened before, remember?" And it had. B-17s that landed in Germany with badly wounded aboard were often crewed with Germans to mix in with American formations, reporting on altitude and speed for antiaircraft weapons below, or even sliding in close to another B-17 and then opening up with all available weapons on the unsuspecting victim.

"He looks like he's going to land!" called out a gunner.

"His gear's down!"

The Fortress descended steadily. "Look, he's got one feathered..."

"Another one's windmilling; the prop's just going around uselesslike."

"He's crazy. This is a farm field, not a bloody runway!"

The B-17 continued its descent and made a perfect approach to the plowed field; the men saw it flare, and then they scrambled behind sandbags for cover as the Fortress's landing gear thudded against the ground. The bomber rocked as it rolled past them, hurling up freshly plowed dirt.

"Watch it!" a gunner yelled by reflex. A landing gear leg began to buckle in the soft ground as a tire dug in, the wingtip struck ground, and the Fortress swung about wildly, then rocked to a stop all in one piece save for the propeller that struck the ground. The three-bladed prop sheared from the engine, but the two engines that had been operating normally continued to roar.

They stared at the airplane. *Nothing happened.* The B-17 rested in the field, two engines running. No one moved. No hatches opened. The gun leader called in by radio to his command post. They fired back questions: identification numbers, symbols, insignia; anything to pass on to the Yanks. "All right," came their orders, "they *may* be Jerries. If they are, you know what to do."

The gun leader shrugged. Brilliant orders. If they're Yanks, make them welcome. If they're Germans, capture them. If they don't wish to be captured, shoot them. *A, B,* and *C.*

Two men went to the Fortress; one stayed behind with his antiaircraft weapon leveled at the airplane. The two men at the airplane peered in through the Plexiglas and the waist compartments. They waved for the third man to join them.

"Not a stir, not a peep," one gunner said. "Just those two engines whaling away like they're supposed to."

"Are you telling me we've got a machine that just landed by itself and there's no one aboard?" asked the leader.

"Look for yourself," one of his men said. "This thing's got a bloody ghost for a pilot, *because there's no one in that thing!"*

The senior noncom called in his report again; his call was passed on to the nearest operations center, at Cortonburg. This went to a British officer at Erps-Querps. Twenty minutes later the officer, John Crisp, raced to the scene. He and the others walked slowly about the Fortress, the two engines still running. "Cripes, look at the damage. This thing's been hit with everything the Germans could throw at it."

Crisp tried to open the lower front hatch. It was locked from the inside. He went back to the bomb bay. The doors were closed and secured. Every hatch was locked from *inside* the bomber. Crisp went to a waist-gun position, its fifty-caliber machine gun jutting into the open air. "Help me up," he ordered. The gunners boosted Crisp to the open gun position, and he eased his way into the Fortress.

He called out loudly. "I say, is there anyone about?" He felt foolish, but then he felt amazed. No one answered. He leaned out the waist position and helped the three gunners aboard. John Crisp told them, "I want one man always with another. Got that? Do not go alone through this aircraft."

Crisp fired questions in rapid fashion at the gunners. Had they seen *anyone* in the aircraft? In the nose? In the cockpit? Anywhere? Each time the answer was negative. Not a soul had been visible.

They went through the Fortress from nose to tail, all the while with both engines still rumbling. Finally Crisp returned to the empty cockpit, his sense of eeriness growing. He moved his hands gently across the unfamiliar controls, experimenting as he went, and finally worked the controls that shut down the engines. The deep rumbling died away, and a blanket of silence followed. They continued their search. In the navigator's log-

B-17

book Crisp read the notation, *Bad flak.* Other documents lay about, including the secret identification radio calls for the bomber for that mission. Crisp was surprised to find the still-secret Norden bombsight in its proper position in the nose, uncovered and obviously in recent use.

The search baffled them more every minute. They found bars of chocolate lying about, several of them partially eaten. Then several fur-lined heavy jackets and six parachutes, all ready for instant hookup to chest-harness clips.

Then there was nothing more to do except pass on as much information as possible to the Americans. Crisp went to Evenburg and advanced headquarters of the Eighth Air Force Service Command, providing full details of everything he had seen and noted. It took a while for the bizarre report to make its way through channels, but finally word reached Brussels, where the main headquarters of the forward operations command of the Eighth Air Force was located.

Immediately a maintenance team was on its way to the lone Flying Fortress in the plowed field. The official report of their inspection indicates that the B-17 had taken a terrible beating from German flak and fighters. Two engines were chewed up. Large sections of aircraft skin had been torn away. Bullet and cannon-shell holes were everywhere.

Then the mystery deepened—although at first it appeared the mystery had been solved. Eighth Air Force *found the crew from the bomber.* The crew couldn't understand all the questions thrown at them. According to the pilots and aircrew, the Fortress was losing altitude steadily, and under orders from the pilot, everyone bailed out over Belgium.

Why abandon the still-flying airplane? The response was that the windmilling propeller had set up tremendous drag, making it almost impossible for the pilot to maintain proper control of the B-17. When the two remaining good engines began to backfire and choke up, losing power, that was it. The bell for bailout rang through the airplane, and out everybody went. The crew reported the pilot had the airplane on automatic pilot before they abandoned the ship; the crippled bomber was in a steady descent as they went out.

What about all those parachutes? Again the crew had an answer. They always carried extra chutes, ready to be snatched up and used. Why so many? Again the answer seemed plausible. The chutes were packed one atop another. If they took flak or bullets from below, the bottom parachutes took the damage and left the upper ones in good shape to be used. It made sense.

That's where "sense" began to dissipate. In short, too many "plausible explanations" went out the nearest window when a tighter review of events was made.

First, *no one explained how they bailed out.* The hatches were closed from the inside. The bomb-bay doors were closed. Climbing out the waist positions was just about impossible without injuring or killing several crew members, and none of the "survivors" had said a word about going out through the waist openings. Could they have climbed up and gone out an upper hatch? Yes, with a virtual guarantee of smashing into the tail. Scratch that explanation. What had seemed so easy to understand was now an even greater mystery than before.

Then there was the matter of the two good engines. The crew said they were backfiring and choking badly and losing power. It would seem, then, that the very act of the crew abandoning the airplane somehow brought those two engines right back to full and smooth operation. That *could* happen. Engines do strange things, and more than one pilot who left his faltering machine and took to his parachute later heard his pilotless machine rev up to smooth, full power and send the abandoned plane off into wild gyrations.

And then, finally, *there was the matter of the landing gear being down and locked.* The more we reviewed this individual case, the more suspicious *we* became that someone was yanking someone's string. First we had a mystery that defied all rationale; an abandoned airplane, suffering severe battle damage, one engine dead, another dead but windmilling (from the force of the airstream) and only two engines operating, and a crew that bails out of that same airplane through hatches that remain closed from *inside* the ship...and after all this, the Fortress managed to continue its steady descent and *then* lift its nose and flare for a landing (and this is a tail-dragger—with a ground-hugging tail wheel—*not* an airplane with a tricycle gear) *and land.*

This is something like a reverse operation; the explanatory sting, so to speak. To the everyday, normal, average reader, hell, the explanations fit. But to those of us who've flown B-17s and other heavy iron, considering what happened and at what point in this flight, *something stinks.*

There's the hook in here. If you have a B-17 with two good engines, one dead and feathered, and another dead and windmilling—stop right there. A prop that's windmilling and causing tremendous drag means that engine is kaput. Funeral material. So you want to feather the blades, have them point knife edge into the wind for absolutely minimum resistance. Having the blades present frontal area, without power, is like putting up the barn door to create drag and control problems.

So here we are, the bomber unable to maintain altitude, a nightmare of drag and *asymmetrical* drag combined, which means the airplane driver is having one hell of a time maintaining directional control. The last thing this guy needs is any more drag—*and then he drops his landing gear while he's still well above the ground, and they're bailing out?* What that gives the pilot is a whole bunch more drag. His airplane needs more power (which it's already lacking) and it descends faster (which it's already doing against the pilot's best efforts) and everything starts going to hell in a handbasket a lot faster than before. Now consider those engines. The two working engines were backfiring and "stuttering," to quote one of the alleged crew members. That means there was even *less* power available than with both good engines howling at full throttle. It also means there's every chance those working engines would not only cut in and out but would fail altogether, and then the best B-17 ever built is swiftly becoming a Steinway piano instead of an airplane!

So the gear comes down, the drag increases greatly, a bad situation becomes a real nightmare...why put down the gear?

Well, after all the foregoing, the airplane without a living soul aboard makes an incredibly smooth landing, its few bounces the result of the furrowed field rather than poor control, and it is rolling across the field, and stops finally when a gear digs in and swerves the machine around. And those two cranky, stuttering, backfiring engines keep right on running. (Okay; we'll buy that. The Fortress is now nearly at sea level, which means denser air and more oxygen, and it could have been just what the two remaining engines needed to gasp back to life. It is highly improbable, but it *has* happened a goodly number of times to other airplanes, and we accept we'll have to buy the package of those engines.)

But the rest of it does not fit, especially the gear coming down, at altitude, from a drag-crippled airplane. And why drop the gear if you're bailing out? The attempted "fit" gets worse.

One explanation was offered that dropping the gear would increase controllability. The creation of more drag would help keep the airplane under better directional control. Nice try, but not likely. When you're riding that thin edge of fighting the balance between drag and speed, trying to keep your bird from tearing out of your hands, and you're already too slow and you can't even maintain altitude, the last thing you want to do is throw out a couple of drag-creating skyhooks.

Someone, somewhere, for some reason we have never fathomed, except to get rid of a nasty report that was unexplainable and unacceptable to higher headquarters, twisted around what *really* happened to bring in an abandoned, pilotless airplane to a landing on a field where even a human pilot might have found the going too tough to handle.

So the mystery that was explained became a mystery doubled. And the odds are, we'll never really know all the details.

Consider this, as well. If the pilot didn't lower the landing gear, and the odds are he didn't, *who did?* Well, the next immediate possible solution is that the gear, because of battle damage, fell down freely.

That's a nice try, too, but it won't hold water. Because, you see, when the British officer climbed into the cockpit, and this was later verified by our Air Force technicians, the gear was down *and locked*.

It's vexing, but Time is one hell of an eraser.

One of the most frustrating elements of recording these pages of history before they disappear into legend that can no longer be confirmed, because the participants or the eyewitnesses have died or can no longer be found, and the records themselves are lost or destroyed, is that on many occasions there appears a mystery so confounding, so strange, that the record keepers refuse to place in the archives the events as they were recorded or sworn to. They simply refuse to do so, on the basis, as we've already heard that "if I put this down on the record, they'd carry me off to the banana farm." So they don't.

Fortunately, not all pilots, crew members, eyewitnesses, or historians feel that way, and they simply "tell it like it is." This next "moment out of history" is one that has been erased from the official records (as far as I can determine). To those people who don't believe the records are lost, burned, destroyed, or deliberately deep-sixed, let me assure them of the facts. When I was historian for the Fifth Air Force in Japan, headquartered in the Yamato building in the heart of Nagoya, I had the time to go deep into the subbasements of our headquarters. There I found a stack of charred old footlockers. We got them open and found a treasure of historical records: Fifth Air Force histories that everyone believed had been destroyed in a Japanese bombing strike when the Fifth Air Force was fighting out of New Guinea early in World War II.

All this history had been considered lost. What we found were the "flimsies," the thin carbon-paper copies of records that told of events we'd never known—including one air battle when a lone pilot in a P-38, by circumstance in the air on a test flight, was informed by frantic radio call that more than a hundred Japanese fighters and bombers were on their way to attack Seven Mile Drome. The lone P-38 pilot had combat experience and one confirmed kill to his credit. But to attack enemy planes with the odds better than a hundred to one? That was crazy....

His name was Lieutenant William Sells, and he did the crazy. He hauled that thirty-eight into a wingover and ripped straight into the Japanese formations. They watched in amazement from the ground—as they rushed more fighters into the air—as Sells attacked bombers head-on, scattering formations, and making ramming passes at Zero fighters scrambling out of the way. The ground observers confirmed *six* fighters and bombers shot down by Bill Sells, who was himself badly wounded, his P-38 shot up to flying wreckage. He stayed in the fight until he was out of ammunition, made one long pass at high speed through the Japanese, and dived away from the fight.

Bill Sells was faint from loss of blood and from shock but brought his P-38 around to land. American fighters were on the runway, and they gave Sells the signal to "go around" to circle and return for another landing approach.

His time ran out. The P-38, with its pilot faint and by now perhaps falling unconscious, slid off on a wing and plummeted into the jungle. Bill Sells died in the explosion of impact.

An incredible story, a feat worthy of the Medal of Honor—and it lay buried for years in an old footlocker in the subbasement of a building in Japan.

So for whatever reason or reasons, we lose events, episodes, and our history.

Again, I've gone through this preamble because I do not have the documentation for this next episode. I heard of it many times. I spoke with crewmen who were at the British airfield when it happened. Without backup my first decision was not to include what follows in these pages. But I spoke with so many people, *in the right place at the right time to know,* that, with this notice to the reader, I can now relate one of the most incredible moments in the air war of the early 1940s.

Another mission nearly completed. Thousands of bombers returning from the plunge into German airspace. Fortresses, Liberators, Mitchells, Marauders, Havocs, Invaders, Halifaxes, Lancasters, Stirlings, and still others. Our attention moves quickly from them all to one airfield in England, home base to the Boeing B-17 Flying Fortress.

Anxious ground crews drift outside to watch the bombers returning. The head count is the single most important thought. How many went out? *How many will return?* Because when certain hardstands remain empty, the ground crews also feel the terrible loss. That plane, its pilots and crew members, were all part of a tightly knit family, and now the relationship is scoured violently with permanent loss.

There are also the bombers that return with a special announcement. As these ships enter the pattern to land, they fire off dazzling flares that arc high over the bombers—flares that signify *wounded aboard.* If at all possible they receive priority position for landing. As soon as the bomber taxis to its permanent stand on the field, the medics rush to the machine to attend to the wounded, to save lives.

So it was this day, for this particular Flying Fortress. She slipped into the pattern, and men on the ground pointed, and ambulances rolled, as the flares arced high and bright. Medics reached the hardstand, watched and waited. The bomber eased to the runway, rolled steadily, and turned off the exit strip to reach the assigned hardstand. The Fortress wheeled around neatly. The B-17 has noisy brakes, and the ground crews and waiting medics heard them squeal and rumble as the bomber rocked to a halt. Then, in the cockpit, the proper controls were moved and switches thrown, and four propellers slowed to a halt.

Immediately the ground crew was in the airplane through the aft fuselage hatch. They rushed in, looking for the wounded, and they froze. Several men whitened, their faces in shocked disbelief.

No one in the crew of ten men of the bomber moved.

Every man aboard the Fortress was dead.

The medics rushed from one to another, looking at each other with still-growing disbelief.

The bodies were cold. The crewmen of the bomber, according to an official report, "had been dead for a period of time that was a great deal longer than the few minutes it took to conduct the approach, land, taxi from the runway, and park on the hardstand."

Mechanics swarmed through and over the B-17. The disbelief expressed within the fuselage with ten long-dead men, in an airplane that flew and landed as it did, and taxied to its own parking hardstand and then shut down, was repeated by the mechanics.

"The fuel tanks," reported the crew chief, "were literally bone dry."

Word spread swiftly. Other men drifted to the hardstand from where the impossible reports spread through the bomber group. They watched ten lifeless bodies removed from the B-17. Men pointed to the gaping tears and rips in metal from German guns and cannon, but nothing could explain the dead crew, or how the airplane ran with all four engines thundering on empty fuel tanks.

As the last body was carried from the bomber, the B-17 burst into flames. The fire raced through the aircraft fuselage and its wings, a literal explosion of flame as though the ship were soaked in fuel.

The B-17 burned to charred wreckage, virtually consumed by a fierce, raging, "impossible" fire.

Postscript: *No comment.*

COINCIDENCES A BIT TOO FAST

The letter arrived on the 26th of February, 1989, addressed to me from Robert W. Norman of Chicago, Illinois. A quiet and unspectacular letter, but which on study and after further research is one of the best examples of sliding along the thin edge of our reality to some other reality we find so hard to understand.

The very frankness and underplayed simplicity of Bob Norman's continued exchange with me is its strength. He wrote in his first letter—

Twenty years ago, as an architectural student at Texas A and M, I was given an assignment to go out in the field to do some sketching. Having heard of some old B-25s sitting out in Rockdale, I drove over to have a look. There, on an unattended, windswept runway out in the middle of nowhere, I found the four planes I'd heard about. Only one was airworthy; the other three were kept for spare parts for the one flyable bomber.

After maybe a half hour of drawing, I heard a metallic rattling over my shoulder. I turned to look at the one airworthy bomber. The airplane had been locked and fully secured. I was the only person there, and I was some distance from the ship. I stared at the suddenly opened access door under the flight deck. I was amazed to see also that the telescoping ladder had run out toward the ground and was fully extended.

I assure you, not a soul was within miles at the time. Though startled—scared might be closer to it—*I took the incident as an invitation to climb aboard.* After ten minutes looking around, I left the aircraft as I had found it, pushed the telescoping ladder back into its locked position, closed and secured the hatch beneath the flight deck, and returned to my sketch pad and stool. Nothing more occurred.

That called for some specific questions, and I put them to Robert Norman. He replied (along with his sketches of the B-25)—

With respect to the actual incident there's little to add to my original report. But I will absolutely verify, as to the hatch handle and the ladder, both seemed to be in perfect order, because when I exited the plane, I pushed the ladder back up and closed the hatch. Everything was *secure.* In fact, the whole aircraft was intact as far as I remember, not like any picked-clean skeleton in a boneyard. That's what those other three B-25s were for.

I do recall picking up a small piece of broken perspex off the ground that day. Though the day was cool and windy (it was *always* windy out there), and the vegetation all around was a universal shade of brown, under where this broken fragment had been acting as a miniature greenhouse, all was in fresh bloom. It's funny what you choose to remember.

Nothing seemed amiss aboard the plane. I recall that small tunnel running under the flight deck to reach the nose compartment. Years later, when reading a description of that tunnel in *Catch 22,* it all came back to me.

One thing I never forgot was that plane's number. It was 246. I can hardly forget it; I *sketched it.* And though I never again returned to that lonely airstrip and her planes, the incident has never been far out of my thoughts these past twenty years.

Well, the years passed since that moment when I was "invited" aboard that B-25, and for the longest time my life and my world stayed normal. But in 1984 I visited England, and it was as if Time got all twisted up, and another series of strange events took place. Since my boyhood my father spoke of a prewar sailing buddy of his who had gone on to command a bomber group of the Eighth Air Force. I checked on Joseph A. Moller and turned up his old group: the 390th Bomb Group (H) based at Framlingham, Suffolk. Now I'd to England many times before June of 1984, but this trip found me in Felixstowe, so I hired a car and drove out to the old strip.

Near Framlingham I saw a wind sock sticking up above the crops and turned in off the road. Though most of the old base has since reverted to farmland, a small flying operation still existed. At the base stands a restored World War II tower housing the museum collection of the 390th Memorial. Since it was a weekday and the field was closed, I almost gave up and started back to my motel. Then I saw a small notice in the window, referring visitors during off-hours to contact the farmer operating just off the end of the strip. I found the place and met Mr. Percy Kindred, who had been at this station during the war and had known Colonel Joseph A. Moller. I explained my relationship with Moller, and Kindred was kind enough to provide me a tour of the museum.

This is where coincidence came rushing in out of nowhere...

Only three days before my visit, Colonel Moller (whom I had never met) had *also* been at this same field! He signed the guest book just ahead of me. Despite my explanations that I'd never been here and had never met Moller, Percy Kindred stared me right in the eye, locking his gaze with mine in a startling and penetrating look. Then he said: "You were here during the war." At first I took this to be a question. It wasn't. And Percy Kindred was adamant about what he'd said. Well, I wasn't born until 1948, three years *after* the war was over. But Kindred was elderly, and perhaps his sight was failing and he confused me with someone else. That certainly made sense.

Alone again, I set up my camera to take some pictures. I'd treated this camera with consummate care ever since college. It had *never* failed me; not a jam, not even the smidgen of a problem. This time it jammed solid. Something weird was going on. The camera not only jammed, without any reason we could ever determine, but it never again took another photo.

After poking about a bit, I returned to my car to leave and switched on the radio. I froze; out of the speaker, in the style of music popular to that long-ago war time, came the song, *As Time Goes By.* Or perhaps it was *Till We Meet Again.* I'm sure only that it was one of these two songs, and it drifted to me from somewhere far beyond a radio speaker.

Now I'm aware that none of this is too significant by itself, but I found each coincidence coming a bit too fast, and Kindred's insistence he knew me from wartime shook me up, so strong had been his conviction.

Later I spent some time in deep discussion with a friend who is also a successful and professional psychologist. Neither he nor I tried to make out anything more than what I'd told you. But to my surprise he didn't dismiss a thing. *He* brought up the matter of spirits, and he said that if in truth these "spirits" exist, these old warbirds and airfields are their perfect haven. Nor was I alone or even rare in my experiences, which, he added, were really quite mild.

And ever since, other events have cropped up, usually related to England, that not only make me question what is really going on, but how much more there is I myself don't know.

All right, let's remain in England for a while.
First we'll go to Tangemere.
Hang on.

Chapter 11

—BEGIN WITH TANGEMERE

he first letter came in from Jim Gray, a member of the Experimental Aircraft Association, and at the time of this writing, a pilot for more than forty-six years. Once again I must take the moment to emphasize the extraordinary experience and background of the people presenting material for this book, *and signing their names to their statements*. It's called "standing up and being counted."

Jim Gray's initial details were enough to put a chill in the room. "My friend, Eric Marsden," he wrote, "from Horndean in England, is a trustee and 'volunteer' at the Tangemere Museum on the old B of B RAF station. Eric has been instrumental in bringing the museum to its present state of completeness and interest. He has built many of the displays himself and is an author with excellent credentials. He was in the RAF, a leading aircraftsman, from about 1939 through 1945.

"My wife and I visited Tangemere in 1985 and were not only impressed by the progress being made but also had a vague feeling of tragedy and doom when we wandered into the area where bits and pieces not formally added into the collection were kept in storage: that is, not yet made ready for display. There were all of the relics of battle there: torn pieces of aircraft, partial cockpits and turrets where obviously men had died in combat or been grievously wounded. It was a place dark, dreary, gloomy, and full of 'ghosts.'

"I didn't realize at the moment how true, and prophetic, was that feeling....

"My story, brief as it is, concerns some workmen who were building displays at night in order to get things ready for the coming visitors at the soon-to-be opening for the season. Two men, working together but otherwise alone, experienced some 'ghosts.'

"Working on a display one night, they heard a bumping in what I call the 'Gloomy Hall.' Knowing that nobody should be around but themselves, they suspected someone might be trying to break in. They started down the hall and saw a three-foot length of four-by-two (English version of our two-by-four) *pogo-sticking down the hall toward them*—without *any* visible means of locomotion.

"They said loudly, 'All right, chaps, enough is enough!' whereupon the two-by-four subsided and fell to the floor!

"The second episode was with, apparently, the same two workmen, one of whom had placed his hammer next to a piece of work on the floor. When he looked back to pick it up, after a moment's inattention, it was gone. He asked his fellow where it was, and the other workman asked, 'Is this what you're looking for?'

"The hammer had somehow become lodged on a nearby table!

"The workman whose hammer had disappeared called out: 'Okay, chaps; you win!' They picked up their tools and never came back to Tangemere at night. Would you? *Would I?*"

Well...

Anyway, a letter dated 31 January 1989 from Eric Marsden arrived several weeks later.

I read that letter several times, and I offer it to you now without changing a word. It is the marvelous stuff by which legends are given substance, and I, and others, are grateful to Eric Marsden for bringing this before all of us....

Thank you for your interest in the odd phenomena that have occurred at Tangemere. I have shown your letter to our management committee, of which I am a member, and it is agreed that we should send an account to you....

First, you should have a briefing on the museum. It has been set up and run by volunteers, mostly ex-RAF, but also ex-army, merchant navy, plain civilian, and, of course, wives. The chairman, and one of the founders, is Jim Beadle, ex-brat (Halton apprentice, RAF); treasurer, Len Jepps, ex-Queen Victoria's Rifles, went in the bag at Calais, 1940, and had a very interesting POW career. Secretary, Bernard Hammond, ex-Sussex Yeomanry, Dunkirk, North Africa, Italy—a "tankie." Curator, Andy Saunders, younger enthusiast, aviation archeologist and magazine contributor. I joined in the second year: ex-RAF volunteer reserve, flight mechanic and fitter on Hampdens, Hurricanes (Battle of Britain), and Halifaxes, then Mobile Oxygen Plant, RNZAF and USN in Solomons. (I sorted out the oxygen problem, which was killing F44 pilots in the Black Sheep squadron, as well as others.)

Len Jepps tells the events that occurred first—this before the museum was thought of.

The RAF Station, Tangemere, was closed down in October 1970. The old NAAFI (Navy, Army and Air Force Institute, equivalent to your Post Exchange) became the property of Tangemere Parish Council. Round about 1978 Len Jepps was chairman of the parish council, and therefore played host to official visitors. The old NAAFI was now the village's community center, and a party of visitors from West Germany was making a visit to learn about English village efforts in this area of community work. In the evening, after the official business, the visitors were being entertained to drinks, etc., in the bar, when one of the men asked Len about toys and model kits that he had seen on sale in the town. (Len has pretty good German, from his five-year stay as a POW). Was there no problem in England, reference the swastika, he mentioning the ban in Germany, and was there not in England hatred of the Germans from the war, still, and did not these toys prolong the ill feeling? Len pointed out that children will play cowboys and Indians, and you can't have cowboys on their own, and anyway, there was little or no ill feeling anymore, the war was over, and the ill feeling had been for the Nazis. *As he was saying this, his jar of beer took off from the table alongside and hit him in the chest.*

This caused a certain amount of surprise, but whilst Len was being mopped dry, and the floor swabbed, the group stood to clear the area, and one of the ladies put her sherry glass down in the middle of a group of glasses on the nearby table. To everyone's wonder *it began to rock, until*

*it fell over, and then proceeded to wangle its way between the other
glasses until it fell off the table—and the table was level.*

At this point the German ladies indicated they would prefer to leave. It
should be clearly understood that Len has German friends, including one of
the staff of the stalag in Poland in which he was "held" as a POW. (Len had
a couple of German trucks and official escort, with which he traveled as far
afield as Czechoslovakia, delivering clothing to stores and other goods to
other prison camps—and of course collecting all kinds of goodies, including, on one occasion, a brand-new large radio set in carton, which he carried
into camp in full view of guards: after all, he had an escort!)

The second "Tangemere story" concerns the airfield itself—the main
runway. Told me by Len Jepps also. People from the village regularly
walk their dogs around the perimeter track, and before the great storm of
1987, along the runway. (Since the storm a huge bonfire, over one hundred feet long and twenty feet wide, from trees felled by the storm, burned
for three months, and as is the way of country districts, gradually became
transmogrified into a rubbish dump.) Many people, including Len Jepps's
son-in-law, and Len himself, had reported a curious feeling as they walked
the runway in the late evening; they felt sure that coming in from behind
them was an aircraft, and, specifically, a Lancaster. They also felt it to be
in trouble. One chap received such a strong impression that he went home
and painted a picture of what he saw—a Lanc with a couple of dead
engines, drooping ailerons, etc. Again, this was before the museum was
set up. When Len became involved with the museum, he discovered that
*exactly such a Lancaster had come into Tangemere and blew up as it
touched down.* Must have had a hung-up bomb or something similar. (I
have spoken to a chap who lived nearby at the time, and who remembered
the explosion.)

An odd follow-up to that story came to me in 1984. A group of traveling people, or gypsies, had occupied the end of the runway with their vans,
caravans, and trucks. They were always moved on by the local policeman,
who lived in the village, but he always did it with maximum diplomacy,
being one of the old-fashioned wise kind of bobby. I had shown him the
painting of the Lanc, which was then in the museum, and filled out the
story for him. My wife and I were on duty on the Sunday, and he came in
and asked if I'd go with him and tell the gypsies the story of the Lancaster,
which he thought would cause them to view that particular site with disfa-
vor in the future and encourage them to leave immediately.

So I told them the story, and being generally of a superstitious nature, one or two promptly announced that they were going to leave. Others pooh-poohed the whole story—until one lady said that she for one believed such things, ever since they had parked on an old airfield in Kent and her husband had wakened her in the middle of the night to say that they were leaving—because *twice that night he'd been wakened and turned in bed by a nurse!* They left and found later that they had been parked on a hardstand that originally had been the site of the Station Sick Quarters (hospital), now demolished. So, she said, "I believe such things, and we are going." And they all left. The station mentioned by the lady was probably Hawkinge, now long gone and become a housing development.

The next story concerns two "sightings." We have in the UK a government scheme for providing some training in crafts by paying unemployed people to do work of a socially advantageous nature, rather than simply providing a "dole." One winter, three or four years ago, we had two such folk at the museum, carrying out carpentry work; a chap in his late twenties, and a young woman about twenty or twenty-two. On one occasion the young woman arrived at the museum first, in the morning, and on opening the main door was surprised to see "a man in a gray uniform" standing just inside the door, to the left of the entrance. When she spoke to the figure, it simply faded away. Not wishing to be laughed at, she made no mention of the event. A few days later the young man, working in our Battle of Britain Hall, by the top fire door, and working at floor level, looked over his shoulder and saw a "tall figure in gray." Since no one else was supposed to be there, he asked the "man" what he wanted and was surprised to see the figure fade away. When he spoke of this to the girl, she told *her* story.

The last two reported events were perhaps "poltergeist" in nature. I got this report from Bob Shears, one of our carpentry volunteers. Working late one evening, during the winter shutdown, Bob was alone in the Tangemere Hall. Timber for use was stacked near the model of the station at one end, and Bob was working at the other end. He had gone to the timber and cut a piece of two-by-two, leaving the cutoff on top of the pile. Back at his job, sixty feet away, he heard the sound of wood hitting concrete and looked up to see the two-foot-long cutoff "coming down the hall toward me like a pogo stick! So, I went *home,*" says Bob.

Last, I think "GD"—Grant Davis—and Bernard Hammond were involved. Again, in the Tangemere Hall, working on the central partition that runs lengthwise down the hall, they were using the empty shop counter as a bench. (Once again, during the winter shutdown.) The countertop was fairly clear, so, having marked a piece of wood to length, they put the pencil down on the counter—but on turning back to pick it up, to mark the wood again, they found the pencil missing. Having accused each other of mislaying the pencil, they searched the counter and immediate area, to no avail. Whereupon Grant Davis announced loudly to the void, "Oh, come on, fellows! Stop messing us about; we've got work to do!"— *and in that instant the pencil reappeared on the countertop!*

A number of visitors, not knowing these stories, have reported being aware of "presences" in the Battle of Britain Hall, sometimes so intense that, without knowing anything about such past events, they have fled in fear from the Hall.

We have also had *dogs that refused to enter that area.*

A local psychical research group spent a night in the museum and reported readings consistent with the presence of psychic phenomena.

But that's it; I'm sorry we can't give more precise dates or names of probable "origins."

I wasn't letting loose of Eric Marsden that quickly. The events he reported, especially the feelings about a crippled Lancaster bomber coming into Tangemere, are not uncommon in the airfields of England. That's very important to our wide-canvas look at such events at these British airfields and former airfields, where tens of thousands of planes and hundreds of thousands of men worked, flew, and too often died, either staggering back from combat or in accidents. When Jim Gray and I were going over researching the story of Tangemere he impressed upon me not to let Marsden "off the hook, until you get him to speak of himself. I don't know how much he'll admit, but the attempt will be worth it."

Eric Marsden didn't exactly *want* to leave his third-person relating of Tangemere events, but we prevailed, and it was worth it a hundred times over. Marsden finally explained...

My own psychic experiences have been only "premonitions," such as planning to go to a flying meeting and then on the day being reluctant to go. On the first occasion, I didn't go and got into severe trouble with the whole family—it was at Syerston, near Nottingham, on the day the Vulcan (a huge jet bomber—author) crashed and burned on landing, in front of the crowd.

The next time involved country with which you're familiar and have done some flying of your own, especially when you brought in that lovely old Catalina—this was, of course, at Yeovilton. I did not wish to go, that "feeling" again, but we did go, me driving very reluctantly—and saw the pilot of a Harrier being shot through the canopy of his Harrier by his ejector seat, after parking the aircraft. Horrid, bloody mess.

The other was to be chatting with Neil Williams, at Old Warden, where I used to be a helper. I suddenly "saw" Death in his face and said immediately afterwards to one of the other helpers, "Neil will be dead within the next year or so."

And he was.

During the war it was quite unnerving on occasion to have this sudden feeling about aircrew, but in those days we didn't think much about it, because the chop rate was such that one could have made random guesses and been right oftener than not.

ECHOES

England is one of the more extraordinary graveyards of the world. Not that a body count of past lives means very much, for that's a reality virtually anywhere in the world. But for the most part, especially as world population has increased, death functions in its same old way, and the great scythe swings steadily to claim its number. No fuss, no bother.

But *something* changes this prosaic march of death. Something that for most of us is a vast gray unknown. There are some among us who may perceive more clearly, offer more sensitivity in wavelengths about which the rest of us know naught. These people maintain a strange and inexplicable link with a past that seems, with phantom figures, with sounds-that-can-no-longer-be, and even with animals and machinery, to be recurring over and over again.

In researching this book, and this is important for the reader to understand, I rejected more than 90 percent of the material almost immediately upon first study. We haven't been looking merely for *ghosts,* but for events as well as phantoms that in our prosaic, everyday, dreary world, should not be happening. So something special *has* happened, *is* happening, and may *continue* to happen, on the basis of whatever energy field brings such things to pass. But because human nature is what it is, and because imagination, fear, superstition, and peer pressure can do startling things to the human mind, every attempt has been made in this book to exclude "it is reported," "the theory is…" or "it's most likely that…" And so on. Where documentation or references are missing, this book readily admits that fact.

It is a great temptation to go through the many hundreds of incidents, reports, stories, reviews, and studies in our hands and snatch the most gripping of such events and display them here for your study and review. But that's not the way to go.

To me it is not the tumultuous event that marks that world or dimension beyond us, but the subtle, the quiet, often the unspoken.

England during the Second World War became a charnel house of airmen burned, cut, maimed, bruised, wounded, slashed, ripped, torn limb from limb—and many who died. Tens of thousands of men, most of them young and eager and bright, of many nationalities and religions and backgrounds, joined this great gray mist of death.

We don't know who they all were, and we will never know. That, my friends, cuts to the heart of it. It's not all neat and orderly and properly notated and filed simply because it's in our immediate past. And these omissions sometimes bring us much perplexity today. It is as if—and few theories, or convictions, are stronger than this one—until certain souls are laid to rest and their spirits in peace, they're going to hang around and scare the hell out of us. Time and again this seems to be the pattern involved with phantoms, apparitions, ghosts, whatever you wish to call them.

Is this the way it really is? I don't know. I lack the insight, the knowledge; whatever it takes to know.

But I do know there is something terribly unsettling about certain markers in our histories. Something jars the soul and the mind when we come to the tombs of unknown soldiers. Something has been taken forcibly from us when a bomber explodes and not even a shred of one body is ever found. A ship goes down, and dozens or hundreds of thousands of men die within minutes (but at least they return to where life began; small solace for those who wish past lives and loves laid to rest!).

In Newport Cemetery at Lincoln, England, lies an all-too-familiar headstone. It seems utterly forlorn, lonely, a sense of being forgotten pervades its space. The inscription on the stone reads: *An airman of the Royal Air Force Killed…Known unto God.*

Almost all military forces, all nations, in one way or another have such memorials. *This* one, however, really cuts to the bone. What remained of the pilot of a British fighter plane is interred here. The airplane was seen to crash on landing. It could hardly be avoided. The fighter came down, something went wrong, and it veered out of control, tumbled, and then burst into flames as the wreckage slewed off the runway. The fire was so fierce, it melted much of the airplane and its single pilot; what the medics and the graves people could do, they did. They interred what was left and placed the marker at the head of the grave.

The problem isn't that no one could identify the pilot from the remains.

The problem is that neither the pilot nor his fighter plane, on the day the crash and fire happened before hundreds of witnesses, were ever reported as missing then—or since!

RECOGNITION

Linton-on-Ouse airfield sprawls across the countryside of North Yorkshire in England. It's a typical British installation of the Royal Air Force. It played its role during wars and between wars and remained an active air-base down through the years. And it didn't have any ghosts or phantoms, any apparitions, either of past people or dogs or machines. Almost a rarity in England. Everything quite normal and everyday, thank you.

Until the late summer of 1988, that is. *Then* the ghost appeared. An apparition *so* visible, in an operational control tower on the field, that "all hell broke loose among the on-duty personnel."

The first to see the ghost was assistant air traffic controller Brenda Jackson, of Oldham. She knew nothing of ghosts in the control tower. Not until Brenda stared at a figure in World War II flight gear *gliding* past the door. No one else was on duty. No one else was in the tower.

So when she saw the apparition, Brenda did exactly what any sensible woman would do. She screamed. Loudly. An ear-splitting shriek.

Several RAF personnel came running, feet pounding up the stairs to the tower deck. "I've seen a ghost!" she screamed again.

The officers stared at her. No one spoke for a few moments. Thinking back to that first post-ghost encounter, Brenda Jackson remarked wryly: "They thought I had gone mad."

Two weeks later, while perhaps not yet confirming the sanity of Brenda Jackson, the RAF officers on duty at Linton-on-Ouse no longer doubted she'd seen a ghost. The ghost appeared again, this time not gliding past a door, but staring directly at Brenda Jackson and then vanishing.

But not before she let out a howl once again, drawing the instant attention of Flight Lieutenant Mark Byrne. No doubt he muttered under his breath something on the order of, "Oh, no; not again," or "What is it this time?" He confided those were his first thoughts, but he dismissed them quickly.

Lieutenant Byrne also saw the ghost. That took the apparition immediately out of the hallucination category and confirmed the good eyesight of Brenda Jackson.

"Brenda shouted to me," Lieutenant Jackson reported officially, "and I saw this gray shadowy figure. But," he went on with a grimace, "then it disappeared into thin air!"

By now an investigating team was trying to track down the identity of the ghost. Brenda Jackson and Lieutenant Byrne had seen enough detail to make this possible, and within a few days the operations staff was sure they'd pinpointed the source of the ghostly figure.

Warrant officer Walter Hodgson. He flew from Linton-on-Ouse in the Big Deuce. His bomber was shot down over Germany, and he finished out the war as a stalag POW. After the war he returned home, but good fortune eluded the man who'd survived a war. In 1959, only fourteen years after war's end, when he was thirty-eight years old, Hodgson fell ill and died. It was an unexpected ending for the man who had been decorated for bravery in battle and was also one of the more daring prisoners involved in a huge breakout of the German prison camp (he was one of the "true story" characters in the film *The Great Escape*). But the ball bounces without aim, and pursuant to the request of his will, Hodgson was cremated and his ashes scattered along Runway 22—the same runway from which he so often took off and landed during the war.

But why his sudden appearance? Then they had it. A memorial plaque to Hodgson had been mounted outdoors near the control tower. Then the plaque (for a reason not explained) was moved inside the tower.

Explanations came from higher and higher levels of officialdom. Now it was the turn of squadron leader Mike Brooks: "At the time of the first sighting (of the ghost) last summer, we moved a plaque, donated by Hodgson's family to his memory, from the outside of the tower to the inside.

"Perhaps moving it upset his spirit."

Now that's a pretty heavy statement for an RAF squadron leader on active duty to make! All the more credit to Brooks when he next heard from RAF headquarters, which felt the wandering ghost was getting far too much attention. But how do you get rid of a ghost that's the apparition of a *hero?* Why, contact the dead man's widow of course. Which is just what the Royal Air Force did, inviting Mrs. Hodgson back to the airfield "to see if she can make contact with the restless spirit."

Squadron leader Mike Brooks made it official to the family: "Mrs. Audrey Hodgson and her family can visit the station at night to see if they can make contact with Walter."

Audrey Hodgson sent a message to the Royal Air Force women working the control tower. "Don't be afraid. He won't harm you. He just loves the place so much."

Apparently, that was enough.

Neither Walter Hodgson nor his spirit was ever seen again.

TIME TRAPS

In the early morning darkness of 4 August 1951, at the seaside village of Puys, a quiet coastal community close to Dieppe, France, "a gap appeared to open between the present and the past." Those were the words of a British historian who was asked to try to explain how the fury and sound of a battle that had taken place nine years before could be heard nine years later, by two British women on that date, vacationing at Puys. The women were sisters-in-law and especially close; they had gone to Puys for a quiet rest.

Then it was four o'clock the morning of 4 August 1951, and the women awoke, startled and disbelieving with the uproar that crashed through the open windows of their room. Not until later did they recall that Dieppe had been the location of a horrifyingly disastrous "practice invasion" of the French coast, back on 19 August 1942—and then they learned that Puys was one of the actual landing beaches.

On that terrible morning of 1942, British and Canadian troops in a joint operation slammed into the beaches about Dieppe, and into the German-occupied port itself. Dieppe lay in Normandy, and this would one day become one of the major landing areas of the full-scale invasion of Europe (on 6 June 1944). Dieppe wasn't intended to land a force on the French coast and strike inland. It was a test, a probe, what the historians preferred to call a "rehearsal" the invasion to come. As a rehearsal it was an unmitigated disaster. The Germans chewed the strike force to shreds. The attacking force put ashore 6,086 combat troops. The Germans killed or wounded no less than 3,623 of those men.

Time passes; the war ends. Then it is the morning of 4 August 1951, and the two women are trapped in a tunnel of battle. They were so bombarded by the sounds, they wrote down the times of events and the details of what they heard.

It was something *very* unusual...

At just about 4:00 A.M. the women began to hear the shouts and cries of men, as if they were shouting loudly to be heard above the sounds of a storm. Immediately thereafter, in the distance, they heard gunfire, exploding shells, and then the shriek of dive-bombers plummeting earthward.

(At 3:47 A.M. nine years earlier, the lead ships of the strike force began to exchange fire with German ships patrolling the French coast. On shore German soldiers shouted and called to one another as they rushed to their defensive positions.)

At 4:50 A.M. the thundering sounds of battle heard by the two women cut off as if a switch were thrown. An uncanny silence followed.

(At 4:50 A.M. the gunfire of the attacking force stopped. 4:50 A.M. was the scheduled zero hour for the first troops to hit the beaches at Puys. The attack was now seventeen minutes behind its original scheduling. In the confusion of the delay, all gunfire that was scheduled to be lifted from the beach *was* lifted, so that the invasion fleet would not fire on its own men.)

The women strained to hear anything from the silence; it lasted seventeen minutes. Then precisely at 5:07 A.M. they were bombarded by long rolls of thunder, rising in crescendo to waves of explosions. They heard aircraft engines screaming as dive bombers plummeted from the skies, and against this background they could hear the faint cries of men, nearly overwhelmed by the battle clamor.

(At 5:07 A.M. the first wave of assault boats and landing craft slammed into the beaches at Puys. Running late, the troops were desperate to get ashore and out from under withering enemy fire. The seventeen-minute delay was proving lethal, and the British threw everything they had into the protective barrage for the men. Swift destroyers raced perilously close to the shore to hurl direct fire at the German defenses, and waves of fighters and light bombers attacked at point-blank range buildings along the water's front believed to house heavy German forces.)

At 5:40 A.M. the hotel room went crushingly silent, as if once again a switch had been thrown.

(At exactly 5:40 A.M. the British bombardment by warships ended.)

At 5:50 A.M. a long roll of distant thunder drifted into the hotel room, growing steadily louder. The women recognized, unmistakable to them with the war ended only six years before, the sound of bombers in formation, many more bombers than they had heard prior to this moment. Beneath the massed engine thunder they heard other confused sounds, as if from a distant battle.

(At 5:50 A.M. a fresh wave of British bombers with heavy fighter escort came to Dieppe at high speed from their home bases to relieve the fighters on station. By now the Luftwaffe was out in full cry, and violent air battles spread swiftly over the beaches.)

At 6:00 A.M. the sounds faded slowly from the hotel room. By 6:25 A.M. the ripping thunder of battle and aircraft engines was barely a background sound, interrupted only by barely audible cries of men. At 6:55 A.M. silence in the room.

At 8:30 A.M. at Dieppe and the beach landing zones, the German defenders took full control of the battle. The British and Canadians, bloodied and savaged, withdrew as fast as possible from the devastating German firepower. All survivors of the attacking force surrendered to the German army.

Postscript: Although the sounds of battle, the cries of men, and the thunder of aircraft engines at times was so loud, so fearsome, it seemed to shake the entire hotel, only these two women in the entire building heard anything.

When silence fell at 6:55 A.M., the time curtain closed again. Puys and Dieppe faded forever, at least for these two incredulous women, who had somehow tuned in to the past.

RF 398

First there was the Avro Manchester, a whopping giant of a heavy bomber produced for the Royal Air Force mission of hammering German cities after the outbreak of the Second World War. The Manchester was sleek and held great promise as a powerful instrument of destruction. It featured two huge engine nacelles; but its appearance was misleading, for the Manchester had *four* engines. Each engine mount bore two engines mounted together to drive a single propeller, so that you had a four-engined airplane with two pairs of engines each driving a single big propeller. It was an ingenious arrangement that stank. The airplane was as much a whopping failure as it was a whopping giant.

The Manchester in each engine mount had two Rolls-Royce Kestrel engines; mated with a common crankcase, they were given the name of Vulture, a brilliant foreboding of the machine's future. The Manchester was in shape a beautiful machine but often lit up brilliantly in flight from the fact that its vulturous engines failed often and led to wild engine fires. This annoying problem, along with a growing host of others, kept the airplane from ever becoming truly operational, brought the RAF to cancel the "filthy thing" after only forty-eight bombers were placed on operational status, and produced the official explanation that the Manchester was a disaster.

The head of the RAF went with his staff to the Avro company to fly "in the damned thing." They made several teeth-gritting runs about the field and then pointed earthward with but a single-word command: *"Land."* Back in the office of Roy Dobson, the unlucky fellow who had designed the treacherous aircraft, Dobson had what we like to call a "brainstorm." On his desk was a model of the Manchester, which he had already mentally consigned to the scrap heap. But now, impelled by his moment of shining intuition, he held up the model of the Manchester. He yanked off a wingtip and in its place stuck an extra wing panel and an extra engine.

When he finished fiddling with the model, he had a machine with a much wider wing than the original, and instead of two-paired Kestrels-cum-Vultures, he said: "Stick four Merlins on that wing, and we'll *really* have something."

Take one awful machine, suffer its flames, gather for a gloomy meeting, and then have one man with a brilliant afterthought, and you have the beginning of a production line that spawned no less than 7,366 of one of the most successful heavy bombers ever built—the Avro Lancaster.

When things go from bad to good and then to very good, they move along an upward curve that usually heads to even better, and that's the route of the Manchester-cum-Lancaster to a later replacement, the Avro Lincoln, which soldiered on with the RAF after Germany collapsed in 1945.

After its own period of service, the Lincoln began to yield to still-newer designs. Turboprops and powerful jet engines opened the door to greater performance and sounded the retirement bell for the quickly old ships like the Lincoln.

Which includes Avro Lincoln RF 398. The airplane was parked on a remote hardstand of an RAF airfield and virtually abandoned. For thirty years the big four-engined bomber deteriorated slowly in the weather extremes of heat and cold, and from the worst destroyer of all—neglect. Then history began to become a buzzword, and a clamor rose to "save the old machines for posterity!" The RAF decided to place the Lincoln in the museum hangar at RAF Cosford, Shropshire. This particular aircraft, RF 938, had never itself shown a record of combat but was considered worthwhile to represent the developing line of British bomber development.

In the huge hangar with other planes, the Lincoln each night, during its restoration period of some eleven years, was kept safely behind locked doors. Each night the power was cut, and the old plane waited in darkness for the next day.

It was *supposed* to wait in silence through each night.

It didn't.

Guards passing outside the museum doors stopped to listen to strange sounds from the other side of the locked doors. They heard men shouting to one another, engines surging in power, propellers changing from fine to coarse pitch, staccato blips of Morse code signals, cockpit voice callouts as switches and levers snapped and banged, and even the hangar doors rolling open and closed.

A guard opened an entry door and peered in. No question: the uproar was coming from Lincoln RF 398. No one was in the airplane. No one was in the museum. The guard heard the faint sounds of machine gun and cannon fire. He blinked; he knew 398 had never been in war service. He slammed the door shut, locked it, and called the museum authorities.

The story spread swiftly. It appeared that for nearly eleven years Lincoln RF 398 had been a whirlwind center of hauntings, bodiless voices, thundering combat action, and other sounds. No one, outside the small group affected, had ever talked about it. Now, with higher authority on the scene, they not only related what they had heard, but admitted that many of the workmen had refused to go near the airplane at night, and wouldn't even touch it by day.

As official investigation pressed for details, they became ever more startling, and each detail was sworn to and confirmed not by one man, but by *every* worker in the museum at RAF Cosford. Men who were still willing to work on the airplane, for example, would on the day of a violent winter storm enter the freezing hangar. Icicles stretched perilously from the roof. Inside the hangar it was almost as cold as outside, where it was merely cruelly bitter. When the workmen entered the Lincoln, they found the airplane's interior comfortably warm and in the seventies! There was no heat in RF 398, the ship was not exposed to sunlight, the *other* aircraft were freezingly cold. But not RF 398.

On other days, when the hangar doors had been opened and the usual blustery winds of England swirled dust through the hangar, something happened during the night when the shop was closed down. The workmen entering the hangar in the morning stared in disbelief at the planes. They were covered from nose to tail, from wingtip to wingtip, with dust.

Not RF 398, shining a glossy and lustrous black, without a speck of dust, as though the bomber had just been polished.

Ivan Spenceley, an investigative reporter from Chesterfield, Derbyshire, found the stories too inviting to ignore. He received permission to go through RF 398, and he did, from one end to the other. He found nothing unusual during his visit. But when he left the Lincoln, he hid his battery-powered tape recorder inside the bomber. And he concealed it within the cockpit. Then he stayed with the museum staff as they locked all the hatches to the bomber, then padlocked all entrances to the hangar itself.

The next morning he was at the hangar doors as they were unlocked, and standing by the airplane as they unlocked the hatches, and he was first into the cockpit to retrieve his tape recorder. Terry Treadwell, my fellow researcher in England, confirmed this series of events.

In Ivan Spenceley's own words:

"When I played back the recording, I shuddered. It was as if the old girl had suddenly taken to the skies. Human voices are clearly audible, but it is impossible to make out what they're saying. It's eerie."

The administrator of the museum, John Francis:

"I can confirm the hangar was empty when the recording was made because I locked the doors behind Mr. Spenceley. The noises are a mystery. I've got an open mind about it all, but the ghostly stories come from level-headed people who stick by what they have seen and heard."

And then a group of workers refused ever again to enter the Cosford Museum. They had watched a ghostly airman, in full flight gear and battle jacket, walking through the hangar. *That* wasn't so bad, but they could see airplanes *through* the unexpected airman from an unknown past.

Chapter 12

═R̶EAL LIFE

There's this young kid up in a Piper Cherokee in the Midwest, lolly-gagging around on a day with wonderful puffy white clouds surging higher with each passing hour, offering the kid with the still crisp pilot's ticket in his wallet a whole new playground. The kid is good, and he's making the most of it, swooping and spiraling and soaring amidst the building cloud mountains and rushing down the canyons. It's marvelous stuff, and soon some of the bigger cumuli are churning into dark boomers-to-be, but not yet. Now they still have vertical walls brilliant in the afternoon sun. In another hour or two, this sky won't be friendly. The white clouds will darken, and they'll shove seven and ten miles high and begin to close ranks, and their lower ramparts will lose all their friendliness and spit tongues of lightning and dump Niagaras on unsuspecting pilots. But that's still another hour or two, and right now is *glorious!* The youngster races along the edge of a high cloud canyon wall, and he has enough speed to stand the red-and-white Cherokee on its wing and fly a curve that matches almost exactly the curve of the cloud. He'll come out on the other side and roll out to look for another playground before they all become elusive.

The Cherokee goes up on its wing, and the youngster eases in some more throttle to compensate for his lift sliding off to one side; he balances speed and lift and gravity so he'll have enough of what he needs to play out the vertical-wing slide. Now he boosts around the cloud; there, he's free of that wall and a great open space is before him and *omigod!* Directly in front of the shocked pilot is a biplane doing just what he's doing, flirting with wind and sun and clouds; but unseen by one another as they rushed and danced in the air, they ended up heading directly at one another, perilously close.

Both pilots did what pilots do at this sliver juncture between life and death. Stamp on right rudder, yoke all the way over and suck it back in the gut to slam through the tightest break to the right possible. They almost didn't make it. They flashed by one another but not without scraping wingtips. An inch farther apart, and they wouldn't have touched. An inch closer together, and they might have torn loose their wings. But they came *just* close enough for wingtips to scrape. The shocked-terrified youngster in the Cherokee had a blurred look at what he swore was a Nieuport...a Nieuport 28? A World War I biplane fighter? It could be; people were rebuilding and flying every kind of antique these days. He put aside his thoughts. He had maneuvered so violently, he'd kicked into a spin, and he chopped power and kicked rudder opposite to the spin turn and let the yoke forward freely, and the Cherokee came out. With control back in his hands, he swung about desperately, afraid he would see wood-and-fabric wreckage fluttering to the ground below. *Nothing.* He went down beneath the clouds, and he circled the area in a wide pattern, searching for smoke or wreckage or anything, a sign of where might be that Nieuport. *Nothing.*

He tapped in the right frequencies on his radio and called the nearest field and reported what had happened, giving the time and his location. If that other plane had crashed, at least help would be on the way. Then he swallowed as he looked at the fuel needles starting to edge toward the Big E, and he flew to his home field and landed. He repeated his story. The field operator came out to look at the Cherokee wingtip. Sure enough; some paint had been scraped away. But no one had reported a plane down. No one knew of a plane or pilot missing.

The young man's friends hooted and laughed. Told him he scraped his wingtip on a runway light or a fence post, and he'd come up with all this blather just to cover his clumsiness. He took their jeers good-naturedly, and he didn't press the point anymore, but he damned well knew what he had seen and what he'd *felt* when the wingtips brushed.

A couple of months went by. The locals were part of a flying club that looked for old airplanes to rebuild. You never knew what some farmer might have in his barn. They'd even found a Grumman F4F Wildcat, its twelve-hundred-horsepower engine still as good as new, stored in a barn by a farmer who quit flying twenty years before. So when you got a lead or a hot tip, you chased it down.

"I heard there's some old fighter plane in a barn." The word passed, a group drove off into the country, found the farm, talked to the farmer, who allowed he did have an old plane in the hangar, but it had been there so long, it couldn't be worth anything. To the people who restore these things, *nothing* is impossible. They'll take a basket case and turn it with hard work and money and volunteers into a sweet flying thing again.

They went into the barn and gaped. There it was. A Nieuport 28 from the First World War. Or rather, what was left of it. Tires flat; just gone. Fabric rotted off the wings and tail. The engine seized and tight. Everything covered with dust and straw and bird droppings. It hadn't flown in twenty, maybe even forty, years. But they were overjoyed. They touched the old ship, thrilled to her ancient lines.

They walked around the left wing. They stopped and they stared. Jaws dropped.

On that wingtip of the Nieuport—that sagging old unflyable wreck that hadn't been airborne for years—was a smear of red-and-white paint that looked impossibly bright against the drab wingtip. They knew about the kid in the Cherokee; they'd laughed about his story. Yet someone had the presence of mind to scrape off some of that brighter paint. Another pilot stood in the cockpit, leaned down to one side, and reverently brought up a musty, cracked, yellow-weathered old logbook thick with dust.

There are two endings to this story, and they are both true.

They sent the paint to a laboratory to determine its type and age. They also sent, separately, a scraping from the Cherokee.

The paint samples were an exact match.

They read the logbook, especially the last entry. They brought it carefully to another laboratory to confirm its age. "About thirty years, maybe forty"' was the answer. "The paper, its condition, the ink that was used. Oh, it's real, all right, and it's old. Very old."

They felt the cold chill settle on them all. That last entry had a pilot's notation on the line where he wrote the date and the time spent aloft. The pilot of that Nieuport noted he'd had a near collision. With the strangest "red and white machine of a type I had never seen or heard about before."

HARDSTAND TWO EIGHT

"13 June 1989."

"Mr. Caidin, I'm writing in response to the notice I read in *Professional Pilot Magazine* about the *Ghosts of the Air* book you're now writing. First of all, I've got to tell you that if I hadn't been a fan of yours for many, many years, I would *never* have responded with this letter, but I figured it was the least I could do for the many hours of enjoyment you have provided me.

"I am currently a flight engineer in Air Force Special Operations at Hurlburt Field in Florida. I've been a crew member on various types of C-130s since 1974. Again, if this wasn't going to you, especially, I'd never write this letter with what it contains. My only request is that I remain anonymous due to my sensitive work in what we'll just call special operations. I don't want to screw up my responsibilities or have the head-shrinks pounding the pavement after me."

(The source, the people, have been confirmed by the writer. In deference to his request, all true names have been eliminated from this copy. In every other respect this is verbatim. M.C.)

First, some background. I used to be stationed at Pope Air Force Base, North Carolina, with the 317th Tactical Airlift Wing. They had a mission of airlift support in Europe with two other airlift wings. These "rotations" lasted sixty-five to eighty days and were flown out of England and Germany. In the early 1970s a crew chief stole a C-130 from Mildenhall RAF. The Herc was parked on Hardstand 28. Due to personal problems at home and involuntary extensions of the TDY (temporary duty), the guy flipped out. Then one night, while alone at his aircraft, he called for a fuel truck and topped off the tanks. As dawn approached, he called for taxi clearance to the end of the runway for a max-power engine run. He started the aircraft entirely by himself; this involved pulling power, chocks, and then backing the airplane from the hardstand with reverse props. As he approached the hammerhead for run-up, he just kept on going and took the active for a successful takeoff.

The official air force position on what happened next is that as the staff sergeant flew out over the North Sea, he lost control of the aircraft and crashed. Speculation is that he didn't properly set the gyros for the compass system and was headed off in the wrong direction. All they ever found of the C-130 was a main gear tire.

C–130

Now this brings us to the weird stuff. Since that C-130 incident *the ghost of that crew chief is still at Hardstand Two Eight.* While I was on "rote" to Moldyhole during wintertime 1975, a good friend of mine (also a flight engineer) told me that while he was preflighting an oh-dark-thirty launch, the external power cart quit as if it ran out of gas. This power loss trips relays and a switch in the cockpit that has to be reset. As my friend went down the stairs, out of the darkened aircraft, the power cart suddenly restarted. Don't go by this one too quickly; this was an old MB-3 cart that took two hands to start. And when it restarted, the power came back on in the aircraft.

That means switches were flipped, and buttons pushed, on not only the power cart but the aircraft as well. As a flight engineer I could go into the electrical impossibilities of this, but I won't. I'll simply emphasize that this is absolutely *impossible.* And, for the record, my friend, Les, was the *only* one at the aircraft.

Another Hardstand Two Eight story soon came in from another crew chief, a very close friend of mine, the kind of relationship in which each guy trusts the other absolutely. While preparing his C-130 for a dawn takeoff, he completed everything early and decided to catch a quick nap before the crew showed. The bunk on an E-model C-130 is on the flight deck, and the crew entrance door is plainly seen. Wayne said the back end of the plane was all closed up with the doors pinned from the inside. The only way into the aircraft was through the crew entrance door.

Wayne said he had just dozed off when he heard the unmistakable sound of tie-down chains falling on the metal cargo floor. Thinking he overslept the crew show, he ran to the back and found numerous chains lying about the cargo compartment and hanging out of their stowage bins. Wayne said he picked up everything and tidied it all up, somewhat pissed that someone was playing practical jokes.

He said he hadn't thought of it at that time, but any practical joker leaving the cargo compartment would have had to have passed directly by him. Since he was awake now, and it was almost time for the crew to arrive, he sat down on the edge of the crew bunk on the flight deck to make sure the forms were in order, and as he did so, *he again heard the chains hitting the floor.*

Wayne said he was out of the plane in about two steps and was waiting outside when the crew showed up. He said he didn't go back inside the aircraft for the rest of the night.

The air force quit parking aircraft on Hardstand Two Eight for quite a long while, several years, in fact. Some say it was due to complaints of a nearby farmer (prop blast, too much noise; that sort of thing), but the rumors are that late takeoffs and ground aborts from this particular parking spot were all too frequent. I remember the hardstand being used as an AGE (aircraft ground equipment) storage area for quite awhile; then later, in the late seventies, in fact, it was again used for aircraft parking.

The rotational squadrons deployed to Europe enjoy quite a remarkable safety record. In the fifteen years that I have been flying C-130s, there have been only two catastrophic C-130 crashes while the units have been deployed to Mildenhall, and these were several years apart. Both aircraft were new C-130H models from Dyess Air Force Base in Texas. Both aircraft crashed in Turkey.

Both aircraft had departed for their missions from Mildenhall RAF, Hardstand Two Eight.

C-130

We have another incident with another C-130 that gave her crew chief some kind of instant religion. This man crewed a C-130 at Woodbridge RAF, also in England, during the early seventies. Woodbridge was used as a crash base during World War II, as best I know its history. One night the line truck dropped off this crew chief at the aircraft, and as it drove away, he noticed a specialist or other mechanic already at the aircraft. He set down his toolbox to unlock it and was near the nose of the Hercules when he stood up again, looked up to the darkened cockpit, and in the faint light saw a figure sitting there dressed in leather flying gear, goggles, and oxygen mask of the type worn during the Second World War.

I'll tell you that he departed that area *quickly.* Another time, while sitting in the cockpit of his aircraft, he looked out across a dark parking ramp, and through a light fog he saw an entire crew bag-dragging their gear under a flightline light pole. For those moments they were under the light, they stood out unmistakably, and as they kept walking, they disappeared into the night. He stared after them a long time. In the midst of all these modern Herc transports, that crew was dressed in World War II flying gear.

We come now to the final episode; not my story, but told to me by my aircraft commander when I was flying at Pope Air Force Base. If you're a pilot, and someone who's flown the C-130 yourself, you know just how tight the crews get and how much absolute faith they've got to have in their pilots. That says it all. I must keep my word and not use any names here because of what happened.

One of our pilots was on TDY, temporary duty assignment, to Europe. He woke up in the middle of the night, fighting his way out of a bad dream about his college roommate, who was stationed at Guam flying WC-130 weather ships, the tough Typhoon Chasers. His dream was about his friend being in an airplane crash.

He was so shaken by the dream that he immediately called the aircrew command post to ask if there had been any aircraft accidents. They replied in the affirmative; there had been a crash, but they didn't have any details about it as yet. "All we know," he was told, "is that we just received a message, and it tells us very little, that a C-130 is missing somewhere in the Pacific."

This pilot, his dream haunting him, then proceeded to tell the controller a list of specific details, all of them from his *dream*. He told the controller that the missing aircraft wasn't a cargo C-130 but a WC-130 weather ship; he gave the controller the *number of the aircraft* and the name of his friend who was flying in that plane.

Everything he said was correct. That day (remember—it was nighttime in Europe) an Air Force WC-130 had been lost without a trace while tracking a typhoon in the Pacific. The pilot who had clawed his way up from his dream also had said that he had "seen" the WC-130 come out of the clouds, with his friend struggling at the controls, and it struck the water left-wing low. Everyone was killed instantly, and the WC-130 sank almost immediately. They never fund a trace of the crew or that airplane.

CONNECTIONS

The letter was dated 9 February 1989, sent to me by Steve Sanchez, membership number 227276 of the Experimental Aircraft Association. Steve Sanchez mailed the letter from Bridgeview, Illinois. On this date he had been at his local airport. Nothing special. A quiet day, and then—

"I was eating lunch and reading my January issue of EAA's *Sport Aviation*," wrote Sanchez. "I had just finished reading your article about your upcoming book, *Ghosts the Air*, and as my lunch period ended, I got up to leave.

"It was then that my eye caught a pamphlet on the next table with a picture of two aircraft flying cockpit to cockpit. I picked it up to find an interesting story I felt should be brought to your attention. Needless to say, the coincidence of the two sent a chill up my spine, *as I felt that I was meant to find it.*

"The pamphlet is of a religious nature, but the story is in keeping with what you may be looking for. This is the reason I am forwarding it to you."

The "mysterious pamphlet" lying on the table of a small airport in Illinois told of a remarkable incident high over the Pacific Ocean in November of 1976. Marine Attack Squadron VMA 513 was ferrying seven Harrier VTOL jet fighters from Iwakuni, Japan, to Marine Corps Air Station Yuma in Arizona. Their route of flight took them over Guam, Wake, and Hawaii. The long distances to be covered demanded good weather, huge extra external fuel tanks, perfect navigation, and skill in rendezvousing with tankers at twenty thousand feet to refuel in flight. The seven Harriers flew in two flights, four aircraft leading and three trailing one hour behind the first flight. The Harriers would cruise at thirty-three thousand feet and descend only for tanker rendezvous and refueling in the air. The entire mission went beautifully—until it started to come unglued about fourteen hundred miles off San Francisco.

The promised good weather fell apart; huge thunderstorms loomed along the flight path, and the Harriers were plunged into difficult instrument conditions. Making matters worse was the fact that between Hawaii and California the Harriers absolutely had to complete another in-flight rendezvous and refueling. The Harrier pilots dodged the worst of the storms and flew as precisely as they could, with abruptly changed courses and altitudes. These Marines were hot; they did it all just as the book says it should be done.

And barely in time. One of the pilots on this arduous transpacific trek by fighters designed for short-range operations was judged as one of the very best in the business. Major Robert L. Snyder, USMC, had been selected to demonstrate the stunning performance of the heavy jet fighter able to take off and land vertically, fly sideways, hover, back up in the air;

in short, perform as men had always dreamed of performing, though not until the Harrier did they see their dreams come true. Bob Snyder flew before literally millions of people in conjunction, at air shows, with the Blue Angels, Thunderbirds, Art Scholl, Bob Hoover, the Confederate Air Force, and other attractions that "packed 'em in."

As soon as Snyder completed his critical refueling, his Harrier and the other three jets in his formation stabbed into violent thunderstorms. The airplanes were bounced and slammed about violently in what the pilots considered one of the "wildest rides" they'd ever known.

When the planes broke out into limited visibility, but free of the violent thunderheads, Snyder found his airplane sliding back from his formation. The weather conditions were so poor that the Harriers were actually in instrument conditions, yet Snyder threw all his concentration visually on the other three Harriers, now ahead and above him. Snyder's plane, loaded heavily with fuel, lacked the extra thrust and speed to overtake the other fighters, and he still faced thirteen hundred miles of ocean before California.

He needed to get to thirty-three thousand feet while still keeping the other planes in sight. Once he was at the same cruising altitude, and free of the need to climb, he could use his power to catch up to the other Harriers. So he was balanced between climbing with limited speed, in rotten weather, *and* keeping the formation in visual sight.

He began to lose the contest. The other Harriers steadily diminished in size as Snyder failed both to climb and to overtake the formation. And then, concentrating on the other planes, by now straining to keep them in sight at all, he discovered he had failed to keep a careful scan of his instruments. He *believed* he was flying wings level and climbing. Apparently, as he recalled, he wasn't doing that at all. In fact, he was in much greater trouble than he realized.

"Suddenly and to my astonishment, I was canopy to canopy with another AV-8!"

He stared in disbelief. *The other Harrier was flying inverted, holding rock-steady position, the canopies almost touching, in instrument conditions at thirty thousand feet.* It was so wild as to be considered absolutely impossible, but the other AV-8 Harrier was right there with him. Snyder kept his eyes locked on the other pilot; he noticed the man in the other place kept a calm and steady gaze on Snyder.

The entire scene punished reality. Immediately what *could* be possible had to be considered. Was Snyder seeing a reflection of his own Harrier in his curved canopy? That possibility came and went swiftly, for Snyder could see the other pilot still retaining that calm, steady gaze, while Snyder's own thoughts were obvious in his facial expressions that were hardly *that* calm.

There was always the chance of an inversion-layer mirror image. As wild as was that kind of scene, it *was* possible. An airplane flying directly atop an invisible layer of air sandwiched between an upper and lower layer of differing temperature acts as if it's riding the top of a mirror in the sky. One of the more famous incidents emerging from this phenomenon is a film clip of two Douglas DC-8 four-engined jetliners flying perfect belly-to-belly formation. Of course nothing of the sort was happening. One DC-8 flying straight and level skimmed that mirroring inversion layer, and its reflection was absolutely perfect. The camera records reflected light; bingo, film proof of the belly-to-belly formation that didn't exist. But that had to be dismissed from this moment, the two Harriers were flashing through clouds within which the inversion-layer mirror image couldn't exist.

Snyder moved his gaze from the other plane to his instrument panel. A sense of shock hit him. He discovered that the world he knew only a few moments before had changed drastically. Not only was he not flying wings level, but he had been hit hard with vertigo—full spatial disorientation—and *he* was now inverted and had fallen back to twenty-four thousand feet.

Immediately he half rolled. He looked for the other Harrier; it was gone. Snyder felt it was impossible that he had moved through his own formation, but that other Harrier left him little other choice but to believe this was what had happened. His plane under control, he started climbing again and established radio contact with the DC-9 navigation plane flying ten miles behind him to "radar guide" the Harriers across the ocean.

Snyder was caught by surprise when the DC-9 radioman told him his own flight was still five miles in front of his own aircraft and in level cruise at thirty-three thousand feet. Now he had another question he had to ask himself, and he *had* to have an answer.

"If they were five miles ahead of me and level, and the other flight was an hour behind me, then who was this 'fifth' aircraft flying on my wing at twenty-four thousand feet?"

Minutes later he rejoined his formation. As he slid into position, the original flight was complete: four Harriers.

But there had been that fifth airplane that had brought him to realize he was suffering vertigo and plunging toward the ocean...*a fifth airplane that did not exist.*

Major Robert L. Snyder was a hardened U.S. Marine Corps jet fighter pilot. *Consider all these factors.* He had been a pilot for thirteen years. *He flew five hundred combat missions in Vietnam.* He was selected as one of the outstanding jet-fighter pilots in all the U.S. Navy and the Marine Corps to demonstrate the unique qualities of the AV-8 Harrier VTOL jet fighter. He was dispatched by the Pentagon to demonstrate skill and performance with the Harrier throughout the country. *He was one of the best of the best.*

Now he faced a judgment he felt he could no longer avoid. That fifth Harrier simply could not be. Nothing in the normal train of events could make it even remotely possible. Yet the fifth Harrier had appeared. Its presence and Snyder's reaction to that presence snatched him from the jaws of death, plunging out of control through storm clouds to smash into the ocean.

And nothing in life could explain what had happened. There was but one other conclusion to be drawn by this man of such outstanding record, courage, and performance.

"I knew that something supernatural had just happened in my life."

At this time in his life, Bob Snyder wrote in a pamphlet describing his incredible experience that "I knew about God, and I knew about the historical Jesus, but I had long since removed all knowledge of God from my life and was quite happy with the direction my life was moving. I had no spiritual involvements, and my dealings with life were 'matter of fact.'" Never again for Robert L. Snyder. He stated his feelings simply when he said, "God performed a powerful miracle in my life when I least expected it, and for the next year I sought for an explanation of what I had seen."

Whatever he sought, he found. He retired from the U.S. Marine Corps. On the day he took off that for that transpacific flight, "I was an agnostic at the time."

Never again.

Bob Snyder found a new course to follow.

THE SEVENTH MAN

The Boeing B-17 Flying Fortress, the unparalleled "Queen" of bombers through the Second World War, was far more than "just another airplane."

All great machines develop their own personalities. Pilots and crew blend with metal and gasoline and weapons and the flying characteristics of their machine. They discover, as they become a tightly knit unit, that a distinctive aura begins to embrace the humans and their creature of metal. The Fortress seemed almost made for such a relationship.

Born in 1935, the product of an era when "hands-on flying" mated man and machine in their unique relationship, the Fortress also kept ten men within shouting distance of one another. Sweat and oil intermingled, the smell of new leather mixed with the acrid bite of explosives, and the world could be either serene drifting through the sky or struggling through natural maelstroms or the stormy hell of flak and fighters.

That era left us decades ago, and in its place came the crash and thunder of the jet engines, the new swept-wing shapes, and bombers that dwarfed the suddenly ancient Flying Fortress. One of its successors, well down the line of development, was the huge Boeing B-52 Superfortress. In this new age of jets and power systems, of swept wings and overwhelming size, of soaring into the stratosphere and speeds nearly three times greater than the past, it seemed the spirits and souls, the camaraderie of men-and-machine, was found wanting. Air combat seemed drained of its intense emotional impact. The very forces that gave us tremendous speed and altitude appeared to bring a cut-and-dried feeling about the great new war machines. If they took damage that gashed and cut their winged form, that very damage meant a quick end to the sleek new warbirds. It would seem this was the new way things were to be. But as time passed, and as the stories told by individual men rather than by headquarters-issued press releases began to circulate among us, we discovered that we had not really lost what had been so vital to us in the past.

As you will find in this incredible tale of a B-52 bomber flying Vietnam combat. John L. Frisbee's story cuts right to the quick of what happened that 27th of December, 1972. After reading Frisbee's report, I spoke extensively with Captain John Mize, the pilot of that Superfortress bomber. As I suspected, there was even more to tell than what Frisbee had reported. Captain Mize elected not to go into further detail. As he explained to me, "having that Seventh Man aboard was more than enough for all of us, for all our lives."

For a bomber with a six-man crew, well, so it is, so it is.

The following excerpt reprinted by permission from *AIR FORCE* Magazine. Copyright ©1990 the Air Force Association.

John D. Mize bent his B-52D into a sharp turn away from his objective, a surface-to-air missile (SAM) site, VN-243, near Hanoi. It was his fourth Linebacker II mission and his 295th in Southeast Asia. The 27th of December, 1972, was the ninth day of the "eleven-day war" that finally brought North Vietnam to the truce table, led to the return of the POWs, and lowered the curtain on direct American participation in the Vietnam War.

Seconds after bombs away, Captain Mize, copilot Captain Terrence Gruters, and gunner T Sergeant Peter Whalen counted a barrage of fifteen SAMs headed their way. Already they had evaded several SAMs in the target area, but not a mass firing of this size. Fourteen of the missiles missed, but the fifteenth exploded with a tremendous concussion between the Number 4 engine and the fuselage. Shrapnel hit Captain Mize in the left thigh, lower leg, and hand. Sergeant Whalen and radar navigator Captain Bill North were wounded in the legs. The cockpit was filled with debris.

Before Captain Mize could react, two hundred tons of aircraft plunged toward the earth, with all four engines of the left wing knocked out, engine Number 1 on fire, navigation and engine instruments inoperative, and most of the power boost for flight controls gone. Only one alternator, the radio, and cockpit lights were functioning.

With virtually no power boost, it took a superhuman effort by captains Mize and Gruters to regain control of the shattered bomber. After a rapid damage assessment, Captain Mize knew they could not make it back to U-Tapao in Thailand, where the Twenty-eighth Bombardment Group was based. "The question was," says Mize, "how far we could get before we had to abandon the aircraft." Whether anyone had flown a damaged B-52 with all engines out on one side, using only needle, ball, and airspeed (the latter erratic and undependable), he didn't know, but they would give it their best shot. "Everyone knew what to do," Captain Mize said. "They were absolutely professional in every respect."

As soon as the bomber was under control, navigator Lieutenant Bill Robinson gave Captain Mize a dead-reckoning heading from their last known position to friendly territory. Separated from the other bombers in Ash cell and with no defensive systems operational, the B-52 limped westward toward Nakhon Phanom (NKP) in northern Thailand. How long would the badly damaged left wing hold? What other structural damage had the aircraft sustained? No one knew.

In order to maintain bailout altitude, Captain Mize repeatedly descended fifteen hundred feet, then climbed back one thousand feet. Over northern Laos their desperate situation began to deteriorate still further. The bomb-bay doors fell open, one side of the landing gear began to cycle up and down, and other electrical systems went haywire. Forty-five minutes after they were hit, it was time to bail out, but navigator Robinson calculated they were over jagged mountains. Another thirty miles would put them over flat land near NKP—if the burned and battered left wing held.

As they approached NKP, Captain Mize felt "a kind of death throe" run through the B-52. He called each crew member, ordering him to bail out. Co-pilot Gruters, Sergeant Whalen, radar navigator Captain Bill North, and EWO Captain Dennis Anderson (the last two, from the Seventh Bombardment Group, were substitutes on the mission) went out on order, but Lieutenant Robinson's seat would not eject.

Lieutenant Robinson told Captain Mize that he would go out the hole where the radar navigator had ejected. Since there would be no contact with Lieutenant Robinson after he left his seat, Captain Mize, knowing the left wing could go any moment, told Lieutenant Robinson he would stay with the aircraft for three minutes, giving the navigator time to bail out. Before that time was up, all electrical systems failed, signaling the end of that B-52. Captain Mize called Lieutenant Robinson once more. Getting no response, he punched out as the aircraft went down. All crew members were picked up by rescue choppers within a few minutes.

For his superb airmanship and for laying his life on the line to assure Lieutenant Robinson's escape, Captain John Mize was awarded the Air Force Cross, the first SAC man to receive that medal. The other crew members were awarded the Distinguished Flying Cross for heroism, and all six received the Purple Heart for wounds and injuries suffered in their night bailout.

Now retired and living in Oscoda, Mich., John Mize believes "there was a Seventh Man aboard" on that memorable night. Who could argue the point?

Chapter 13

=HERE—AND GONE

May 1941 saw frenetic activity day and night to prepare the new airfield at Hibaldstow in Lincolnshire. Air battles were still in full swing between British and German pilots. As quickly as the Hibaldstow runways were ready, the RAF moved in Defiant bomber interceptors of Number 255 Squadron.

Soon the slow and clumsy Defiants without forward-firing guns, only a single aft turret with four machine guns, were removed from front-line duty to be replaced with more agile fighters. The war ended, the RAF closed and abandoned the field in 1945. Nature went wild; buildings collapsed, bushes, weeds, and trees grew everywhere.

Seven years later several pilots drove to Hibaldstow; a tug of memory. They viewed with mixed emotions what had once been a bustling, thundering combat field. Now the wind sighed through trees and tall grass as though an airfield had never existed. The men walked back to their car, then turned for a final farewell look where there had once been runways.

They froze. At the far end of the field, gear and flaps down, engine rumbling with her throttle back, a Spitfire Mark IV floated down for a landing. It crossed the edge of the airfield—and before their eyes the Spitfire vanished.

The men never returned to the airfield.

Memory draws like the pull of invisible chains. Every Englishman who ever flew knows the name of Biggin Hill, one of the most vital airfields and RAF installations of the Battle of Britain and the air war that followed ever deeper into Germany.

The old pilots come to Biggin Hill. It's quiet; they like those moments. A hush falls over the field. Then: "Listen!" a man calls out quietly, urgently. The sound; there's no mistaking the cry of the Merlin engine as a Spitfire races across the field.

No airplane is visible; the sound fades as it ghosts off into the distance.

Some men see into the past, or see what the past brings to them. More than thirty years after the last shot of war fired against a savaged Germany, the airfields of England long submitted to time and abandonment, several former pilots and mechanics visited East Cowes. The airfield was still an active facility but usually quiet at night, except for intermittent sounds of airplanes being prepared for flight the next day, or for the security teams making their rounds.

The visitors, and the permanent station personnel, are drawn to look up into the sky Someone, several, many people are pointing at a parachute drifting earthward. *The figure in the parachute is headless. He's been seen before.* Just before touching down, usually, but sometimes after feet hit the ground and the chute folds, the figure vanishes.

Outsiders who hear this story laugh it off as ridiculous and the work of overactive imaginations.

Obviously they never talked to the security dog working guard duty one night. The animal looked into the sky; the *animal* saw the headless figure descending beneath the parachute. Perhaps he saw more than that.

The well-trained security dog tore loose from his handler and fled, howling. When they reached the animal, he was completely berserk and had to be put to sleep.

An elderly gentleman, veteran of the air struggle over England and German-occupied Europe during the Second World War, drives with his son to Church Broughton. They park outside the field, release their two dogs from their car, and begin the long walk across the airfield. A father taking his son back in time, pointing here, pointing there, the dogs walking with them. It is dead silent.

It remains dead silent, not a whisper, when at the far end of Church Broughton a twin-engined bomber rushes in across the treetops. It tears directly at them, barely a few feet overhead, and at high speed races across the field. *It does not make a sound*, and then it is gone in the distance, diminishing to a dot, then lost from sight.

The dogs have gone wild, howling and racing frantically from the airfield.

He stopped alongside the narrow British road late one night at Hemswell, an RAF field that had been operational for more than sixty years and now, in 1978, had been shut down for just over a year. Derek Harrison left his car by a hedge to look across what had been virtually a monument to British military aviation. A cool evening, quiet, wind sighing across the tall grass and the hedges along the old runways.

Harrison heard music, somewhere far off in the distance. It seemed to be coming from the airfield itself. He recognized the tune: *The Missouri Waltz*. He reasoned that sound travels far at night, and the music could have been coming from miles away, no matter how much it *seemed* to be coming from somewhere on that deserted airfield.

He strained to hear the sound more clearly; abruptly the music stopped. Harrison grinned at himself. It could even have been his imagination. He stood quietly. Utter silence. Then his heart felt as if it had jumped in his chest.

This time there was another sound, and it *was* coming from one of the abandoned runways. A military aircraft, obviously of its own time, unmistakable from the coughing bark of its ancient radial engines, rumbled and backfired to life. The engines smoothed out and were run to high power, the propellers screaming. Then the power backed off, and the engines settled down to a smooth rumble.

Suddenly, in fact abruptly, without warning, bright lights exploded garishly from the center of the crossing runways; immediately after, a heavy truck roared onto the runway. The truck slowed, it seemed, alongside the airplane. Then laughter, calls of men to other men, sounded clearly. Boots crunched on gravel, and heels thudded on hard surfaces, and then—

Absolute silence.

Postscript: It's happened several times. No one even tries to explain it. It just happens, if you happen to be there at the right time on the right night.

There are times, as we have seen, when ghostly aircraft do not wait for the passage of years before making their appearance, especially, as records of such events will show, when a message of great, even imperative, urgency is given. In late 1939, before the Royal Air Force had built up its strength in pilots and aircraft in order to take on the power of the heavily numbered and aggressive German Luftwaffe, much of the air fighting was of a desultory nature: probes, feints, and attacks of limited strength. This period went into the history books as the "phony war," when a great deal less than an all-out effort was expended against the enemy.

It was a time of lethal sparring, and the jabs and blows, however "phony," still claimed the lives of men and the destruction of their warplanes. A lead force in this period operated from Mildenhall in Suffolk, flying Vickers Wellington bombers of Number 149 Squadron with the mission of destroying the powerful German radar installations on Heligoland Bight.

This was still a time of the British sending out bombers in daylight, an incredibly foolhardy thing to do in the Wellington, which might be considered a grossly paunchy Colonel Blimp of an airplane with defensive firepower so weak the German fighters proved quickly just how much of a mockery it really was. Furthermore, there was precious little fighter escort available to protect the vulnerable bombers, and in those days radio silence was almost a holy commandment. The bombers left, and those on the ground at Mildenhall began the long sweat until the bombers returned— or failed to return.

The mission was so set up that the Wellingtons would strike during daylight and then run for home with darkness closing in about them. The date of our immediate interest was the 18th of December, 1939, and daylight time was about the shortest of the year. To bring the bombers back in safely, the ground crews laid out rows of flare cans filled with paraffin; when their wicks were flamed, they gave the incoming pilots a clear stretch of parallel lights along the landing runway. The Wellington pilots aimed for the parallel lights; as they were ready to begin power reduction and flare, the ground crews lit off a Chance light to cast its bright yellow beam down the runway.

Of the nine Wellingtons launched this day from Mildenhall, two had failed to carry out their mission, returning with various mechanical difficulties earlier in the day. The seven still in the air faced an absolutely rotten return. The temperature had plummeted to well below freezing, heavy cloud cover cast a thick gloom over the earth, and it began to snow. Yet, in the lowering gloom, one Wellington (best known to its crews as *Wimpy*) came home just past five P.M. Two more straggled in. Night fell; no sign of the other four. The snow thickened, the clock ticked inexorably, and now the four Wellingtons were more than an hour overdue.

The operations staff considered calling in the ground crews, all this time waiting to light off the flares for the overdue bombers. By now it had to be judged they were down.

Another thirty minutes; that was it. The ops officer heard something. So did the other men. An airplane coming in directly to Mildenhall. By the sounds of it, the machine had been chewed up; the familiar drone of two powerful engines was now a choking, backfiring cough rather than smooth power, which meant engines in distress, on the razor edge of failing.

"That ain't no *Wimpy*!" a mechanic called out.

"Light the flares!" the ops officer shouted. The runway leapt into flickering relief, the Chance light cast its baleful glow down the strip— and the men on the ground stopped in their tracks, gaping, struck with disbelief.

Floating slowly into the light of the flares and the reflection of the Chance light was an ancient, fragile mishmash of winged fabric, wires whistling in the wind, bicycle tires, and the open cockpit of an FE.2b from early in World War I. They watched the FE.2b level off, skimming the runway, and in all the lights there could be no mistaking the helmet, goggles, and scarf as the plane clattered by. A gloved hand thrust suddenly from the cockpit. An object was flung to the ground, and the pilot went to full power, the clattering and banging a sound these men had never heard before.

Then it was gone.

Men rushed to the object on the runway. It was a handwritten message tied to a wrench.

Wellington aircraft N2961, code-signal OJ-P, *was down*. Not shot down over the continent. The Vickers bomber in its struggle to return to Mildenhall had finally lost its ability to fly, and the pilot ditched in the sea forty miles from the nearest air-sea rescue outfit. A ditching at night in a bomber either badly damaged or out of fuel is almost a guaranteed death sentence.

As it turned out, N2961 was lost with her entire crew. Then, *why,* and *how,* could they comprehend the clattering FE.2b and its incredible appearance over the Mildenhall runway.

Sometimes there's a tenuous connection, a thread so thin it's invisible, but much stronger than steel.

Number 149 Squadron, flying the Second World War, now flew Wellingtons.

More than twenty years before, operating from airfields in France by British pilots, Number 149 Squadron, flying the First World War, then flew FE.2b biplanes.

A tenuous connection that had never quite been severed.

Nineteen eighty-one; RAF Swanton Morley in Norfolk. An airfield in service since 1939. Former home to Bristol Blenheims, Douglas Bostons, North American Mitchells, and de Havilland Mosquitos. Now stood down to minor flying, a station just short of caretaking status.

The father of an RAF airman stationed at Swanton Morley has come to visit his son. During the day the younger man, Greaves, is on duty. His father takes the moment to walk through the quiet airfield and then walk along the perimeter of the field so he can see it all and yet not be in anyone's way. Mr. Greaves, with his dog on leash, is thoroughly enjoying the quiet time.

Suddenly the dog barks, a strange and shrill cry, as if the animal is extremely upset. Greaves turns; the dog is barking madly at an RAF airman, clad in an overcoat and wearing a forage cap, running wildly down the runway. A wind suddenly picks up. Now the sounds of the running man are clear, his boots crunching on the gravel beneath him. Greaves turns in the direction the man is running. He gasps; at the far end of the runway a bomber has crashed, its tail jutting well above the runway, the nose section crushed and burning fiercely. Flames leap upward, and black smoke boils outward.

But Greaves hasn't heard a sound except for the airman running on the gravel. Greaves starts to run after the airman. In the intensity of the moment, he fails to notice there isn't any gravel underfoot; the runway is solid surface.

He stumbles to a halt. The burning aircraft seems fainter. As Greaves watches, the smoke thins, the flames become transparent, and crashed bomber and running airman fade into nothingness.

The runway is empty.

The dog howls mournfully.

PERSONAL ENCOUNTER

Don Brereton of Thornton, Liverpool, in Merseyside, United Kingdom, exchanged a series of letters with me; I was determined to stay after Don because of his extensive service in the Royal Air Force throughout the world, and because I had heard that this man had something very special to relate. Even his letters were especially refreshing as he brought to light certain attitudes rarely encountered today.

"You already know I am ex-Royal Air Force," wrote Don Brereton, "and part of my service was in the mid-1950s when in Malaya, where we had a little war with communist terrorists. Pity what we did failed to gain more attention; we actually *won* that mix-up! Perhaps I failed to pay as much attention as I might have to the natives and their tales of the spirit world; they were a very superstitious lot, and they firmly believed in spirits then, as they do today, but I never was able to gain any details with sufficient depth to pass them on to you. Better none than rumor grown out of hand.

"So Malaya is a matter of intense interest to me, but it is grit and mud and heat and combat, and *winning,* with most of the world knowing nothing about it. It was really very similar to the war in Vietnam *except,* as I say, we came out on top and did in the terrorist organizations. I kept detailed reports in a diary and even wrote a book, of more than three hundred pages, to pass on to future Breretons so we won't be forgotten, nor will what we did fade unnoticed into history (although my own sons, aged twenty-six and twenty-four, haven't shown any interest whatever in reading it).

"But what you have sought, the events that took place in UK, *are* very real, and also very much beyond the pale of events common to our daily world and our lives. I managed to take several photographs of the Polish grave..."

But we're getting ahead of what Don Brereton had to say, and let it be told in his own words:

I am in the Royal Observer Corps stationed at the Royal Air Force Station Woodvale near Southport. We have an underground bunker on the station. I have never before related this tale to anyone. Odds are they would have judged me daft, or that it was a dream, or simply that I'd made it up. But it was as real as anything else in my life, and I've had enough time in the rough to have a most solid grip on reality.

It happened during the annual all-night exercise in 1988. I came on duty at midnight with two other Observers who, for the sake of convenience and respect for their privacy I will call Jim and Fred.

The weather was warm for the time of the year; indeed, that winter was particularly mild through the entire season.This night had been quiet. Not much activity anywhere. No synthetic bombs to be reported, and our fallout readings were running steady.

We took it in turn to have a doze. As dawn approached, Fred was taking his turn on the top bunk. Jim was operating the radio, and I was twiddling my thumbs. After drinking my umpteenth cup of tea, I had the urge to go upstairs for a call of nature. As I got near the top of the shaft, I heard the sound of an aircraft flying low overhead. Our bunker is situated just inside the perimeter wire of the station. I called down to Jim, asking him what he thought it was, as it was too early for Woodvale's aircraft to be airborne.

Jim, however, was busy reporting our instrument readings to group headquarters; his attention to his work kept him from hearing my questions. I turned back to the outside. The engine note sounded much more powerful than the locally based Bulldogs and Chipmunks of the university squadrons. I thought that it may be one of the twin-engined planes that from time to time visit the station.

However, by the time I reached the top of the shaft, the aircraft was nowhere in sight, and I could no longer hear the sound of engines. It was that time between night and day when the light of the sky is a bit misleading; much of the world seems to hide itself in the shifting of one form of light to another.

Well, I kept looking into the sky scanning carefully for our mysterious visitor. Suddenly I got the feeling that someone was watching me. I felt myself go cold, and the hairs along the back of my neck stood on end.

I looked around and almost immediately saw a figure standing by the crash gate leading onto the A565, which runs along the side of the airfield. I peered into the gloom trying to work out just who the figure was. I could see plainly that it was a man; then I saw more detail. A man in uniform. I thought at first he was either our officer on a surprise visit, or one of the airfield security staff on patrol, or even one of our Observers who had decided to come on duty, though we weren't expecting anybody.

By now my eyes were becoming accustomed to the half light, but somehow, and I thought immediately this was strange, the figure before me wasn't becoming any clearer to view. Well, by now I could make out that the uniform had a blue color to it and had flashes on the top of the arms. He had on some kind of light-colored sleeveless jacket. He wasn't wearing a hat, but he held something in his right hand, and although I couldn't make out what it was, I assumed it was his headgear. All of this took but a matter of seconds. Then I shouted out to him.

I would hesitate to say I remember my exact words from that moment, but certainly it was something like: "Can I help you, mate?"

Up to this point the uniformed figure had been looking directly at me. But when I called out to him, he turned slowly and began to move away. He walked into the bushes that abut the perimeter fence at this point and just seemed to *merge* into them. I stood looking at the point where the figure had disappeared, for what must have been an entire minute. Then I thought, This won't do!

This broke the spell, and I ran quickly down the slope on which I'd been standing, to the place where I'd last seen him. There was nobody there. And somehow, for whatever reason, I knew there wouldn't be anybody there. I seemed to come back to earth, gather up my senses, and I remembered the need that had brought me out of the underground post. After I finished, I started walking back. And I kept looking over my shoulder a number of times. I don't know why, but I felt very vulnerable. I also wondered what Jim would think or say when I told him what had happened. That stopped me in my tracks. *He'll think I'm making it up,* I told myself. So I decided to ask him only if he had heard the aircraft engines that I'd heard as I was leaving the post. And if he had not heard the sound of engines, I'd leave well enough alone; I would not tell him about the mysterious figure I'd seen. Yet somehow I knew that the engine sounds and the uniformed figure were linked.

As I came back down into the post, Jim turned to me and asked, "What kept you?" I started to answer, but he was on his feet, and he added, "I want to go myself."

I nodded assent and looked over to the bed where Fred was still asleep, then decided to ask my question of Jim. "Did you hear the plane going over as I went up the shaft?"

He looked at me with surprise. "What plane? It's too early for the station aircraft to be up. Was it something overflying us?"

I shook my head. "I don't believe so. It was a lot more powerful than the local planes, by the sound of it. I didn't actually see it."

Jim shrugged and started from the post. "Well, no matter. I didn't hear anything, anyway." He went up the shaft to the outside.

That did it in. I made the decision to keep what had happened, what I'd seen, to myself. And I wouldn't even talk about the unseen plane that had overflown our station.

In the ensuing weeks I tried to put out of my thoughts the figure I'd seen. It wouldn't leave me. I was fair to going mad, wondering not what, but *who,* it was. Then, in December, I found a documentary book that contained an excellent and detailed history of RAF Woodvale. And at the back of this book was a section dealing with graves that related to Woodvale.

One item leapt from the pages at me. It told of a terrible collision between two Spitfires flying a dawn patrol from Woodvale. Of the two pilots involved, one was killed.

He was a Polish Squadron leader. *Now,* as memory rushed back, and missing pieces of memory began to fit, I "saw" that strange figure in a new light.

The light-colored sleeveless jacket…of course; a Mae West life jacket! The pilots all wore them in their fighters. And the shoulder flashes at the top of the arms? How I wished to have seen those more clearly. They were letters, not numbers, and the Polish fighter pilots all wore that flash that read POLAND at their shoulders.

Postscript: On 9 January 1941, while on a dawn patrol flying a Spitfire fighter plane from RAF Woodvale, Squadron Leader M. J. Wesolowski, of the free Polish forces flying with the Royal Air Force, died in a collision with another Spitfire.

Squadron Leader M. J. Wesolowski was buried in Our Lady's Church, School Lane, Formby, near Liverpool, Merseyside.

Chapter 14

IT'S *STILL* THE BERMUDA TRIANGLE

I don't want my readers to believe, even for a moment, that we waltzed across an easy-gliding floor into the contents of this book. Far from it. It takes a pretty solid backbone to stand up and be counted by saying what you know and what you believe, despite all the hooters and naysayers always ready to pounce upon anything alien to their orderly, pinioned little lives. Even pilots don't always make it. We consider ourselves a very special breed of cat, just about *all* of us, and we are. So are the guys and the women who go out there and climb mountains or wrestle sharks in *their* environment, or hang-glide, or whatever it is that is something so special it separates us from the great mob of the undistinguished. Does that sound opinionated? Heavy on the ego?

You bet! As I've said earlier in these pages, a man can tell all the tall stories he wants on the ground, but if he lies to his airplane, it will kill him. And in our business it doesn't take long for us to flush out the snake-oil men in their shiny brown shoes, or the tellers of stories without substance to them.

No apologies to anyone.

But there *are* people, including pilots, who don't believe *anything* that's even remotely associated with what you have already read in these pages and will continue to read a bit more. Most often these people of negative thought, or simply those who have never really broken from the mold, are made of sufficiently stern stuff to come forth and challenge us. Some of them even go so far as to allow the use of their names. *That's* rare.

One such sent me a letter dated 16 January 1989, a professional civilian and, from everything I can determine about the man, a skilled and experienced military pilot. Let me get that down on paper immediately. This letter from Joseph A. Thomas of Arlington, Virginia, is simply a statement of, "I don't care *what* you say; I'm not going to believe it." That's *my* statement to encapsulate what *he* said, so in all fairness I'll reprint his letter here.

I read your request in "Pro Pilot" for accounts of bizarre events that may have befallen any of us in the aviation field.

I'm a 43-year-old commercial-instrument former navy pilot with a lifelong interest in airplanes. I've worked for the FAA, and I've managed the aircraft finance division of General Electric Credit Corporation with a staff of pilots. I fly several times a week as pilot-in-command of a fleet of several general aviation aircraft based at Dulles.

As a member of the "Quiet Birdmen" and many other aviation organizations, I've had numerous conversations with Yeager, Crossfield, Halaby, Rutan, Bader, and other legendary pilots.

I've seen all the airplane movies, read all the Ernie Gann books, built hundreds of models, hung out at the Air and Space Museum, often fly commercially to Europe and the Orient, and yet...None of this good-deal stuff you are going to write about has ever happened to me or anyone I've known. Just doing our jobs.

Gee, that's *swell,* Joe. If you ever get around to reading the first-person statements of Don Cochrane, or the official combat files of the Eighth Air Force, or Judge Kenneth Bacon, or G. T. McDowall, well, you can always deride Captain Robert J. Hanley and *his* incredible record *and* first-person reports, right? Or we can cast out John T. Gell and Eric Marsden and Walter Hodgson, to say nothing of Don Brereton and Robert Osborne and, well, you get the idea, I'm sure. And there are so many *more!*

I don't want to be unfair to Mr. Thomas. I invited him to "have at me" or "have at it" and chew up anything he liked. I offered him all the space he might want to decry and ridicule anything he wished. I wrote him back on 19 January 1989 with these offers, and I added, to be fair and equal his own statements, that (at the time) "I'm a sixty-one-year-old commercial pilot and an FAA Ju-52 Examiner with a lifelong interest in airplanes and have been flying since 1944. I've worked for the FAA as consultant to the flight surgeon, for the Office of Air Safety, and for the Public Affairs Office, and have been (among a few other things) flight safety officer for the Fifth Air Force in Japan. I *never* managed any finance office, but I have flown B-25s, B-17s, C-130s, C-118s, and some other heavy iron across the Atlantic, and have flown Messerschmitts, B-25s, B-17s, Ju-52, and other heavy iron in movies, TV, and around the States—and some oddball foreign lands. At times I flew every day for months on end; at other times, out of the air a while. Oh, yes; there's skydiving and ballooning, etc.

"As a member of AWA, AFA, CAF, VAC, SW (it's a long list) and many other aviation organizations, I've had numerous conversations with Yeager, Crossfield, Halaby, Bader, Galland, Gabreski, Johnson, Hoover, Poberezny, Jobst, Doolittle, Lear—it's another *very* long list. I was also chartered by the U.S. Congress as one of the originals for the Aviation Hall of Fame (as a sponsor, etc.) *and* have contributed to and worked with most museums throughout the world.

I've had nineteen people strung out on just the left wing of my Ju-52 at nine thousand feet for the world wingwalk record...and a bunch of other fun stuff. I wasn't going to mention the military, but what the hell... service in the U.S. Coast Guard, U.S. Maritime Service, the Merchant Marine, U.S. Army, and the U.S. Air Force...the latter two in A2 Intelligence in both the States and overseas.

"I have *not* seen *all* the airplane movies...I never built any models...but I did write 140 books and had them all published, in addition to tech manuals, screenplays, newspaper and magazine articles...and managed to churn out such extras as the novel and film, *Marooned,* and write *Cyborg,* which went on to become *The Six Million Dollar Man* and *The Bionic Woman....*

"I don't hang out at air museums...I don't fly commercially as often as you indicate you do (but I do enjoy a good martini at any altitude)... and, I consider your letter and your position so important..."

Well, I tried, but that was the last we heard from Mr. Thomas.

Another gentleman, his feathers ruffled equally as much as Mr. Thomas's, wrote directly to the editor of *Sport Aviation,* the magazine of the Experimental Aircraft Association. This gentleman, whose name was published in the magazine at his own request (issue of 4 March 1989), when I answered him directly, was quite anxious for me not to publish his name in this chapter. But it's a hell of a letter, and we grinningly share it with you now....

> To Whom It May Concern:
> As an EAA member, I have read many articles in *Sport Aviation* that were well written and very informative. Upon reading in the January 1989 *Sport Aviation* a call for stories about ghosts and reappearing dead pilots, I had to write to lodge my complaint. Currently General Aviation is in jeopardy due to increased liability and regulatory restrictions. The public's view of general aviation is distorted believing that private pilots are unqualified to safely operate aircraft. Nonsense about ghosts will further the public's negative opinion by adding that we are now also mentally unstable. I would urge *Sport Aviation* in the future to refrain from printing news items of a questionable nature, or the reputation of the organization will be compromised.

*   *   *

As noted, I promised not to print this poor man's name in this book. I'm not certain behind what woodwork he is hiding to blame liability and regulatory problems on ghosts. Does this include angels? Does God get His share of the clout?

Well, better than my answer were two statements, unsolicited, from other pilots, which speak quite well, thank you, for the rest of us. The first letter was from Captain Tad Galler, whom you met in Chapter 6. "I noticed in a letter to the editor of the 4 March 1989 issue of *Sport Aviation*," Captain Galler wrote, "that EAA member [DON'T PRINT MY NAME!] So-and-So is complaining about ghost stories. Well, he deserves a riposte.

"As far as EAA member [DON'T PRINT MY NAME!] So-and-So, he should be spirited away as a super robot to the outer fringes of the cruise missiles, where he could safely hide in a convenient hole from the Harpies of the public view, by which he is so much terrified.

"At the same time there will be no doubt an opportunity for him to supervise and censor the rank and file of the spiritless and mindless ordinary robots and assorted doodlebugs."

This comment was signed personally by Captain Tad Galler, EAA member number 60771.

There's a reason for presenting this sampling of strong and sometimes heated response by the naysayers on the contents of this book. My reason is to the point: it's just as important for this book to show the attitudes and reactions of the great majority of the pilots as it is to read the material itself in these pages.

Much earlier, and several times since, I have stressed that most pilots who encounter unexplainable phenomena or supernatural events that save their lives are extremely hesitant to discuss the matter or will flatly refuse to discuss it because it is "out of the ordinary." I don't wish to flog the dead horse, but I must stress to the reader, then, that when you encounter the real longtime pilots, the most able and experienced of the veterans, consider that their statements and admissions are made without anything to gain for them, without benefit to them, and *in spite of* the lemming out-cry of "I don't believe that stuff."

A Mr. Alan Sheppard, attorney from Fargo, North Dakota, in response to the letter printed in *Sport Aviation* with its worry-wart hand-wringing stating that talk of ghosts will increase costs of insurance and bring down the wrath of government on pilots, gives us the final word on this matter—

> Letter to the Editor
> EAA *Sport Aviation*
> RE: Ghost Stories
> A chance to defend Martin Caidin! Does he really want or need my help? I must respond to the negative let-ter in March's issue about "nonsense and ghost stories." Please, Mr. [DON'T PRINT MY NAME!], loosen your tie. Armchair flying usually predates the financial ability to get wings. (I know; my plastic money is melted still from private instruction and falls apart dreaming of instrument and float rating add-ons). I doubt aviation ghost stories cause distorted public opinion, as long as the armchair pilot doesn't fasten the book to the yoke, instead of using the approach plates!
> I often reread Martin's three-part account of Connie Edwards's PBY reenactment of the NC-4 Atlantic cross-

ing. I literally got sore sides from reading Caidin's *Rag-wings and Heavy Iron,* and I urge *Sport Aviation* to print excerpts from Caidin's best writing-in stories he collects from pilots. In fact, *please* reprint his request for ghost stories and his address.

The lore of flying includes tongue-in-cheek humor, as well as spiritual reflection upon the wonder of the ground below and technological understanding of the mechanics of the plane.

Martin gets my vote for as much "artistic license" as his brilliant mind and pen may want. Aviation's multiple areas of interest are unfolded in each issue. Keep up the diversity of topics. The chance to try something else was recently demonstrated to me by Bruce Aarestad's ride in his ski-equipped L-4. Just like aerobatics, a peek at the grass on the other side of the fence may reveal an entire aspect of flying I'd never contemplated. Mr. *Don't Print My Name* (which is strange, since you did in the maga-zine), I appreciate your concerns with the public image of general aviation. Unfortunately, they've already seen the series of *Airport* movies. Martin's dry humor can hardly be said to be the cause of the bad reputation, so-called; espe-cially compared to the damage caused by one low buzzing.

LOST

The pilot departed Havana, Cuba, at 1:35 A.M. on a long planned flight direct to Saint Louis, Missouri. He planned to cross the Straits of Florida and then continue on to his destination. Most of his flying would be dead reckoning. This was 1928, and the navigation aids we take for granted today weren't even wishful thinking in those times. And the pilot was well experienced.

As he left Cuba behind and flew over open water, "strange things" began to happen inside and to his plane. They made no sense, and they baffled him. First, his magnetic compass began to turn to the right, then to the left, right again, left again, and suddenly it began to rotate around and around. It was spinning uselessly. *It wasn't supposed to do that.* A mag-netic compass can be affected to give an "off" reading, but they don't spin madly so that they're completely useless. Every now and then a pilot would talk about his mag compass "going wild" or "berserk" and spinning so fast it would even break its container bowl and splash alcohol over the instrument panel. That was almost the situation now.

But not to worry. This aircraft also had an earth induction indicator, about as solid a piece of navigation equipment for its time as one could obtain. You could use the EII for crossing oceans, and many pilots used them for more reliable long-range navigation. But now the EII in this plane went bananas; it began to wander erratically, pointing first one way, and then indicating a course to follow that made absolutely no sense.

In short, *both compasses were now useless.* The pilot had no way to use those instruments to check his heading, or to use timing and dead reckoning to figure his position.

But he was good. He kept flying as steadily as he could, using star references to hold course. *That* went to hell in a handbasket. Haze settled like an instant mist through the entire area. Fog formed to blind the pilot. Above him the stars were now barely visible, and beyond use as navigational reference.

So the pilot went down low, as low as he dared in the dark. He figured that by judging the whitecaps of waves, their size and movement and direction, he would have at least a rough idea of the wind direction, its force and if it had changed from the forecasts. That didn't work; the air became turbulent, it was difficult to see out of the airplane.

Dawn finally began to streak the eastern horizon. The pilot couldn't believe the sky. He later described it as looking like "dark milk."

The sun kept pushing up and the sky brightened so that now he could see the surface below. He was over land! And his compass was starting, just as crazily as it had gone bad before, to reverse its wild behavior. It settled down and now worked perfectly. So did the earth induction indicator.

It took a while for the pilot to locate his position. For several minutes he scanned the shoreline features, and then his charts. If they matched, as they seemed to do, then he was far off course. So far that it exceeded any distance he could possibly have reached with the fuel on board.

The lost pilot?

Charles Lindbergh, flying *The Spirit of Saint Louis* in 1928 from Havana to Saint Louis.

In everything he had ever said or written about his career he did not bring attention to this flight until his final written words for his book *Autobiography of Values,* published in 1976 by Harcourt Brace.

It leads one to wonder. If the pilot had been an aviator with lesser credentials than those of Charles Lindbergh, who would have believed he was "impossibly" far to the north of his predicted path of flight?

STAR TIGER

Okay, here we go into the Bermuda Triangle.

But *not* in the manner you might expect.

We turn back the clock to January of 1948 and the disappearance of the British airliner, *Star Tiger.* It's in the official reports and the books as one of the all-time great unsolved mysteries in aviation.

Star Tiger was an Avro Tudor IV belonging to British South American Airways Corporation. The airliner was a severe modification of the Avro Lancaster bomber, configured to carry thirty-two passengers on a flight from London, with stops en route, to Havana, Cuba. The refueling stops after departing London were Lisbon, the Azores, and then to Bermuda for the last refueling stop before continuing on to Havana. The toughest part of the flight at a speed of about 170 knots was the nearly two thousand miles between the Azores and Bermuda.

It's also an area in which the winds are both unpredictable and treacherous. The last time I flew this route was in Connie Edwards's PBY-6A from Lajes, Azores, direct to Bermuda. Our Catalina had more powerful engines than the standard model, and we had two huge external fuel tanks beneath the wings. And mighty glad we were that we had the extra power, speed, and range, because we ran into unpredicted head winds that began to raise eyebrows in the flying boat.

From Lajes to Bermuda was a flight of some *twenty-three hours, forty-five minutes!*

We had aboard the finest avionics available in the world, from weather printout machines linked directly to satellites in geosynchronous orbit to LORAN and other systems. In 1948 the navigator aboard *Star Tiger* relied on celestial bearings to determine his position accurately. If the weather went foul, the name of the game was instant trouble.

Star Tiger completely vanished with all souls aboard. The official accident report of the British government states that "No more baffling problem has ever been presented for investigation. The Court has not been able to do more than suggest possibilities, none of which reaches the level even of probability."

Let us get right to the flight, which departed London on the 28th of January. It wasn't the most comfortable of journeys for the twenty-five passen-

Catalina

Edwards Archives

gers. The heating system went belly up, and icicles hung from the cabin roof at twenty-one thousand feet because of condensation. Temperature in the airplane was somehow brought up to 34°F, which at least meant only shivering rather than freezing passengers. And a cockpit compass failed.

Everything was repaired in Lisbon. When *Star Tiger* took off on the run to the Azores, the familiar song went to a second verse. The same compass failed again, followed immediately by the heating system. But they made it to Santa Maria, landing in the teeth of a sixty-knot gale. The huge Tudor touched down and came to a dead stop in two hundred yards.

When they next took off from Bermuda, the flight was planned for twelve hours, thirty minutes. They had sixteen hours of fuel on board. For the first half of the flight, cloud cover was expected; at the halfway point it was predicted to clear, so the night flight would have excellent star readings for navigation. There would be a head wind, but it would be at its lowest force at two thousand feet. This would also help keep the passengers a bit warmer, they believed.

For once the cloud forecast held up. Near the halfway point the navigator took his bearings. They were on course, but the head winds were increasing, and the flight would now take fourteen hours. That brought the "required reserve" of two hours of fuel right down to the razor's edge.

Shortly after midnight *Star Tiger* reached 750 miles from Bermuda. But not for another hour or so did they find out that the head winds were now a howling gale and they were being blown off course. They had 550 miles before them. The reduced speed over the ocean surface would add another hour to the flight, which meant landing with *one* hour's fuel reserve.

When they were 400 miles out from Bermuda, they attempted by radio contact to have Bermuda get a bearing on the airliner. After several fruitless attempts they had it. Bermuda radioed: "Your bearing from us is seventy-two degrees. Class One."

Class One meant they were no more nor less than two degrees from course. And they could improve their bearing accuracy the closer they got to Bermuda. The operator at Bermuda settled down. *Star Tiger* would call every thirty minutes.

The airliner did not call. When the time reached thirty-five minutes, the Bermuda operator signaled the airliner. No reply. He tried again several times. No reply. The operator had to work several other aircraft, then got back to calling *Star Tiger.* It was now ninety-five minutes after the last contact.

No reply. Bermuda Operations flashed the alarm that the airliner could be down in the ocean. It could also have suffered radio failure; the alarm was a wise precaution. It was also fully justified.

Star Tiger had vanished. By daylight more than twenty-five aircraft and an unknown number of ships scoured the area where *Star Tiger* should have been. Not a trace was ever found. No wreckage. No bodies. *Nothing.* For five days the official records show the extensive search for the airliner. The records also state they didn't find so much "as a trace of oil."

Charges of "sabotage" were heard. Competition for the Atlantic airliner runs was keen and often bitter. But the claims of sabotage seemed brought up only to fill the vacuum into which *Star Tiger* had disappeared.

I don't believe there's any mystery, though this might seem the wrong book to make that statement. After all, we're seeking unusual occurrences, supernatural events, and ghosts. What better place to bring down the hammer than this case of a mysteriously vanishing airliner?

No way. You see, the difference in this instance is that I flew with one of the search teams dispatched over the Atlantic to look for either the downed airliner or any survivors, or even a sign of wreckage. And there were many fewer aircraft in the last reported area of *Star Tiger* than the records indicate.

Most important of all, the skies over the Atlantic where *Star Tiger* was last reported were violent almost beyond description.

Mitchell Air Force Base on Long Island the morning of 30 January 1948 was closed down tighter than a drum. The weather was so lousy that from the tower the far end of the runway vanished in gloom. All planes were either hangared or tied down securely. Underfoot was treacherous ice and slush. The wind was strong, and it continued to intensify. Headquarters Air Defense Command was about as quiet and shut down as it could get. I had hot coffee and good cigars and a bunch of intelligence reports to catch up with. Perfect day for it.

A captain stuck his head in the doorway. "Hey, hotshot, how about an airplane ride? I need some observers. Very fast. Right now I have an empty airplane. Would you believe all the volunteers have gone underground?"

"Captain, *look outside.*"

"Not my idea," he shot back. "And you don't *have* to go. An airliner went into the drink this morning, and we got a max search effort starting, and—"

"I'm with you," I said

He nodded. "We're taking the C-47. See you in base ops in ten. Tech Sergeant Cabe Jackson is going with us."

At base ops we counted heads. Two pilots and four of us as observers to look for survivors. A bunch of B-25 crews came in; they were also going. The ops chief kept it tight: last radio report from the airliner at 0100 hours. "At 0200 (our time) a ship reported a large aircraft low overhead. They saw the lights. And that's what we got. The best we can make out is that the airliner augered in about 440 miles northeast of Bermuda. It looks bad, but maybe some people got into rafts."

A doubtful B-25 pilot called out, "What's the weather?"

"Bad. Moderate to heavy swells. Strong winds. The barometer is dropping. If you're going to find anybody, *go now.*"

We went. Parachutes (ha-ha), rafts, flares; the works. We watched the B-25s roll to the end of the runway and disappear in the icy mist before they turned. Then they came back, oozing into view as they came closer. They bored off into the sky; in moments they were gone.

We were off the deck like an elevator in that C47. The winds were getting stronger with every moment. And from the moment we left the ground, we bounced. Hard. Skidded sideways, shot up on gusts, plummeted in down drafts. It felt as if we were in a hurricane. *We didn't know it, but we were.*

We'd search a rectangular box area fifty by a hundred miles. Start at one end of the box, swing about in a 180-degree turn, run down the box again. Five thousand square miles seems like a lot of territory, but over an angry ocean, it's spit.

All in all, Air Transport Command and the rescue teams launched fourteen search planes. A couple of coast guard cutters and merchant ships were out in the stuff also.

What we didn't know was that the B-25s that left Mitchell just before us were forced to land in Washington because of violent weather. The other planes also turned back. We didn't know it, *but we were the only plane airborne.* Jackson told me our radio receivers were dead, but we could transmit. So we continued the search. We *should* have turned back. But the captain flying our old crate had spent six days during World War II in a raft on the Pacific. He was *sympatico* with the airliner crew and passengers. We pressed on.

We were airborne about three hours when the world went plain flat mad. The C-47 had come alive and was berserk, pitching and tossing with forces that threw us about the plane. She vibrated and groaned, and the wings sagged under loads they never should have survived. We passed through waterfalls of rain that exploded against us, disappeared, reappeared.

None of us in that C-47 were airsick: *all of us were violently ill.* It wasn't just the hysterical motions around all three axes and the tumbling; it was that it never stopped. Everybody was throwing up, the cockpit was splashed with vomit, one sergeant was strapped in tightly and gripping handholds, his face white, and he was throwing up blood. I'd never known anything like it that could last that long.

I thought of what it must be like on a tiny raft smashed by those winds and engulfed by waves. *If* anyone had survived a ditching, how could they have gotten into the water with rafts? Jackson spotted something, and we went down to about two hundred feet and stared at some wooden crates. Back up to twenty-three hundred feet.

We didn't stay there long because the overcast was coming down. We eased from twenty-three hundred to two thousand and then to seventeen hundred feet. We saw two merchant ships, and an hour later we spotted a yellow life raft. We circled it for ten minutes, trying in that turbulence and rain to focus on the object as it was sucked under water, popped up again, and kept appearing and disappearing. Well, if it was a raft from the missing plane, no one was in it, dead or alive.

The search went on. We razzed one another about puking up our guts, but the razzing stopped as a second man began to show blood from his violent nausea.

Then we *knew* we were going to flat-out *die.*

We were fighting our way back down from an updraft, so we wouldn't go booming up into the clouds overhead, when the C-47 felt as if she'd stopped in midair. The airplane vibrated madly. The left wing dipped, and the next second the C-47 plummeted downward. It felt as if all the air beneath us had disappeared and we were falling in a vacuum. One of the men yelled. It wasn't a scream. We were hanging on for dear life, and he just *yelled.* Maybe he was the only one with enough air left in his lungs at that moment to yell.

Down we went, out of control. The wings seemed devoid of lift. The ocean loomed up at us. Finally there came the wonderful feeling of our bodies pressing against our seats, the wings grabbing lift, starting again to fly. We were still canted over to one side, the left wing pointing downward at an angle of thirty degrees or so.

But...this was crazy. We were "hung up" in the air, hammered by winds that seemed to lock us at low altitude, and I looked through my window, and this was the kind of moment when you kiss your ass *goodbye.*

We were caught in a trough between two tremendous swells. One towering wave loomed above us, and as we tried to climb out of the wind trap, that mountain of water plunged down against us. Talk about déjà vu; the last time I'd seen anything like that was in the Mediterranean in 1945, sailing the old Liberty ship SS *Joseph Hooker,* and we got hit by a tidal wave that scoured our decks, lifeboats and all, like a giant brush. But now we were *flying...*

Then a voice, ridiculously calm. Old Sergeant Jackson looking through his window. "I always wondered if I'd know when I was going to die. Now I know. *Yep.*"

It certainly seemed as if it were all over, with the C-47 moving ahead sluggishly and barely hanging in the air. And we could hear the two pilots from up front, *"Climb, you sunuvabitch, climb!"* and the guy in the right seat was trying to shove the throttles right through the panel, the seconds dragged, that water mountain continued falling, and maybe it pushed a hell of a lot of air before it, because abruptly we were going up like a cork popped from a bottle.

We hit the overcast at seventeen hundred feet. We climbed right on through until we broke out at eight thousand feet and headed back for Mitchell Field, unbeknownst to us the only search plane still airborne.

But as to that airliner disappearing so "mysteriously"?

Uh-uh. The accident review board was in England. They weren't low over the Atlantic in that storm. If they had been, there would never have been any question, never any mystery.

Postscript: *Consider this case solved.*

While we're at it—and doing our best to emphasize repeatedly that we have rejected most material submitted for this book—let's get into this business of "mysterious disappearances" of aircraft that so many people attribute to supernatural rather than perfectly natural (even if misunderstood) forces of nature.

I daresay that those of us who have spent years analyzing such disappearances, chasing down hints and clues and possibilities, know a hell of a lot more about this subject than the armchair experts who seem to use everything save reason in their knee-jerk comments.

Consider lightning. Frankly, I'd rather the reader consider it instead of me. I've been too close to it. I've been hit (the airplane has been hit, rather) many times while flying, and I've had two hits on the ground—one direct, and one through the wall of a house with a roomful of people watching electricity sparkling all about my body. It gets your attention. My left arm was frozen in place for several hours, and it left me with a tingling that demanded scratching everywhere at the same time, but the effects fade away after awhile.

But for years pilots have been told by the "experts" that lightning would never take down an airplane—especially a *large* airplane. I do not understand where these stoneheads come from. That is one of the more patently idiotic statements for *anyone* to make (especially to one who's been in the hot seat). If you're ever that close to a lightning strike, you'll never doubt it can tear up any machine ever built.

And every now and then, it does. Airplanes are hit, and they survive; lightning strikes every day of the year. Most airplanes build up a tremendous static electricity charge when flying in the area of storms. Sometimes that lightning bolt is the lightning being discharged *from* the airplane to the nearby clouds. Sometimes you fly between two big bumpers, and you're the attraction between them, and a charge lets fly, and the lightning passes through your plane to the other cloud. That can do funky things to your hair, the seat of your pants, and your state of mind, but it's *very* survivable.

But then again, sometimes it's *not.* So many planes have disappeared in bad weather that *we do not know* what caused them to go down, but we certainly can figure the possibilities, and the odds work out to violent natural forces rather than supernatural destruction.

Once in a very great while a *killer* strike of lightning is witnessed, and we *know* what happened to transform the airplane into a sudden boiling mass of fire and debris, or to tear off a wing and send it plummeting earthward.

I offer you an excerpt from a book I wrote, *The Night Hamburg Died,* when a massive force of British heavy bombers went out to erase Hamburg from existence. From page 118...

Burr manages to fight the Lancaster in a laboring, grueling climb to 16,000 feet. At this altitude, still fighting every foot of his flight, the lieutenant sets his course over the North Sea, moving on a line that will take his Lancaster—as other pilots will also fly—toward the final massive blow at Hamburg.

There is no respite from this flight. Simply to keep the heavy bomber on level flight demands the constant and unremitting attention of its pilot. It is a nightmare of flying, a mission in which weather surmounts the dangers of the enemy and becomes a foe much more deadly and effective.

At 17,000 feet the bomber refuses to climb any higher. It is no longer constantly within the furious storms; now it floats between giant mountains. Towering peaks loom far above, and beyond them are the stars. The Lancaster drifts through a world in which it is an insignificant mote, a tiny winged machine dwarfed by the immensity of lofty pinnacles, the weather ramparts of nature.

Then, without warning, nature reveals a hidden weapon, one that it has held in check, has refused to play in the stakes of life-or-death. From darkness lit by brief moments of the palest light oozes a strange lightning that clutches at the airplane. It is a lightning without thunder, no jagged streaks blaze through the sky. It is a personal, hellish fire, persistent, frightening, immediate.

The pilot, Burr: "All the metal parts of the aircraft shone with the blue spikes of Saint Elmo's fire.... About a quarter mile to port was another aircraft flying on a parallel course. It seemed to be a mass of flames, and I realized, too, that it must be covered with Saint Elmo's fire: I stared at this flying beacon and...suddenly, as I watched, *a streak of lightning split the heavens. There was a huge flash and burning fragments broke away. The blazing wreckage tumbled into the clouds and disappeared....*"

If you fly in wicked weather, if you chance your life in the big thunderstorms, if you go barreling into and through the thunderbumpers, the odds are you *may* survive, but almost certainly, sooner or later, you'll take a whack from lightning. Some pilots have been in aircraft struck not dozens, but through their careers literally hundreds of times. If the ship is properly grounded, if it can bleed off the enormous forces building within it, if it doesn't take a lightning bolt of 50,000°F right in its guts, why, it will go right on scaring its occupants but surviving.

The point I want so earnestly to make is that many of the so-called experts insist lightning isn't dangerous. Well, that Lancaster we just read about is a sort of unanswerable refutation. The passenger-loaded DC-8 flying out of Rome which took a lightning strike while spilling fuel from its dump ports and exploded instantly is another refutation. The Boeing 707 in the American northeast that had a wing ripped from the fuselage by a lightning bolt makes a mockery of "it ain't so bad."

You see, the yardbirds who insist on these "truisms" really don't know what the hell they're talking about. When I started flying, the "word" was that once you flew above thirty-five thousand feet, *you were above all weather.* This is what they taught pilots. How asinine! They never did any real studies, they didn't fly airplanes up to high altitudes, or they would have discovered those storms build up to fifty thousand and sixty thousand feet without a break. They would have found the really big bumpers breaking seventy-five thousand feet all summer long.

And later, if they'd talked to the astronauts who looked ahead and down to see the tops of the really great thunderbumpers, they would have seen the measurements showing some of these monsters hitting ninety thousand feet. But many pilots bought this diddly-poop of thirty-five thousand feet and went charging through the night at even greater altitudes, when they finally had the planes that could handle the altitude, and they found themselves helpless pawns in the grip of the monsters.

What concerns us, here and now, are so-called mysterious disappearances of aircraft and their crews, without so much as a shred of a clue. Now, I'd like to join the parade that attributes every such loss to something supernatural, but I just can't do it. Tankers that explode and vanish without a trace. Airliners that are here one moment and gone the next. *Unless you know the exact conditions under which an airplane disappears, it must be chalked up to unknown, and this is all she wrote.*

In other words, we don't need to stretch the point. If we don't know, that's the way it should be written down in the records—period.

There was one flight in which *I* almost disappeared, along with a large airplane and the entire crew. This was a night flight out of Mitchell Field on Long Island in a C-119 Packet we were taking to Ohio. The C-119 is a huge lumbering sod of an airplane with two big engines and two tail booms and a propensity for stumbling over itself. But this flight was a piece of cake. We were well under gross weight, the weather was severe clear, a billion stars shone down on us, and we had great food and coffee aboard. For the first part of the flight we tossed heads-or-tails to see who'd drive the bird, and I got third choice. I'd take it later, but for now I was free to walk about the airplane, looking down on the frosted jewelry of city lights. Finally I took a position by a window at the left rear of the airplane, looking to recognize different stars, and I sought and found Polaris, the north star, *and it hit me like ice water right down the back of my neck.*

I looked at Polaris again. No way! It's in the wrong place! A cloud deck slid beneath us, and ground lights vanished, but I knew we weren't over land and headed for Ohio. We were over the ocean and on our way into a huge nowhere that would swallow us up forever, because we had enough fuel to get to just about the middle of the Atlantic, and then everything would go *very* silent as the tanks emptied.

I went forward to the flight deck. "Hey, guys, you know what? We're going the wrong way. Unless, that is, you're trying to get to England."

They laughed and pointed to the nav systems and the compasses. "Sorry, fella, look for yourself," the pilot said. "Just follow the yellow brick road in the sky to Ohio."

"Look outside to your left," I told him. He gave me a look that said I'd slipped a cog here and there.

"What, what?" he said impatiently.

"Find the Dipper. Find Polaris," I prodded him. He did. *To our left.* It should have been to our *right*. He gaped. We were on our way to a point of no return in the ocean.

What were the odds? A million, a billion, a trillion to one that every instrument and navigation system in the airplane had reversed itself. Hey, boys and girls, that is *exactly* what had happened.

We did a one-eighty right then and there. We didn't trust the nav instruments, but we could home in to Mitchell Field, and we did, paying homage to Polaris all the while. If we could have affectionately patted that star on its furry little celestial head, we'd have done it. Finally we reached the edge of that cloud deck, the lights on the ground reappeared, and we canceled Ohio and put down at Mitchell, where every nav system in that airplane was ordered to be *removed*.

Now this is an incident without an exciting moment, without a revelation, without a gory or a heartwarming or any kind of splendid conclusion. But it's a perfect demonstration of how something so basic, so simple, so reliable, can go completely bananas and put an airplane into the drink with no one else around for hundreds of miles. They'd never even have looked for us over the ocean; we were headed for *Ohio,* in the opposite direction.

If I *didn't* mention or briefly discuss the Bermuda Triangle, also known as the Devil's Triangle, the omission would raise a long line of eyebrows. So we'll get in and we'll get out, because there seems little justification in this book for rattling on about the disappearance of aircraft (and ships) under conditions that baffle us all. After studying everything about those vanished planes, we end up *still* baffled.

At times, even when we recover debris and bodies, we haven't a shred of a clue as to what took the airplane apart and hurled it into the sea. So many possibilities, though, fit within the borders of "normal." Vapors seeping from fuel tanks and lines that explode and destroy an airplane in a single blast. An engine that itself explodes and in its violence tears a wing from the plane, sending it whirling so violently into the ocean, there's no time to get out any distress calls, and the plane hits water that's fifteen thousand feet deep, and that's the end of *that*. There's sabotage; a bomb goes bang, and an airplane is gone. It happens; it happens.

Airplanes run out of fuel and don't get off an emergency signal. In the span of one year, *several dozen* of the finest corporate and executive jets, with the best pilots in the business, ran out of fuel over the ocean and went down, and we knew about *these* planes. What prompts professional, experienced, top pilots to allow such stupid things? It happens...

Or you're aboard a four-engined plane and suddenly *all four engines quit*. It has happened, and it continues to happen. The electrical system goes bonkers. The plane at night flies into a cloud of ash from a recently roaring volcano (that happened in late 1989 when a 747 lost all four engines, sustained eighty million dollars worth of abrasion damage and made an emergency run for safety). An airliner is over the ocean, and its pressure hull tears apart; that's an explosion. We lost a lot of planes *that* way, and they never got off a message.

One of the world's best four-engined piston airliners went through a terrible period. The damn things kept catching on fire. They traced it down only after one pilot brought his blazing, passenger-terrified ship down to a safe landing. They put out the fire and traced a fuel leak in the belly of the plane, running through the cargo compartment, that had been ignited by electrical systems. Two of that "model" aircraft were lost without any explanation.

Remember the Lockhead Electra? A terrific ship. Two of them tore apart in the air, but they went down where we could go over the wreckage. No explanation, *for a while*. It turns out the airplane built up a resonance in a wing, a back-and-forth buildup of a vibration that turned the wing into a huge tuning fork—and under the right conditions, the wing *snapped* off. They found the fault, and they cured it.

Few people in our business remember when the old Consolidated B-24D Liberator, a four-engined bomber that was a stable companion to the Flying Fortress, built up an incredible record of disaster. It baffled the experts, confounded the engineers, and killed its crews when the tail would suddenly rip off in flight. No one could figure it out, and we had a real problem on our hands; we needed that ship for combat operations.

The really sharp engineers were called in. They took high-speed films of the airplane taking off. They found that the main gear oleo for the B-24D, with its single huge tire, acted like a great tuning fork in exactly the same resonance range as the tail. A vibration, a humming, built up with tremendous force. If the conditions were just right, which could be mild turbulence, or maneuvers, or simply flaring to land—the tail would tear off and turn the airplane into flaming wreckage.

They added thirty pounds of weight to the tail and completely changed the resonance, and the problem was solved.

Then there's weather that takes planes down. Ice can drag the biggest and heaviest of them all right to the ground. There are pilots who mess around in turbulent air and exceed the loadings of their airplanes and *blooey*—one great wall of debris trickling from the sky. The pilot of a Jordanian 747, convinced that nothing could bother that monster, blithely flew his huge Boeing into the worst part of a humongous thunderbumper. The airplane did not come out of that thunderstorm. Not in one piece. In a few thousand pieces, yes. The storm tore it apart, because winds are violent, explosive, and they contain tornado vortices right in their belly that you cant see until it's grinding a wing in the same way you would pulp a paper towel.

Even the term Bermuda *Triangle* is a popularization. That area in the Atlantic where the mysterious disappearances become so great, under conditions so odd that they beggar answers, is really about a half-million square miles of ocean, with many islands and part of the Florida coastline thrown in. It runs from Bermuda in the mid-Atlantic in what's generally a southwest or west-southwest line to about Saint Augustine on the northeastern coast of Florida. Then it goes almost due south, through the Miami area, to the Keys. The line then extends southeast to Puerto Rico, and from there generally northeast, to Bermuda. What we've just described is *not* a triangle. It's a trapezium—a rectangle in which no two sides or angles are the same.

Now, in the thirty years from 1945 through 1975, a total of sixty-seven ships and boats of all sizes, and no less than 192 aircraft of all types, involving some seventeen hundred people, disappeared in the Devil's Triangle with no known explanation. And this does not include the many more ships and aircraft lost for reasons that were identified.

How could it *not* be baffling and mysterious?

I don't want to get bogged down in the Devil's Triangle, figuratively speaking, because I could write at least three or four entire books on that subject. I've been involved with it that deeply and on a very personal as well as professional basis. So we'll do a wrap on this subject with three incidents. The first is absolutely baffling, and so impossible it's maddening; I wasn't part of that one. The second was terrifying, but not for any supernatural reasons, and I was right in the thick of it. And the third was as calm and smooth as sitting in an armchair at home, but it defied all the rules of flight, electronics, and our "normal world," and I was right in the middle of that one, along with some of the world's best pilots. My wife, Dee Dee, was with me, and that was *her* first taste of what it's like to have the hell scared out of you as a pilot in the Devil's Triangle.

The first incident went into the logs under the date of 28 December 1948. Captain Robert Lindquist and his copilot, Ernest Hill, were just completing a thousand-mile charter flight in their Douglas DC-3 from San Juan, Puerto Rico, to Miami. The twin-engined piston airliner, famed in the military as the C-47 or the Gooney Bird, was owned by Airborne Transport, Incorporated. They had thirty-two passengers aboard, including two infants. One stewardess, Mary Burks. From the position reports, a good flight in the old, reliable airliner.

The records showed that at 4:13 A.M. Lindquist called in to Miami Tower. He could clearly see the great glowing bowl of light that was Miami looming into the sky. "Approaching field. Fifty miles out. South. All is well. We'll stand by for landing instructions."

A lazy, quiet time of night. Radar picked up and locked onto the DC-3 on its long, shallow descent. The weather was good. Some patchy clouds, gentle winds. Everything was letter-perfect.

Several seconds after Lindquist spoke to Miami Tower, the airplane vanished. With Miami dead ahead.

It just...*vanished*.

It disappeared from the radar. No one ever heard its radio again. No one ever *saw* it again. There was a hell of a search. They looked for everything. An oil slick, wreckage, bodies, any small debris, even the telltale signs of converging sharks and barracuda. In the daylight hours the sea was so clear, it would have been almost impossible not to have seen the wreckage of the plane on the bottom. There was *nothing*. Forty-eight ships took up the search. More than two hundred planes scoured an area of 310,000 miles, including the ocean waters, the Keys, the Everglades, the Caribbean, the Gulf of Mexico. Occupants of hundreds of boats in the area were questioned.

Nothing.

It remains vanished to this day. Try not to think of that airplane as an item of history you're reading about right now. Imagine you have a loved one on that DC-3. A husband or a wife, a child; whomever. You'll never see them again, you'll never know what happened to them, and you'll have to suffer all your pain and bitterness without any help because nobody knows a damn thing!

Have I been leading up to a possible answer? Keep this DC-3 in mind until you come to the incident of a National Airlines Boeing 727 on a long final approach to Miami International. Make a mental note. You can make your own "connections" then.

The second incident is much more recent. It involved something called a neutercane. Not many meteorologists know about it. The know-it-all lardheads say it doesn't exist. Those of us who've been caught in a neutercane have unpleasant, even nasty, things to say to these potato brains. They were never in a neutercane, they have no experience with it, so naturally it cannot happen. I would have loved to have had a few of these twits in my Apache when three of us were nailed.

The neutercane is best described as a freak storm of violent intensity that covers a relatively small area. It does *not* show on weather maps because it brews up too fast and disappears even faster. The Gulf Stream seems to have some part in spinning these things to life. The storms are only five to fifty miles in diameter, usually the lesser. Some netuercanes rage for only a minute; other rampage for an hour. But when they do erupt, well, it's every man for himself. They tear apart the ocean surface. Calm waves become huge swells twenty to forty feet high, or even greater. The neutercane spawns waterspouts and tornadoes like gumdrops.

My neutercane number came up on the last day of 1968 when, officially, these things did not exist. Three of us were flying back to Florida from New York in my Apache 2216P, which had been modified and strengthened for air show work so I could "throw around" the airplane and still be both safe and legal. We left New York in bitterly cold weather and punched through scattered snowstorms on the run down south, and finally we were near North Myrtle Beach and Wilmington, North Carolina. We were at a point twenty miles from the coastline and looking for a place to land. Heavy snow squalls had formed behind us, and we didn't want to get trapped. I spoke with Myrtle Beach radio, and they said the weather was likely to frizzle on us, but right now the ceiling was thirty-five hundred feet with broken clouds, visibility seven miles, winds about twenty to thirty knots. In short—cold, gusty, and bumpy, a threat of an angry cross-wind for landing, but nothing to get excited about.

We were twenty miles from the coastline, headed due east and at two thousand feet when *it* happened. Of a sudden the sky before us changed from broken clouds and blue sky to a glazed glasslike white. It was featureless, strange, and it brought a touch of caution tingling through the body. At that moment radio contact with the FAA station in North Myrtle Beach went dead. The nav systems went *kerplooey*. That wasn't a problem (we thought) because we were only twenty miles from the coast.

Then from that glazed sky I saw a strange line from one end of the horizon to the other, rushing at us, like a shock wave. As it came closer, we saw what looked like wheat on the ground bending down before the winds of a summer rainstorm. The sky had become a fearsome, brilliant milky white, and the surface was unbelievable. What we thought were "stalks of wheat" were the high pine trees of the forest laid down almost flat before a terrifying wind! I looked behind us for a fast one-eighty to outrun whatever it was coming at us, but the world behind was all thick, blinding snow and zero-zero visibility. Well, rough or not, at least we could see ahead of us.

It took us forty-five minutes to fly the next twenty miles. We could also smell the stink of real danger, electrostatic charges, the electricity in the air making our clothes stick to skin. In the back Diana's hair floated above her head from electricity We all found sparkling tendrils of blue flame. Well, we were back with good old Saint Elmo's fire. All in all, it's a friendly apparition that's *real*.

That didn't bother us; when that "shock wave" of air, exploding outward from *whatever-it-was* that makes a neutercane, hit us, well, from that moment on we no longer had control of that airplane. Had the Apache not been rigged for wild airshow maneuvers, it would not have survived. I've been *tumbled* in more airplanes than I care to remember; this was as bad if not worse, but it was entirely different. It was so wild, I tried to belly in the ship, gear up, anywhere I could find: a field, a road, anything. But there wasn't any control that lasted more than a few seconds. I'd drop the nose and kill power to aim for a field, and the next thing I knew, we'd be down two or three hundred feet, and then we were standing on a wing going straight up.

I was hanging on to that yoke with my left hand, fingers locked in for dear life, and I was playing a staccato tune with the throttles. We were being thrown about the cabin despite all the harnesses; my head slammed more than once into the overhead. I don't know what kind of compression that instrument panel was getting, but we began to see cracked glass before the gauges, and then the rear right window cracked; we saw antennas flapping wildly before they tore loose. There were times when nothing I did with the controls meant anything; it was idiotically funny and frightening at the same time. We shook and banged and rolled, snapped and jerked wildly; the movements were convulsive, we were battered. Ever see a paint can in a vibrator to shake up the paint? That was us, but at the same time we were being tossed forward, sideways, up and down.

We just didn't know how the ship stayed together. I tried to roll with the punches. That's all you really can do. You could *feel* the airplane fuselage twisting and bending. The metal cone of the afterfuselage was flexing; the tin canning sounds were a mixture of flat cracks and deeper booms, like bending a big sheet of metal back and forth in your hands (and kicking it once in a while). Then there'd be a moment of peace. Hooray! *Then* someone put that ship into a great slingshot and hurled it skyward, where it ran into an invisible hand that smacked it back down.

Well, at that point some *more* fun began. We were, in the sense of crawling, flying forward, inching our way to the coast. Then off the water, surging inland, came a picket-fence line of twisters, long and high and writhing waterspouts white with water and turning darker as they picked up surface debris. It's bad enough to be in close proximity with the undulating rope one or two hundred yards in diameter, spitting blue light and lightning, but it's terrifying with seven of those mothers out there, and you've got to anticipate them in a wild fandango dance from side to side, and the gods are laughing, and you've got only a smidgen of control. We went right by one of those suckers, so close it seemed to be snarling at us, and trees and wreckage spilled away from the column; there was a sharp slap of air, a scream as Diana's head was cut open against the side of the plane, and we were through the picket line.

Directly before us was the town of North Myrtle Beach. A strange fog seemed to hang over it. *It was the remains of rooftops, homes, anything not tied down;* debris, garbage, salt spray, and dirt, blanketing the whole town. The world was still spitting mad when we reached the beach and I tried to turn south toward the airport. At that moment we lost all control. Later the police chief of the town told wide-eyed newsmen. "Hell, yes, we saw him. That airplane came over here tumbling end over end and twisting as it went. It was like a kite cut loose in a thunderstorm."

Look, Ma, no hands. Same effect. We tumbled toward the airfield and I was in a vertical bank. Great! I chopped lower engine power and stamped right rudder, and we dropped. We were almost on the runway when the storm gods laughed and threw us back again to about seven hundred feet in the snap of fingers. Back down again.

There; a copse of trees. I dived for them with full power, got below the trees, the wind was crowning overhead, and I hit all three tires at the same time, stood on the brakes (we didn't roll fifty feet in that wind), and just stayed there. People in the local shop came running out and threw themselves on the wings to kill the lift. I chopped power and yanked on the mixture controls, the engines grumbled to a stop, and ten seconds later—the storm was gone. It was like turning off a switch. Power off; storm gone.

When the storm hit this town, it did about six million dollars worth of damage in twenty seconds. Hey, North Myrtle Beach has a government weather station. Finest equipment there is; computerized, formalized, and sanitized. And they had no warning of the neutercane they said didn't exist but that exploded out of "nowhere" and with such fury it blew that station off the air and wrecked half the town. Made real garbage pie out of the joint.

A plane or a boat caught in such a storm is prime to go *down*, and in that kind of horned fury, the odds are there won't be even a banana peel or a sneaker left to find later. Maybe now you can see why we look with such distaste at the boneheads who've never been in the boiling soup but are always so quick to yell "it's impossible…never happen…it can't be."

It can be, and too often it is.

A brief postscript. The worst pain of this flight came when people climbed into the airplane to pry my fingers loose from the yoke. My fingers were muscle-frozen. I must have yelled a lot because after a while they quit trying and gave me a bottle of bourbon to loosen me up. When the bottle was either half-full or half-empty they got each finger loose one by one, and I was still yelling. I didn't find out until the next day I'd also broken two ribs, but *they* didn't hurt.

THE CATALINA IN THE MILK BOTTLE

We were on the way home from an absolutely terrific jaunt through the Atlantic and the Azores, Portugal and Spain and England and then on to Bermuda, where Karen Edwards and Dee Dee Caidin had the really tough job of holding down two suites in Club Med until we showed up. After several days of hard labor at drinking and bopping, we departed the sunny isles and headed for Jacksonville Naval Air Station in Connie's fantabulous PBY-6A. We had a gang of some of the finest and most experienced pilots in the history of the U.S. Navy aboard, plus a couple of renegades, which I guess included me and Connie.

Now the weather was perfect. We had range up the gazoo. We had a couple of million bucks worth of special avionics gear, as I'd mentioned earlier. We wanted to know what the weather was like, we didn't even have to look outside, we were getting direct printout photos on maps from satellites more than twenty-two thousand miles above us. But the weather was *perfect*. One of those days when you could see forever. The people not flying this leg were doing their best to destroy a couple cases of Budweiser. They sprawled in the back turret compartment area.

The others took turns up front. Dee Dee was in the left seat of the Cat. This was great hand-flying. The Catalina's like a whale. Everything in slow motion. No automatic pilot, so it was hand-flying all the way.

The perfect weather disappeared. One moment Dee Dee was looking straight ahead for umpteen miles; the next, she could see the nose right in front of her, but when she looked to the sides, the wingtips disappeared in what looked like the inside of a milk bottle. Maybe it looked more like the inside of a batch of eggnog. You looked up, you saw a tiny patch of sky; everything else was yellow mud (or eggnog). You looked down, and you saw a tiny patch of ocean, and the rest, you guessed it, was eggnog.

No clouds. No turbulence. No bumps and grinds. But then the magnetic compass began to rotate. It picked up speed and went whirling around as if it were a whirligig. We checked the photo printout from the weather satellite. Hey, this is great. The metsat picture showed us in *absolutely clear air*. The nearest clouds were two hundred miles south of us.

But we couldn't see out of the airplane. Dee Dee was flying needle, ball, and airspeed because at just about that time the metsat print machine died. Well, we didn't need that to fly, but it was the opening bid. The electronic innards of the Catalina, all two million clams worth, shriveled up inside. The LORAN went out. The electronic fuel gauges sogged to fuzzy markings. The long-numbered navigation gear read 888888888. The radios died. Everything still had power, *but nothing worked*. It was still needle, ball, and airspeed. What, you say? Why didn't we simply hold heading with the directional gyro? Because it was trying to imitate the mag compass. We went down low. You could see tiny details of spray, but not fifty feet ahead of us. We climbed up to about eight thousand feet. Lots of eggnog up there too.

About an hour out of Jacksonville we seemed to penetrate a curtain. *Of an instant*, no more eggnog. We could see forever and ever. The mag

PBY Catalina

Martin Caidin Archives

compass settled down. The directional gyro quit its foolishness and steadied. The electronics emerged from their funk, and *everything* worked perfectly.

But for four hours what happened to us is, as any competent engineer or scientist will tell you, absolutely impossible.

Final postscript: No one ever said it better than did Ernie Gann in his magnificent book, *Fate Is the Hunter*.

He said that no matter what the science or the engineering, no matter how thorough the planning, no matter how skilled the crews or how exhaustive the preparations, airplanes go down from causes unknown.

Somewhere in the heavens, wrote Ernest Gann, *there is a great invisible genie who every so often lets down his pants and pisses all over the pillars of science.*

You betcha.

Chapter 15

A Mighty Fortress

O n the 21st February 1989 I received an unsolicited letter from a
Mr. Ted Setzer, president of Stoddard-Hamilton Aircraft, Incorporated, of Arlington, Washington. Before I excerpt passages
from that letter, a few words are necessary.

Throughout the stories in this book, many of them first person and
signed by their contributors, it is clear that *something* exists far beyond the
normal pale of the forces we recognize as affecting our daily lives. We
have become familiar with ghosts, spirits, apparitions, hauntings, and
other events that have included men, women, animals, aircraft, ships,
sights, sounds, and physical forces. But all have in common that these are
events and happenings not part of everyday life, almost universally
rejected by scientists and others who are quick to heap scorn upon anything that can't be trapped in a bottle or measured by some instrument.

We have dealt with "more than ghosts." We have seen Time itself bent
and reshaped to permit the "impossible." But there may well be, and most
likely is, a force, an energy, a power beyond anything we know or comprehend. Different men call it by different names, but they all believe

215

absolutely that they recognize, understand, and are one with whatever is this power beyond the pale.

I have been more than hesitant to enter this arena, to take a stand in such matters about which I am so lacking in knowledge. Yet not to enfold these possibilities in these pages is also to be blind to their existence and to suffer my own excessively hesitant position. So I welcomed this letter from Ted Setzer, which in part I will now share with you.

I have enclosed a copy of *Guideposts* magazine which contains a story you might be interested in for your book, *Ghosts of the Air*. The story by Robert Osborne is tilled "A Mighty Fortress," on page 25.

The Lord God who created each one of us and our amazing planet and universe is a supernatural being. For reasons of His own, He intervenes in certain situations and makes His presence known. I personally believe that God intervenes in our lives more than we realize, but it is the rare instances when we see or feel the evidence that we are left in amazement.

I realize that people hold a certain fascination for ghosts and the unexplained, which is a good reason to write such a book, but I would request that you give our Creator ample representation in your book—this is a great story of airplanes and the supernatural.

On a personal note, if you are a believer in the Lord, I would highly recommend this book for monthly encouragement. If you are not a believer, please take a few extra moments and read the story on page 10. It may just change your mind.

Good luck with your book. I've enjoyed reading your stories in *Sport Aviation* magazine.

In this manner, this incredible personal story came into my hands. I now offer it to the reader with every word just the way it was written and printed in *Guideposts*.

When I was an aerial gunner on a B-17 bomber flying out of England in 1943 we seldom came back from a raid over Germany or Occupied Europe without extensive damage to our Flying Fortress caused by German fighters or antiaircraft fire. That deadly hail of machine-gun bullets and shrapnel caused numerous casualties among crew members, too. I remember we talked a lot about defensive armor and wished we had some. Later on flak jackets were issued and did save some lives. But the most effective shield that ever surrounded me had nothing to do with armor-plated seats or bulletproof jackets. It was manufactured a long way from those furious combats in the sky. But without it I wouldn't be here today.

Let me tell you a little about myself. I was born in the low country of South Carolina, grew up on the hill of Puddin Swamp in the Turbeville community. Our family had a two-horse farm (took two mules to work it), but we lost it in the Great Depression when just about everybody went broke. My daddy had to fall back on sharecropping, and things were awfully tight. Nobody had any money; everything was barter, and there wasn't much to barter. We boys had to fish and hunt to keep eating. I remember being given the old shotgun and one shell—all we could afford—and told to come back with one squirrel or else face big trouble. When we went rabbit hunting, we didn't take a gun at all, just a pocketful of those heavy square nuts that hold a wheel on the axle of a wagon. We threw those, and we got so we didn't miss very often.

My daddy wasn't much for religion, but my mother was. Everyone called her Miss Martha, and she used to say she was going to teach us young 'uns right from wrong if she had to beat it in with a stick. We went barefoot all week, and often shirtless, too, but Miss Martha would round up all the kids on Sunday and see that we wore shoes and went to Sunday school in the old Methodist church down at Turbeville. When the war came, she got all the church mothers who had boys in the service to meet every day and pray for our safety.

Because I weighed only about 130 pounds, my nickname was Mutt, after the smaller character in the famous comic strip *Mutt and Jeff*. When I graduated from aerial gunnery school, my size made me a natural candidate for ball-turret gunner. The ball turret, on the underside of a Fortress, was so small that the gunner couldn't even wear a parachute. You were down there with two fifty-caliber machine guns and nothing else.

Some air crews were lucky. I can't say that ours was. On our very first mission we were shot up so badly that we crash-landed on the English coast. That was the end of our Fortress named *Little Chuck*. We got another named *The Last Chance*, and it almost was. On one mission, after we were hit hard, the bombardier and navigator decided to bail out. The bombardier pulled his rip cord too soon. The billowing silk streamed through the escape hatch and then pinned him against the opening so he couldn't move. He was just about being flogged to death. The wildly flapping chute came and tangled itself around my guns; I couldn't see or do anything. I had to go back up in the plane, cut the bombardier out of his harness and pull him back aboard. I got a nasty slash across my hand from my own knife, but finally somehow we got back to England.

Early in November we were ordered to bomb Gelsenkirchen, a German industrial center in the Ruhr. It was my twentieth mission, and it would be tough. I wasn't flying with my regular crew; I was a substitute gunner on another airplane.

We made it to the target and dropped our bombs; but then it seemed to me that the German fighters—Me-109s and FW-190s—came in like a swarm of bees. I could feel our plane shudder from multiple hits, and when I swung my turret around to look at the engines, I saw that two of them were out. That meant we would be losing altitude and dropping behind the formation, a sitting duck for more fighter attacks.

I didn't hear any order to bail out (actually our communications system was destroyed), but looking down I saw parachutes begin to blossom under our plane. I counted eight of them. There were ten of us in the crew. German fighters were still coming in, but I figured if everyone was leaving, I had better leave, too. So I crawled up in the body of the Fortress and clipped on my chute, which I always kept right beside the turret.

The bomb-bay doors were still open, and I was about to jump when I happened to look ahead and see the pilot slumped over in the space between his seat and the copilot's. It seemed to me that he moved a little bit, which meant he wasn't dead. For a moment I hesitated, torn between the desire to jump and save myself, and reluctance to leave a wounded man to what would be certain death. I guess my mother's lessons about right and wrong had been hammered into me more firmly than I knew. I was frightened almost out of my senses, but I found myself walking along the catwalk above the bomb bay until I came to the pilot. He had been hit in the head either by flak or by machine-gun bullets and was barely conscious. The copilot had left the plane on automatic pilot; we were still flying on only two engines.

I knelt beside the wounded pilot, scared stiff and wondering what to do. I looked through the windshield to see if the formation was leaving us (it was), and as I did, I saw something totally incredible. Reflected in the glass was a picture—a vivid picture—of a group of women gathered around a large dining-room table, praying. I knew who they were, because in almost every letter my mother told me she and her friends were praying. Even stranger, standing behind these women were their sons in uniform. I knew them, too, and I also knew that some of them were dead, killed in action.

As I stared in amazement, the picture faded, but I heard—or seemed to hear—a commanding voice that spoke three words: "Take it back!" I knew it could not be the pilot, who was mumbling incoherently. I knew, too, that I was being ordered to take charge of our crippled airplane and fly it back to Britain.

But how could I? On practice missions I sometimes had been allowed to sit in the copilot's seat and "fly" the aircraft. But this "stick time" was insignificant. I had never attempted to land or take off in a four-engined bomber, much less one with two engines out. But the voice came again, clear and authoritative: "Take it back."

Now I seemed to be aware of a figure standing behind me. I thought for a moment the tail gunner had left his position and come forward. But that was impossible because I had seen eight chutes. There could be only two of us left in the plane—the pilot and me. But again the voice spoke, and this time it gave me the compass heading for England. I think it was 322 degrees.

My reaction to all this, to the picture of the praying women, to the resonant voice, to the inexplicable presence of a third man, was a kind of total acceptance. My rational mind couldn't believe any of it, but I accepted it. I felt as if a strong, wise commander was giving me orders. It was my job to obey them, and I felt the terrible sense of panic and helplessness begin to subside.

I crawled into the copilot's seat, took the Fortress off automatic pilot, and swung it around to the heading I had been given. I still felt the presence of the third man behind me; but I didn't look around. The formation had gone ahead without us. Off to the left at about eleven o'clock I saw a squadron of German fighters queuing up to let us have it. We were helpless, and they knew it.

Then suddenly, right ahead of us, was a towering cumulus cloud. By rights that cloud wasn't supposed to be there; it wasn't on our weather charts. But there it was, and we ducked into it like a hunted deer. Visibility dropped to zero. No fighters could find us in such cover. We flew along steadily, our two good engines pulling us, and when we finally came out of the clouds at about ten thousand feet, we were over the North Sea, and the coastline of England lay ahead of us. A tremendous sense of relief surged through me, and I glanced over my shoulder. Was that figure still standing behind me?

No one was there.

But we still weren't home. When we crossed the coast, I began looking for a place to land. I had no idea how to find our home base, the 381st
Bomb Group, but finally I saw a runway with some transports on it. When
I tried to talk to the tower, I didn't know the proper signs to identify
myself, and they kept telling me not to land. The Germans had been known
to load a captured Fortress with explosives and send it to England with
very little gas, hoping that when it came down, it would blow up something. The radio operators in the tower were women, and I couldn't understand their British accents, just one emphatic word, "No! No! No!" I guess
they couldn't comprehend my Carolina talk very well either, but I hoped
they would figure it was something no German pilot could possibly imitate. In any case, I had to land, because I was running out of fuel; red
lights were showing on all the gauges. I told the tower I would circle once,
and then I was coming in. I asked them to have the crash wagon and the
ambulances ready. Then I swung my big crippled bird in a wide circle and
headed for the runway.

I was flying on only two engines, and the bomb-bay doors were creating a lot of drag, so I was moving at only eighty or ninety miles per
hour. I didn't put the wheels down because I wasn't sure how to do it, and
anyway, I figured it might be safer with the wheels up. So I just eased her
in, holding the nose up and letting the tail kind of sag. When I cut the
power, the tail hit first, and then we skidded along on the belly of the plane,
smooth as glass, almost to the end of the runway, where we just slewed
around and stopped.

I got out of my window and went around and pulled the pilot out of
his window. I put him on my shoulders and walked to the edge of the wing
and jumped off; it wasn't very far to the ground. I was a little afraid of fire,
but I knew we had almost no gas left, so I wasn't too worried. I dragged the
pilot about fifty feet and fell down beside him just as an ambulance came
screeching up. They wanted to put me on a stretcher, but I told them to
take the pilot first. "He's wounded," I said. "I'm not." By now they were
spraying the airplane with foam for fire prevention. Someone said to me,
"Are there any more men on board?" I said, "I don't think you'll find
any." Then a wave of blackness descended, and I passed out.

When I woke up in the hospital, they fed me some broth and said I
was suffering from total exhaustion. I couldn't quarrel with that. The pilot
was badly hurt; he lingered a few days and then died. Before he died, he

signed a letter to our base commander recommending me for a Congressional Medal of Honor. They didn't give me that, but they did award me a Silver Star. And a long leave in London.

When I tried to tell our intelligence officers about the third man who had been on the plane, they smiled indulgently and said something about "understandable hallucinations."

I can understand their doubts, but I have no doubts of my own. I know it was our Lord Jesus Christ who came to me when I was in terrible danger and told me what to do and helped me do it. I believe, too, that prayer put an invisible shield around me that day over the flaming skies of Nazi Germany. It can guard you, too, if someone will just pray for you as fervently as that little group of women prayed for me. So many years ago. In a quiet rural community. On the hill of Puddin Swamp.

[The above first-person story is reprinted with permission from *Guideposts* Magazine. Copyright © 1989 by Guidepost Associates, Inc., Carmel, NY 10512.]

Postscript Number 1: On 11 January 1944 Sergeant Robert "Mutt" Osborne flew as a gunner aboard a Flying Fortress in a strike against Oschersleben, Germany. The B-17 was badly shot up and fell out of control. The crew bailed out; Robert Osborne parachuted safely to the ground, was captured, and spent the rest of the war (seventeen months) in a POW camp in Krems, Austria. He lives today in South Carolina with his wife, Juliette; their five children live in the country nearby.

Postscript Number 2: I've got some time driving the Boeing B-17 Flying Fortress. I've flown her in air shows in the United States. In 1961 I was part of a group of happy madmen who made the last formation flight across the Atlantic Ocean, in a flight starting in Arizona and ending in England (all three Forts were bound to play their role in the movie, *The War Lover*). So I know this big, heavy iron and the muscle it takes to move her around, *especially* at slow speed.

I wrote down this description to show to other B-17 pilots: "A Fortress gets the hell shot out of it over Germany. Everybody bails out except the near-dead pilot and the ball-turret gunner, who, sopping wet, weighs about 130 pounds. The drag on this ship is incredible. Two engines are dead. The bomb-bay doors are locked down and open. The wings and fuselage look like a thorn patch or a garbage dump from all the torn metal. This gunner, who's not a pilot and has never made a takeoff or landing, flies this thing all the way back across Europe, finds an airfield, and bellies in the B-17 as smooth as silk. When the ship slides to a stop, he drags the pilot out and carries him fifty feet away from the plane, and this gunner doesn't have a scratch on him. What are the odds this might happen?"

My first respondent said flatly: "You're outta your gourd. That's crazy."

My second respondent: "Are you nuts? If you put that into a novel, no one would ever accept it. The odds are a million-to-one against it."

My third respondent: "Whatever it is you're smoking, switch."

I didn't need any more. I remember wrestling a B-17 around with reduced power in the pattern. I've flown a lot of heavy stuff. For ten years I pushed a massive Junkers Ju-52/3m around the air-show circuit, and handling the B-17 low and slow in the pattern, with all that junk hanging down, was bad enough on *four* engines.

But with only *two* fans turning? Uh-uh. That was the consensus.

It couldn't happen.

No way!

But it did.

Chapter 16

=A STITCH IN TIME

Would have baffled Einstein.

How true.

Earlier in these pages I mentioned a Boeing 727 airliner on final approach to Miami International Airport and urged the reader to keep that aircraft in mind. Before we continue with this specific incident, I will make the extra effort to assure the reader that this information has been checked repeatedly. I spoke to some of the people involved. Airline captains, friends of mine who aided in research, officials of the Federal Aviation Administration, a literal host of investigators, all pooled their information to bring it together before I put this down on paper. Believe what you will out there, this *is* the way it happened.

FINAL APPROACH

The Boeing 727 of National Airlines (a company now relegated to history) was in the long slot for landing at Miami International Airport in Florida. Everything aboard the flight was normal, and the aircraft was

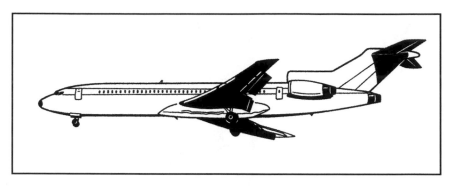

Boeing 727

Martin Caidin Archives

functioning as perfectly as could be hoped. The pilots followed their orders from air traffic control, turning when the calls came and descending on assigned invisible corridors. Miami radar had the 727 and other targets on its scopes.

Suddenly the "blip" on the flat scope that represented the National flight vanished from its electronic position on that scope. One instant it was there; the next it was gone. Several things could have caused the sudden blip disappearance. An electrical failure of the transponder system of the Boeing. An unexpected glitch in the whole radar system. A crew member turning off the transponder that received and boosted back the radar signal from Miami.

Or it could also mean the 727 "was down"; that it had plunged from its approach path, for reasons yet unknown, to slam into the swampy ground far to the west of Miami International.

Immediately the alarms sounded. The reactions are automatic. The word goes out from Miami Approach and Departure, and the tower, for all aircraft in that sector to "look for a Seven Two Seven that's gone off the scope." Pilots strain to see any signs; a reflection of sunlight from metal, a flashing strobe, bright flames, rising smoke—anything.

Nothing. She was *gone.*

Miami Approach hit the alarm signals to the coast guard and other rescue forces. Choppers bolted from the ground and raced to the last-known position of the National 727.

Nothing.

Boeing 727

Fred L. Wolff Archives

Then, precisely ten minutes after the radar blip vanished from the set scopes in Miami Approach, *the blip reappeared before the astonished eyes of the people now crowded around that radar position.*

Reappearance was strange enough. But this was ten minutes after the 727 had disappeared, and now it had *reappeared* in exactly the same position it held in flight when it vanished, both on radar and in flight.

The 727 pilot continued talking with Miami Approach, and then Miami Tower, in an absolutely calm voice. Nothing "unusual" could be discerned from his tone or his words. The still-astounded radar operator worked the 727 in closer and then handed off the airliner to the tower for final landing instructions. The 727 slid in, flaps extended and gear down, and made an absolutely normal landing.

The airliner was directed to park in an area separate from the terminal gate. When it stopped and the doors opened, federal investigators and officials of National couldn't get into that jetliner fast enough. The crew regarded with some astonishment of their own this unexpected and unexplained flurry of activity and barrage of questions.

Then they were told what had happened. "You disappeared from the scope on your descent. For ten minutes there was no radar picture of you people. When you came back on the scope, your position was exactly where it had been. Not only that, but several airliners *flew through* the space you had occupied in those ten minutes. What happened up there?"

The crew—and the passengers who were questioned—were in a different situation. Something incredible had happened to them, and they didn't know the first thing about it.

"*Nothing* happened," the captain insisted. "Nothing out of the ordinary, that is. We were on approach, and we came in, and we got tower, and we landed. *Period.*"

"No break in communications?"

"None."

That only opened the door to another puzzle that baffled everyone involved. A member of the flight crew looked at his watch. He checked his watch against those of the rest of the crew and then against the clocks of the aircraft. They all matched, but every watch and clock on board that Boeing 727 was ten minutes *behind* the watches on the ground.

Where had that airplane gone for ten minutes?

No one knew.

How had it vanished?

No one knew.

Was there any possible answer?

Read on...

Greg Board and I had just landed our B-25 bomber in England. The two of us brought the ship over from the United States for its use as a camera ship in filming the movie *633 Squadron*. We also used the airplane in the film itself, playing a role of dropping saboteurs into Nazi-occupied Norway during the Big Deuce. While we were ratting about with the B-25, we saw this bunch of Messerschmitts also being used in the film, and we got the chance to fly a bunch of wild strafing missions against Mosquito bombers on the ground and also to "shoot up" a bunch of the Mosquitos in the air. Great fun, great drinking, a wild two-day party in Paris, and with us through it all was this great big ruddy pilot, name of John R. Hawke, nick-

John Hawke (right) and Martin Caidin

photo by Bill Mason/Caidin Archives

named Jeff, who had just left active service with the Royal Air Force (he had been based at Tangemere, which we've visited in these pages), where he instructed aerobatics in the double-supersonic English Electric Lightning jet fighter. John was also the heavyweight boxing champ of the Royal Air Force. Stout fellow, tremendous sense of humor, and a born pilot with genius in his fingertips.

That was 1963 and the beginning of some of the greatest fun flying I've ever done. John Hawke and I since that day have flown a variety of aircraft, almost too many to remember, but we did airshows for years in Messerschmitts and other birds of both ragwings and heavy iron. During that time we became as close as two pilot friends can get. John has a worldwide reputation for being both superb *and* lucky, which is the only reason he's still with us, having endured and survived situations that were both madcap and lethal. He can fly *anything*. He's flown hundreds of planes across the oceans of the world—*all* the oceans. This introduction is intended to establish with the reader a man of impeccable credentials, unsurpassed skill, and a great toothy smile, who will forge ahead into *any* situation, just so long as both wings are still on his machine.

John Hawke is also one of the very few pilots I know who has survived not one, but two, time jumps in his flying.

Time jumps?

You got it.

And it will all tie in with a name you're likely to remember for a long time: Kwajalein. But we'll get back to that later. For this moment our interest is with a flight from Fort Lauderdale to Bermuda. John Hawke relates what happened...

UNFINISHED FLIGHT

Well, it was just a jump across some water. Nice little trip. I had a job of flying an Aztec with long-range tanks direct from Fort Lauderdale Executive Airport in Florida to Bermuda. The met people gave me a proper forecast for a send-off; I was told to expect puffy cumulus between four and eight thousand feet, and if I wanted to go higher, I'd find a most convenient tail wind at eleven thousand. Lovely.

But what happened on this flight was something I'd never before encountered. It certainly wasn't what I expected when things began to come unglued. Sort of tatty, when you get right down to it. I was on autopilot, everything as neat as a pin, and I'd crossed the drink a few hundred times already. It was like being at home. Everything was perfect until I found myself staring at the mag compass. I was staring at it, all right, but I couldn't see the stupid thing.

Oh, the compass was still there. But that compass card, that idiot thing, was spinning so fast, it was a *blur.* And I began to feel as if I were passing out. Like slipping under an anesthetic.

That's not the time to contemplate; it's the time to *do.* First thing I did was push my seat way back. If I was going to slop around that cabin like a sack of grain, I didn't want to fall on the yoke. Puts you right into the water, raises your insurance premiums, and ruins the flight, right?

So back I go with the seat and think I really ought to up the trim a bit to compensate. Change of CG and all that. But I couldn't do it. Weak as a kitten.

I put my head back on the rest and had a good look at the sky. It wasn't there. Just creamy yellow *everywhere.* No clouds, no water, no horizon, no blue. Just yellow. And I'm passing out. Last thing I did before I went down the tube was look at my watch. My arm felt like lead, but I fixed the numbers in my head, and the lights went out.

I came back to things just one hour later. Fifty-nine minutes, to be exact. Still flying northeast, if I could trust the gauges. Which I'd have been a fool to do. But I could see the sun now. Northeast I was, all right. But I didn't know where I was. I felt fine, but drained.

I looked up, and there was a lovely contrail. Just beautiful. Got on the horn right off and gave them a call. They came back. I told them I was under them, and asked where in the devil I was.

I didn't believe what they told me. Not at first. I couldn't believe it. *I was seven hundred miles from where I'd been just an hour before.* I'm in a bloody machine cut back to economy cruise and, oh, a ground speed of 180 or so. And in that hour the bird covers a distance of seven hundred miles. It's impossible, of course. But it was true. I turned due west, and I landed in Virginia.

Some years later John Hawke was flying a Riley Dove from Miami to Bermuda. Something happened again. Nobody passed out, but for a while the horizon was gone, and the ocean disappeared, as the airplane became enveloped in a glassy yellow mist. Or what seemed like a mist. He flew on and on and on. The normal time for the flight to Bermuda came and went, and they were still flying. Hawke flew for another five hours, and then the world returned to normal. Bermuda lay dead ahead, and John went down for a normal landing.

On the ground he checked his fuel. The airplane had burned exactly the fuel he had flight-planned before departing Lauderdale. The only problem was that he had been in the air five hours longer than his flight plan called for, but he had not burned one gallon of fuel over that required for the flight.

"That bloody machine gave us five hours of flying and, according to the fuel in the tanks, which I personally checked after landing, didn't consume a drop of fuel for that extra time."

We asked John Hawke if he had any ideas or answers. Remember, this man has flown all kinds of airplanes across all the oceans and continents of this planet. So, based on that experience, did he have any answers to what had happened?

"Hell, no."

Remember: time jumps and Kwajalein.

CLASSIFIED

Some of the more remarkable stories of time twists and the appearance of ghosts—this time specifying the appearance of a human being long departed—have been kept under lock and key and withheld from the world. There are so many such incidents, they would fill several books, but odds are we will never know more than a scant few, and in even those cases where we gain some information, more will be missing than what we find. The specific justification for restricting, or denying, access to such information is an all-too-familiar catchword: military or national security. It is not entirely unjustified. *Not* the appearance of ghosts or any supernatural phenomena, but the installations involved, what they contain, and what they are intended to do.

In the major nuclear powers of the world are heavily guarded facilities where the engines of destruction are stored, held waiting like some terrible disease to ransack all living things. Atomic bombs and the huge hydrogen bombs, meant for use as missile warheads, or carried in huge bombs within the bays of supersonic machines, or at times so monstrous in size and effect, they can be moved only aboard carrier vehicles the size of submarines or ships.

The effect upon people assigned to such installations is at times devastating. Simply being alongside a machine you know can kill twenty million human beings in a single incinerating blast, *and* poison vast areas of the planet, has a crushing physical and emotional effect upon the men and the women involved. It cuts them to the quick, demoralizes them, destroys the perspective they have developed through a lifetime.

There is also a sickness (perhaps it is sanity) that pervades such facilities. Every so often one or more of the men or women working with these infernal devices says: "That's enough," and without another word they walk away from their jobs, never turning back. No threat of court martial, no threat of punishment, can touch them. They are now beyond reach, a sense of horror within their own minds removing them from the world of normal exchange, and they have accepted their own moral decisions so completely that nothing else matters to them.

One such installation of the Royal Air Force, which cannot be identified any more specifically as to name, size, or location, some years ago was placed under the tightest security ever known in England. Normally security is maintained at such installations by specially trained teams whose orders are strict and whose adherence to those orders is absolutely unbending. The consequences of mishandling the weapons about them makes such super-stringent measures absolutely necessary. Within the Royal Air Force these teams were known as the Royal Air Force Police on Special Security Duties.

We know of one such installation located "somewhere in East. Anglia." The place was sealed quintuple-tight with security systems. Anyone found in the installation without full identification required personal cross-checking with other personnel and an unquestioned duty assignment, or was placed under immediate arrest. When such an arrest was ordered, any resistance was likely to result in a barrage of gunfire. The *only* deviation of a security violation that might not result in immediate execution would be the decision to capture the intruder for the purposes of interrogation.

The weapons installation in East Anglia was a security man's dream. A man couldn't *move* without being observed by television scanners. Photocell beams crisscrossed the area, as did invisible laser-beam trips, and because electronics systems can always go dead from power failure, including the battery and generator backup systems, the East Anglia nuclear depot was also riddled with trip wires, movement detectors, and other devices. *And* that old reliable weapon, the trained attack security dogs, their handlers toting automatic weapons. Nearby, helicopters were kept at the ready to move in against any intruders or problems, as were armored cars and other vehicles.

It was not the place for anyone without security clearance to be caught. *But they had their intruder.*

The defense coordinator couldn't believe the first reports from a security lookout in almost dead center of the installation. The lookout reported several people moving through the area; they were unknowns, never before seen by him, dressed in strange clothes, and without any identification.

None of the elaborate electronic systems had so much as twitched.

"He's gone and done himself in," the word flashed. "Completely bonkers, he is. Get a team in there and get him out *now*, and move in replacements at the same time."

Special Security raced to the scene.

The security lookout greeted them with bulging eyes and incoherent shouting. Special Security seized the man, secured him, and started removing him from the area. But he kept shouting, and his voice rose to shrieks. He had become, in the words of the security team dragging him away, "completely berserk."

He kept screaming he had seen *her,* he had seen her racing through the massively guarded complex.

"Who? Who did you see?" they kept asking.

The security lookout, his face bleached almost white with terror, regained sufficient self-control to shriek at the top of his lungs: *"The Queen! It's Queen Boadicea...she's in her chariot!"*

Whatever the security lookout was seeing, he was somehow witness to a sight that went back to the *first century*, for Queen Boadicea was an ancient, powerful warrior of British historical fame. In this period, with violent resistance in the British Isles to Roman occupation and rule reaching full-scale war, the Romans came down heavily on first the Druids and then the Welsh. In typical Roman fashion they smashed the opposition before them, massacring every priest they could find, and then added insult to mass killings by forcing tax payments from the defeated.

Enter Queen Boadicea. Her husband had been the powerful and wealthy Prasutagus, king of the Iceni. After his death Boadicea faced a Roman military force that smashed their way into her castle to collect a major portion of the dead king's fortune they claimed was due to the Roman emperor.

Queen Boadicea met this visit with armed force. Little good it did her, for the Roman soldiers stripped her naked, flogged her brutally, raped her daughters, and then stripped the palace of everything they could carry away. When the fires set by the Romans had been controlled, and the survivors gathered their strength, they encountered a queen raging with hatred and thirsting for revenge.

A neighboring tribe, the Trinovantes, matched her hatred for the Romans. They joined forces, and Boadicea in her chariot, accompanied by her two daughters, led a series of savage raids against Roman garrisons and towns. Boadicea's army, linked with the Trinovantes, smashed into Colchester and leveled every structure of the town. Making good her oath of revenge, her forces tortured, hacked, and butchered every Roman inhabitant they found.

This was but the beginning. The Roman Ninth Legion rushed from Lincoln to put down the upstart queen; again the Romans were routed with a bloody massacre, and Boadicea led her still-growing army toward London.

The Roman garrison wisely raced to the hills rather than be pinned down within the city, leaving London to be sacked and pillaged by Boadicea's forces. By the time she was through, all London had been gutted, burned to the ground. Swiftly Queen Boadicea swung through the ashes of London and smashed Saint Albans.

But now the Roman forces were in motion, and they trapped Boadicea's army in a valley from which there was no escape. A brutal struggle ensued. Boadicea was in fill swing, racing up and down along the lines of her forces, cursing and bedeviling her men to fight. Before the day ended, the Romans triumphed; Boadicea had sworn never to allow the Romans to enjoy the spoils of any victory against her, and she committed suicide on the spot.

And now, in East Anglia, in the midst of a hydrogen-bomb storage depot, she was seen again at full speed in her chariot, followed by men-at arms racing behind her.

"Must have gone off his rocker, poor fellow," commented one of the security officials, and for those easily dropped words, the official was immediately ripped by long-time and close friends of the now raving security man.

It turned out he wasn't any newcomer. He had been in the Royal Air Force for many years, was a highly trained and skilled security weaponeer, and was considered absolutely trustworthy. An official investigation also revealed he had not been drinking, nor did he suffer personal or family or financial problems. But what he had seen—and he never altered one iota his insistence that the ancient British woman warrior had raced through the weapons complex—was quite enough to have him carried off.

Officialdom being what it is in almost all countries, the hapless man was carted off, bound and gagged, to a mental facility. No one believed him. His closest friends and fellow security guards were baffled. They knew he wasn't off his bean—that he *was* reliable, but that something had tripped his mental wires. In the end they accepted that some unknown factor had simply caused this man to lose his marbles.

Done and gone, thank you. Best rid of *that* problem, eh wot?

A week passed. A corporal of the security force shouted for assistance. He pointed with a shaking hand, but *this* man clung to his sanity and had control of his voice, which, if hoarse and strained, was at least fully intelligible. "It's...it's Queen Boadicea...she's in her chariot, the horses racing..."

Officialdom began to crumble. This second security man remained quite in control of himself. They tried everything to shake his story, but to no avail.

He also refused ever to return to the weapons-storage complex.

They threatened, pleaded, reasoned; everything They assured him that in that high tower in the center of the complex he was perfectly safe, that *he* was in command of the defense forces.

"It was she," he insisted quietly. "The queen…"

He never again went to the same place where he, too, had seen Queen Boadicea.

Did her ghost appear again?

No one outside that weapons complex, or in the highest levels of the Royal Air Force, will say a word, will admit to anything, will even comment one way or the other.

Whatever is happening inside the complex; if it still is, remains under the tightest security in British military history.

But it has its parallels elsewhere as we shall soon see.

ABOUT THAT STITCH IN TIME…

First question—

Is there something we can reach out to touch, or to grasp that can explain, or *try* to explain, certain of the more specific incidents and phenomena we have encountered in these pages?

For example, the navy jet pilot seeing his own plane and himself flying in tight formation—

A Hurricane fighter pilot having to abort his night landings because of an ancient biplane from another war cutting him off on final approach—

A heavy bomber, shot to wreckage in the air, unmanned, flying itself hundreds of miles to its home airbase, flying the entire pattern, lowering its flaps and gear and landing—

A bomber racing across a field without a sound, then vanishing—

The figure of a long-dead pilot appearing in the cockpit of an airliner descending to certain doom, and telling the pilot at the controls to veer from his navigational beam, *now,* and saving everybody in that airplane from flaming death—

A fighter plane from an old war, its top speed not much greater than the landing speed of World War II fighter planes, yet appearing in their midst, leading an attack against the enemy, and outspeeding the modern fighters—

An ancient Nieuport and a modern Cherokee brushing wingtips in the air, when it is absolutely certain that Nieuport hasn't left the ground in decades…

And so many more.

Airmen long dead walking through airfields, seen by dozens of men and women...ghost airmen, *yet visible, even speaking to the stunned watchers.* And at different times. And no one has ever yet come up with a *mass,* simultaneous hallucination!

The warning from—whoops! I almost said, from the *past.* But I don't know that! I'm not even certain what really *is* the past. The arrow of Time is still a bafflement. It's a lot like gravity. We know what gravity does, we know its strength, we can measure its force, predict its effect, but we don't know what it *is.*

We don't live in the present, because there isn't any present. It's like riding the rolling edge of the incoming surf. If you think of *this* instant, this moment, the moment you think of it places it in the past. You cannot think of *now* without the use of memory. So there's what's happened, and what's going to happen, and something you cannot grasp in between, and we call it "the present" because we haven't got any other name for it.

Are all these connected somehow? Is Time a dimension? Many dimensions? Or is it just a moving sidewalk on which we travel for a while and are then bumped off into some limbo of "way back then"?

Don't shrink from this headache. I don't have the answers to that. Nor do I propose metaphysical answers. But I *do* have two particular areas to share with you and then turn you loose yourself to seek your own answers. First, there's—

THE QUANTUM CONNECTION

Now stay tight with me on this one. It won't be for long. And it's not *my* conclusion. And it's not anyone's *theory.* It's baffling, troubling, a complete refutation of what we know or believe, and yet it's absolutely *real.* After you read this brief section, and you go and have a very stiff drink, come back to it and play with it in your mind.

Quantum mechanics is real. It's a definite branch of science. It isn't simply theory. But like Einstein's relativistic offerings on the dinner table, it's a hell of a lot to swallow.

When you get down into the subatomic world, just about everything we consider normal gets tossed into a cocked hat. The arena of quantum mechanics is a screaming paradox of "normalcy."

Now, what we're leveling off at is what quantum mechanics does. Stated as simply as I can squeeze it from a limited vocabulary, quantum mechanics tells us how matter behaves, not in our world, but in the sub-atomic. Way own there, man; *way* down.

When you get that far down, deeply into the atom, and you bust everything up into even tinier particles, so that in comparison even the infinitely small atom gains a comparative size of Mount Everest, logic just throws up. At the level where quantum mechanics takes us, the basic units of particles of atoms lose their "normal" behavior.

We expect particles to act as particles and waves to act as waves. If we have a hammer, we use it to drive a nail into a board. We don't point a flashlight at the nail, switch on the flashlight, and expect the light to drive that nail into the board.

Nor do we point the hammer into a dark room and expect it to light up the room. The hammer and the nail are to us particles (or a collection of particles). The light from the flashlight, or heat from the sun, or electro-magnetic waves, *are* waves. That isn't too bad. Particles are particles, and they behave like particles. Waves are waves, and they behave like waves.

In our world. Not way down there. At the subatomic level of quantum mechanics, those particles are not particles. Nor are they waves. *They act and perform as if they are both, and at the same time, and that is what they are.*

In fact, if you listen to the physicists describing this alien universe (which is still ours) of quantum mechanics, the physicists will tell you, "Well, at this level, we can't say for sure that matter exists."

What the hell does *that* mean? In any language it sounds like a cop out.

"Well," drawls our scientist guide, "the best I can tell you is that matter has a certain tendency to be real, you know, a *tendency* to exist. But since particles and waves function as both, even if they're completely different, we judge all this to be a matter of mathematical probability."

I *knew* it was a cop out. But wait—

The first rule to understand is that in this smaller-than-micro universe of subatomic behavior, all the rules we know in *our* world, our macro world of unbusted atoms, of cells and molecules and good stuff like that of which we're made, well, forget the rules. No more. They're gone.

It's going to be tough to believe (ghosts are easier—really), but experi-ments prove this to be true. Our physicist says: "Take an electron. Now that's matter. But it also has an *anti*matter twin, which in this case we'll call a positron. If this electron, which is matter, and this positron, which is antimatter, bang into each other, they annihilate one another. Boom! No more electron and no more positron. But remember what Einstein proved; you can never destroy matter or energy but only convert it. So when these two particles annihilate one another, we get *real* magic, subatomic magic, so to speak, on the quantum level.

"After the collision we find that two photons have been created, and they whip off in different directions. Now even in our world photons can be proved to be matter and they can be proved to be wave. But stick with these two photons that sprang into existence from the collision of the electron and the positron.

"Forget everything else and just picture them in your mind. They're speeding away from one another at the speed of light. But there's more to it than this. If we don't see…well, let's call it Photon One…if we don't see it, if we don't observe it, then it's really not real. It doesn't have the values or the properties we assign to particles. No real velocity, no rate of spin, no electrical charge; nothing. It's real, but it's not real *until* we can observe it."

More aspirin, please. This physicist is saying that what's real isn't real because we haven't observed it yet. It's something, but it's nothing. Hey, don't look at *me*; this is the world of quantum mechanics. So let's all ask the same question: What happens when we do observe this exists-doesn't-exist Photon One?

"Well, instantly, the act of observation collapses its wave function. It has new values assigned to it."

"That's nice. Who assigns values, and what kind are they?"

"Well, the moment we observe Photon One, it acquires a spin, for example."

Take a deep breath now and hold it—

"But what's remarkable," continues our physicist (who gets. silly with laughter when you mention the word *ghost*), "is that at the exact same instant that we look at Photon One and give it its spin and some random values, which we may not be able to measure, anyway, now we have to consider Photon Two. It may be trillions of miles away. It may be billions of light-years away. But the instant we look at and change Photon One, then Photon Two, *instantly*, will spin in a direction exactly opposite to Photon One."

Why?

"We don't know."

How?

"We don't know."

That's a hell of a theory. Be nice if you could prove it.

"Oh, we've proved it. Again and again and again. We've done lots of physical experiments to prove it, and they do."

But that means you have one of these photons at one end of the universe and the other photon at the other end of the universe, billions and billions of light-years apart, and they will always know what the other one is doing and will react instantaneously to what the other photon does?

"Uh huh."

But to have that happen, you must transcend Time!

"Uh huh."

Or you're saying that Time doesn't really exist until we look at it?

"Uh huh."

Or think about it?

"Uh huh."

Are you telling us that there's a connection between each and every part of the universe where Time is absolutely no factor, and that because we also are made up of subatomic particles...that this ability also includes our subconscious?

"Of course."

Then, clairvoyance...seeing things in the future, because the future doesn't exist, is possible?

"Absolutely. The rule of quantum mechanics, of all physics, is that nothing is ever *lost*. It is *somewhere*."

The universe has tremendous forces. Black holes with gravitation fields faster than the speed of light. Falling into a black hole twists the very fabric and space of Time. That means that we're traveling through Time. But whatever Time is can bend or twist or ripple. Can past and present and future, which exist only when and if we affect them, come together? Can one blend with the other?

"Oh, sure."

If such a twist or ripple does happen, then the two become one?

"Absolutely."

That means a life form from the past can join us now?

"A life form. Physical matter of any kind."

A man?

"Certainly."

A machine?

"Yes."

An airplane?

"Absolutely."

Sounds?

"Of course. Sound is only an overpressure in a fluid or solid medium. It's got just as much physical substance as an elephant."

Thank you. Let me repeat one thing. So a life form from the past could join us now? Right now?

"You got it."

So in the world of quantum mechanics, life form is spelled *ghost*.

AND NOW...KWAJALEIN

What if we could actually observe scientifically, that is, confirm beyond all question, that a rip in Time, a bend in that elusive thing we call Time, actually has happened on this planet of ours?

It has.

Think of all those "incredible" and " impossible" incidents and events of which we've read. Now these and many, many more incidents are *impossible* under the physical conditions and restrictions we know on this world. But they *could* be possible if the physicists are right. They could, and they would, be possible, even in the strict world of physics, if we could confirm variations and/or disruptions in Time.

Like, if someone recorded cesium-clock variations or disruptions at these moments.

Such a variation, and return to normal from that variation, in a nuclear-decay timing system that is accurate to a tenth of a millionth of a second per year; *would have to represent a fracture in Time.*

A Time Jump. A rupture in the fabric of Time that opens and closes. You can't measure such a jump with ordinary time-keeping systems. If you could, and you could prove them, *then you know that the Time Jump is not only possible, but real, and with us all the time.*

That would be proof that biological entities and mechanical artifacts can, will, and do shift in and through Time.

It's been proved.

The first recorded shift in Time was measured during the period from 23 November 1973 to 10 January 1974. The Cesium Time Generators on Kwajalein Island in the Pacific Ocean recorded the shift.

Let me tour you through Kwajalein, a small atoll in the Pacific that has long hosted an American naval base. Within the bowels of special structures on Kwajalein is a small but elaborate and dedicated timing system so precise that by comparison a surgical laser beam is a rusty hacksaw.

The Master Timing Center functions about an equipment core of three Hewlett Packard 6201 Timers, Cesium Beam Standards.

Next step in the equipment needed to track to the millionths of a second incoming warheads, anti-ICBMs, satellite passages, and deep-space probes is a standard, one megahertz output frequency connected to the input of a Datum 9110 Time Code Generator.

Each Time Code Generator is interconnected to an alarm and transfer panel, Datum Model 9550.

(Stick with me. You want hard, specific data on what *may be supernatural events and ghosts* in our real world—this is it.)

The alarm and transfer panel compares the generator outputs, placing the primary generator on-line for distribution to user sites. The panel compares the three generators, decides if they agree in outputs, and maintains the primary generator on-line when they all agree.

There is much more to even this basic breakdown, though it's complex and brain squeezing for these pages; but the data, the schematics, the technical details, are kept in a bank vault. They are very real. Suffice, for this moment, to say that the timing center on Kwajalein, the most precise such system in all the world, compares *its* output with the United States Naval Observatory in Washington D.C., *with a millisecond correlation.*

Loran C and Time Interval Counters bring that accuracy to plus or minus ten microseconds of USNO; next in line is final correlation by orbiting satellite, established to plus or minus one microsecond of USNO.

The Cesium Standard has a long-term stability of plus or minus two parts in 10^{12} per year. The MTC time accuracy is plus or minus 12 microseconds per year, and Time Code Regenerators have shown that their output can be controlled to better than plus or minus five microseconds per month of MTC.

Now we return to that period from 11-23-73 to 1-10-74 on Kwajalein.

Suddenly, impossibly, shockingly, the Cesium Time Generators on Kwajalein lagged those of USNO by three-tenths of a microsecond (in the subatomic world that's a whole bunch of centuries, by comparison). This first lag lasted for a month, until 21 December 1973. On that date the readout between Kwajalein and underground USNO installations in Washington matched again, inexplicably.

Scientists keep absolutely quiet outside their own circle, for they were facing the reality that on earth, at that period, there were two different times. Two different time frames. On the surface there existed one frame; in deep, underground facilities there existed another. Two people, one in each facility, now lived in different time universes. They wouldn't biologically notice the differences in microseconds. *But the equipment did.*

For three days after this first jump, things were normal. On 24 December 1973 the lag jumped to 1.1 microseconds. Two days later, on 26 December, the recorded time lag was 1.2 microseconds. On 4 January 1974 the lag was measured at 1.1 microseconds. Six days later it decreased to 0.4, remained that way for another month, then snapped back to normal.

It's happened again. We don't know how many times, but it happened again, and, of course, it happened before. The time jumps are like radio waves. We didn't invent them. They were always here. We simply learned how to detect and to use them.

But now we had proof that *something* happens to space-time, like a shift into a different dimension. Perhaps into many dimensions. Shifting back and forth through bends and curves and twists. Will the government admit to what happened with the master timing systems on Kwajalein? Even if we show them the breakdown of the dates and all the technical information of their own equipment?

Of course they won't. They won't even acknowledge any queries of any kind.

Because if they did, they just might prove that Queen Boadicea really did race in her chariot through that base filled with hydrogen bombs in East Anglia...

Chapter 17

="IT COULD HAVE BEEN ME"

I have always failed to understand why it is so difficult to identify a UFO.

Unidentified Flying Object.

That's what UFO says, and that's what it means. In the same category we'll find another nonmystery called the IFO. That's also simple enough. It means Identified Flying Object. We *know* what it is and beyond any question. The identification is positive. You could even call it absolute (or it wouldn't be an IFO).

So the question that remains is *what* is *un*identified, when that object under discussion exhibits so many characteristics of a mechanical artifact that at one and the same time it possesses shape and performance beyond anything *we* have ever built and flown, and, if its shape and performance are real, and it *is* a machine of some sort or another, it doesn't fit into any niche we can either understand *or accept.*

Therein, the problem. Now we're not going to get into any controversy about whether or not UFOs are real, *because they are.* Unless someone or some group or organization has a hell of a lot more specific data, or even hardware in hand, that we don't know about, we're left with that old saw of a riddle in an enigma. We have hard sightings visually and via radar tracking. We even have photographs, videotape, and film.

We have everything save a satisfactory answer. So we're not going to draw conclusions. Too many skilled, professional, veteran pilots and aircrews have encountered inexplicable objects in the sky simply to dismiss them in the cavalier fashion that usually attends a discussion of this subject.

That's as as we go in these pages, except to do what we've done from the very beginning of this book: bring you an encounter with an unidentified object in flight by a highly experienced, extremely reputable, skilled, and intelligent pilot. Lane C. Morrow is that pilot, and he tells it like it is. No embellishment; just the facts of his experience.

Before we get into the words of Mr. Morrow, I do have a final word to say. When I wore the blue suit of the U.S. Air Force, with an assignment to A-2 (Intelligence) I was part of a team that investigated UFO sightings. We did a hell of a lot of investigating. We were able to dismiss perhaps 95 percent of all reports we tracked down, and we did some very fine nit picking in our searches and research. I've pursued strange objects in the sky while flying everything from bombers to jets. Some of those episodes were real doozies; most had rational explanations, but a few were left in the category of "damned if I know what it was." I make this point because my own experience in flight and research brought me to select the report of Lane C. Morrow as one that should be shared with other pilots and our readers.

He tells it like it is, you judge it any way you like.

Sydney, New South Wales, Australia, about nine o'clock at night, 7 September 1972. I'm taking the last load of passengers on board at Mascot International, for the final flight of the day, to Cootamundra, New South Wales, about two hundred miles northwest.

The Ansett Airlines passenger officer comes on board, pushing gently past a bunch of Japanese men in business suits, who are engaged in what I perceive to be polite but slightly animated conversation.

As the passenger officer enters the cockpit, I can tell there's a bit of a problem, by the look on his face and the muffled tone of his voice. It seems the Japanese never wanted to go to Cootamundra, but were bound for Coota, where an interpreter was to meet them to carry on their business. Would I take them to Coota?

Sure. Why not.

That's the situation at the moment. I depart from Sydney Airport with a load of Japanese businessmen (who've come here straight from Tokyo). We're short of seats in the airplane, so one Japanese passenger takes the copilot's seat right next to me. It's perfectly legal, and the government permits our airline to fly aircraft that operate below a specified takeoff weight with only one pilot on board.

It's a nice night, the weather is good; in fact, the visibility is exceptional, and I can see and recognize towns and cities that I know to be in excess of one hundred miles distant from us at our cruising altitude of eight thousand feet.

Switching over to Sydney Air Traffic Control Sector Discrete frequency, I listen to the crew of the Airlines of New South Wales Fokker F-27 that departs Sydney Airport at the same time we do every night. They are bound with passengers for Wagga Wagga in New South Wales. They're reporting level at eighteen thousand feet, ten thousand feet above me, on the same track. In a few minutes they'll turn for a direct flight to Wagga Wagga.

Everything goes smoothly. Approximately thirty minutes into the flight I see a very bright light coming from an object directly to my left and apparently at my altitude.

The autopilot is engaged, everything hums along beautifully, and my mind isn't cluttered with the usual questions about whether I should be ragging ATC for a higher or a lower altitude to get out of head winds or some other weather situation. I scan the instruments; it's all the way it should be, my passengers are peaceful and quiet, so I'm free to concentrate on that bright light.

Several minutes pass, and my curiosity about this light grows. It is still out there, and I'm aware now that it is *too bright*. It's like looking at the flash of an electric arc welder. That surprises me because despite the dazzling intensity, it doesn't seem to hurt my eyes. It's obvious, also, as best I can tell, that whatever is that object, it's flying in formation with me, although I can't determine how far away it is from my own aircraft.

Slowly but surely the light appears to be closing the distance between itself and us. Now there's sufficient definition to see red and green flashes coming from the top and bottom of the blob of white light. I sigh with relief; it certainly appears to be just another aircraft of some sort.

But then a warning note intrudes into my thoughts. Something is wrong here. Seeing the red and green flashes at the same time means I am looking at both wingtips at the same time, and that means that other ship is banking toward me at an alarming angle. I'm bolt upright in my seat now, because if that thing is capable of any real acceleration while turning—

I'm ready for anything, and I've switched off the autopilot and have the controls in my hands and my feet on the rudder peddles, ready for any sudden maneuvering. I intend to keep out of the way of whatever-it-is out there.

Several seconds later I'm still looking at the bright white blob of light with the flashing red and green strobes, still on my left, and still apparently at my altitude and matching my speed. *It's been turning in toward me.* I feel uneasy about what is happening.

My immediate assessment was that I believed that other machine was on a collision course with me. But, and this was strangest of all that, that simply was *not* happening.

By now I was convinced something was dreadfully wrong with my perception of what was actually taking place, and I should, at a very least, perform the maneuvers that I know about, have practiced for years and am quite capable of performing as the pilot of my aircraft. In brief, get the hell away from whatever it is that seemed to be heading steadily toward me.

Once again I confirm the brilliant lighted object (whatever it is; I still have no real grasp of it) is real, and not any illusion created by my aircraft, by clouds, or by any unusual weather conditions. The night is severe clear; it couldn't better for flight, and that light has been curving in its path. There's no doubt. Something out there is flying under control and at the very least has become extremely disturbing to me.

Now the object again changes its position relative to my own aircraft. I can't believe what I'm watching, because the damn thing is moving up and down, forward and backward, and at velocities I simply cannot understand or believe. If my eyes aren't playing tricks on me, and I have not gone around the bend, I am witnessing an object in flight that is moving at thousands of miles per hour, with instant acceleration in any and all directions!

By now I'm starting to question my own sanity. I seek steadiness in my instruments, in my flying. Everything is absolutely by the book. Well, there's that Japanese fellow next to me, and I prod him and point to the light. "Do you see that?" I ask. "Do you see that bright light out there? Tell me what *you* see."

The more questions I asked, the more he clasped his hands, bowed his head up and down, smiled broadly at me, and chanted, "Ah so, ah so."

Big help. He doesn't speak my lingo, and I can't understand a word of his. So I shout. "Does *anyone* in this group speak even a little bit, just a *little bit* of English?"

A whole bunch of more "Ah so, ah so."

"Look out this window! Do you see that thing? It's a goddamned spaceship! For Christ's sake, you're looking at something from outer space! Tell you're seeing a flying saucer out this window right now!"

My Japanese businessman looks pained, unbuckles his seat belt stands up, bows deeply from the waist up, and trundles back into the cabin. A *real* big help.

All right; I decide to just calm down and live with the idea that I am looking at a real, live "flying saucer," and nobody on this whole damned planet knows it but me.

For the next twenty minutes I study the thing with intense care as we continue to fly along in loose formation. From what I can tell, which is at best difficult at night, it seems to remain about a half mile distant. I'm also aware that I have no reason for choosing this distance of a half mile, because if it's twice as big as I think it is, then it would be a mile away, and on the other hand, if it's half as big as I think it is, it's getting *very* close. Well, what the hell, if I continue this line of thought, I'll have a hell of a headache. I make a snap decision; *I'll* try to get closer.

I've got the autopilot back on again, since we were having such a nice formation jog these past twenty minutes. Using the turn control knob on the autopilot panel, slowly I dial in a left turn. We bank gently to the left, and I concentrate on the object. Whoops; maybe I should have left well enough alone. The object suddenly bolts forward and upward at absolutely incredible speed. If I'm any judge of speed in flight, *and I am,* that thing has boosted away at thousands of miles per hour. *In seconds it has gone so far, I've nearly lost sight of it.*

Well, now, perhaps I can assume the object is gone. Vanished. Good riddance! Relief washes over me. Then, confusion. How could I be so intensely interested in the thing—even to the extent of trying to get closer to it for a better look—and then feel such relief the instant I *think* it's gone?

No more questions. Here it is again, swooping in with that incredible speed and sudden deceleration. The object is now much in the same position it held before, about a half mile (a guesstimate) off to my left, but perhaps five hundred feet higher than my altitude.

Okay, time to get in touch with the real world. I punch the radio transmit button on the control yoke.

"Sydney, this is Mike Whiskey Hotel," I call out.

Immediate response. "Mike Whiskey Hotel, Sydney, go ahead."

"Ah, yeah, do you have any reported traffic in my area?"

"Negative; no traffic reported in your area."

"Okay, ah, you still got me on your screen?"

"Negative. You dropped off a couple of minutes ago."

"Whiskey Hotel, thanks, and good night."

"Mike Whiskey Hotel, Sydney, confirm your situation normal."

"Ah, that's a roger, Sydney. Thanks; good night."

"Mike Whiskey Hotel, contact Wagga FSS upon arrival circuit area Cootamundra, and good night, sir."

Rats! Not only a waste of time, but I almost had to give ATC a story to satisfy them that I'm not in some kind of trouble out here. Well, I don't *think* I'm in any trouble.

The silence is broken again; this time it's that Fokker F-27 of the Airlines of New South Wales.

"Sydney, Foxtrot November Juliet leaving flight level one eight zero on descent to Wagga."

"Foxtrot November Juliet, Sydney, roger, vacating one eight zero, contact Wagga FSS, good night, sir."

Aha! I think I just might get someone else on this, if that spaceship will just stay with me a bit longer....

I switched my number-two communications panel over to the Wagga frequency and hear the Fokker reporting in to Wagga. He's acknowledged and told to report passing through eight thousand feet, and again when ten nautical miles from Wagga. I do some fast calculation and figure the Fokker will pass eight thousand feet at about the same time he's ten miles from Wagga, and that will put him twenty miles from me. Too far away for us to spot each other, but *not* too far for them to spot the intense light coming from my companion. I wait.

Once again the Fokker breaks the silence. *And* proves my calculations to be correct.

"Wagga, Foxtrot November Juliet is ten DME passing eight thousand."

"Foxtrot November Juliet, Wagga, roger, report circuit area."

"November Juliet, roger."

Now it's my turn. "Foxtrot November Juliet, this is Mike Whiskey Hotel."

"Go ahead, Hotel. This is Juliet."

"Yeah, would you guys take a look in my direction? See if you can spot some unreported traffic."

"Sure. Hang on a moment."

A brief silence; then: "Sorry, Hotel, can't see anyone out your way."

"Okay, Juliet, thanks. Good night."

Damn! I'm getting nowhere with this situation. Wait a moment; maybe I *am* crazy. Maybe I'm just imagining all this crap about this damned spaceship. Thousands of miles per hour, indeed! *I'm* the one who is rude to everyone that even mentions the words f*lying saucer* to me. I have my own ideas and beliefs that there are other forms of intelligent life out there in that vast universe, *but,* and I know the buts about this, they're just too damned far away to get *here,* unless they started several thousand light years ago, and they knew exactly where they were going, and why.

Now it's time to begin my descent into Coota, and it occurs to me that I may yet have a chance to show somebody else my playmate, after all. There are still a couple of cards to deal in this game.

"Cootamundra, this is Mike Whiskey Hotel inbound, go ahead," I call by radio.

"Roger, Mike Whiskey Hotel, Cootamundra has no other traffic, visibility is unlimited, wind calm."

"Okay, thanks. Say, would you do me a favor and step outside and watch me come in? I think I saw some sparks coming from my left engine and would like you to confirm that for me, if you would, please."

"Sure thing, mate!"

I start down *and the thing starts down with me.* I'm trying to get through my checklist early, while keeping that thing in sight all the while. Now we're entering the circuit area, and I've got to make a big sweeping turn to the right to get lined up with the downwind runway, so I'm sure that even for a little while I'll lose sight of my "company" out there. But I *don't* lose sight of it, because it simply speeds up to what must be four thousand miles per hour, and it scribes a big arc around the outside of my turn, which takes it right over the airport.

When I finish the turn and continue downwind to set up my base leg turn, the thing continues across the airport to the other side and lands gently atop a little hill about a half mile from the runway, lighting the trees and bushes around the top of the hill as though it were ten-thirty in the morning, instead of ten-thirty at night!

I try to keep my eyes on it through my base leg and final turns, but now I'm getting so close to the ground that I must give full attention to the landing. The runway rushes under the aircraft, and I put us down as quickly as I can, without jostling my passengers. As I roll off my speed, I look up quickly, toward the hill, just in time to see the object lift off and then streak across the airport and disappear quickly in the direction from which we came. My rough estimate of its speed was between five and six thousand miles per hour!

Now it's going to be *my* turn....

As we taxi in to the terminal, the interpreter and a baggage handler emerge from the building to meet the aircraft. I look around the terminal area for the guy I talked to earlier by radio. He's standing by the fuel pumps, about fifty feet away, looking at me, with his arms just hanging by his sides. As soon as he sees that I've spotted him, he makes a gesture by pointing his finger at his chest, then at me, indicating he wants to talk to me right away.

I hold up my palm to him, signaling for him to wait a few moments until I'm through with the commotion of deplaning passengers and baggage. When that's done, I run through my shutdown checklist and secure the cockpit, lock the aircraft, and walk to the fueling area where the man who'd watched my arrival was waiting impatiently for me.

The words blurted from him. "Did you see it? Good Lord, man, *did you see it?*"

Time to continue playing the game. "See what?" I asked as blandly as I could.

The other man's face twitched and his hands clenched and unclenched as he fought to control his emotions. He then described to me *precisely* the sights and events to which I'd been witness in the air and during the landing; his viewpoint, of course, was restricted to that moment when he went outside his office to watch me land. *He* insisted the brilliant object was moving at speeds of up to six thousand miles per hour. That caught my attention because this radio operator was *not* a pilot, and I didn't judge him as capable of gauging accurately speeds of more than seventy or eighty miles per hour.

Finally I related to him all the things I'd seen and my experiences in flight, and that I'd been in visual contact with this strange object for half my flight from Sidney to Coota. His face twisted, and then relief seemed to flood through him, as though he'd just received confirmation (which he had) that *he* wasn't crazy. I told him why I'd withheld any comment of my own until I heard his observations. He nodded agreement. "I can damn well see why you did that," he muttered.

But as quickly as he seemed to relax, he again showed great agitation, an unsettling mixture of fear and awe. He wasn't sure at this moment but felt compelled to report the incident to someone. To whom he didn't know, but *somebody* in an official position *must* be told. He seemed near panic at not having made such a report of seeing the "impossible." By now, however, my own apprehension was growing about *any* further reporting, even with this hard-won witness at my side. Despite corroboration I still don't have a feeling of solid credibility. I looked at his name plate. "Let's sleep on it tonight, Russ. I'll call you from Sydney tomorrow after my final run, and we'll discuss it then, okay?"

He hesitated, then nodded assent. It didn't take a mind reader to understand that without my support for *his* "outlandish sighting," he was strictly on his own and as likely to be considered a candidate for the funny farm as had so many other people who'd reported "unexplained things in the sky."

I was up early and at the field as quickly as I could to go through the routine of weather checking and filing my flight plan by telephone with Wagga Wagga FSS. I went through a thorough preflight of the aircraft, boarded my passengers, and at 6:45 A.M., right on schedule, flew off from Cootamundra.

To me this would be an easy day's work, flying legs from Coota to Sydney, with quick turnarounds to Williamtown, back to Sydney, again to Williamtown, then over to Scone, and back to Sydney. The weather is absolutely perfect along all my routes, the aircraft is humming to perfection, traffic is normal, passengers march on and off my aircraft like well-drilled tin soldiers, there's nothing to distract me, and life is terrific.

By midafternoon, back in my apartment, I made my decision. It would be silence. I stuffed my whites in the laundry bag, hung up my uniform, got into comfortable shorts and a T-shirt, mixed a rum collins, flopped into a favorite chair, and made the telephone call to Cootamundra.

"Russ? Lane Morrow here. G'day, mate. Look, about what happened last night? I've decided that we'd better just forget the whole thing, okay?"

For an answer I got a sharp, snapped, *"No."* It was not okay with this man, who was still in that same emotional upset I recalled from last night. He runs on quickly to tell me he's going to report what he saw, as well as what *I* encountered, to the UFO Society, and be damned if he had or lacked my support. But he was also going to identify me as the pilot of the aircraft involved and repeat what I'd told him.

I shook my head; I didn't like this, but it was out of my hands now, and I didn't want this man churning any of his emotions at me. "You do what you feel you have to do, Russ, but I really think you're making a big mistake." I couldn't touch him; he got more adamant with every word, so I cut him short, said good-bye, and hung up.

Suddenly it's clear to me why I'd decided not to report the sighting. Fear. Plain and simple fear. Russ, on his part, also felt fear, and for that very reason he wasn't willing to suffer in silence. Now he was afraid his own fear would drive him crazy. I know how he felt. Those were *my* emotions while I sought desperately for someone last night to bear witness to what I'd seen.

Only now my fear is different. I'm afraid I will lose my credibility, and that affects everything I do in the life I lead as a pilot flying passengers for my living. There's something that cuts at you when your credibility suffers; my friends will still be my friends, but with a little hint of smirk in their smiles from then on. It's called being patronized. As commercial pilots what we then suffer is compromise with credibility, and that's a bummer.

It is so much of a bummer that if this kind of report, about my claiming to have seen those weird lights and instant accelerations and an object hurtling at many thousands of miles per hour, made the newspaper, I was on my way to being branded a Grade-A nut. To my employers that was the first step toward booting me off the line.

As bad as the newspapers with their bent for sensationalism might be, and they are, word-of-mouth rumor in Australia travels at electronic speed throughout the entire domestic airline system. Once I got the boot from my airline, I wouldn't be able to get a flying job anywhere else in Australia, and despite my spotless and top record as a pilot, I'd be branded immediately. It's the kind of stigma that doesn't let go. It wouldn't just follow me but precede me at every step.

It would also mean that if I wanted to continue commercial flying, I'd have to leave Australia. At that time such a move wasn't even in my thinking. I tried to figure a way to clamp down on Russ talking to the UFO Society, or his superiors, or to anyone. But that meant coercion or some nonsense like that, and it isn't in my book of personal rules of how to live. So I resigned myself to "whatever comes along, well, I'll see just what it is when it gets here."

A week passes. I show up this morning for my scheduled flights. First I check my mail in the small groundfloor office in the Ansett Terminal building my company uses for operations and dispatch at Mascot. One item in the box gives me a little twinge; I *know* it's from the UFO Society because the nondescript envelope is its own dead giveaway.

As casually as I can, I drop the unopened envelope into a wastepaper basket. But not *so* casually that I fail to attract curiosity on the part of Tony Masling. At that time Tony was the Dispatcher/Operations Manager, and *he* had earlier placed that same envelope in my mailbox, along with all I the company memos, current Notifications to Airmen, and other printed paraphernalia that pilots find on a regular basis in their mail slots.

Now Tony Masling and I are damned good friends. He's the son of J.A. "Jack" Masling who founded the airline I work for. That friendship paid off. Tony didn't let his curiosity get out of hand.

Another week passes, I arrive at the Ansett Terminal building for setting up my scheduled afternoon and evening flight legs, and this time Tony calls me aside. "Someone's called to speak to you, mate," he advises. I ask his name; Tony doesn't know. He hands me a slip of paper. "But he left this number for you, says you can get him anytime day or night."

I nod and take the paper. "Thanks, Tony." I shove the paper in my pocket and dismiss it from my thoughts. I'm not about to call any mysterious strangers.

Another week goes by, and this time the curiosity and interest levels are climbing rapidly. "Hey, remember that bloke who called last week?" Tony asks. "The number I gave you? Well, his nibs has been here. Walked right in to flight-ops, said he hadn't heard from you, demanded to know if I'd given you his message, and then wanted your home number *and* your address."

I knew Tony hadn't given him a thing; we're pretty tight when it comes to personal privacy. "What happened?"

"Showed him the way out, that's what happened," Tony said immediately, as if anything else would have been out of the question. "But listen here, Lane, this is getting a bit out of hand, wouldn't you say? Who the hell is this cat? And *why* are you going to such trouble to avoid him?"

Tony wasn't prying. He was letting me know as easily as he could that if I was in any trouble, all I had to do was to let him know, and he'd come charging in to help.

So I lied to my friend. "He's a pushy sort. You know the kind of salesman bastard I mean. Wants to sell me some beachfront property in Surfer's Paradise in Queensland." Tony laughed. Surfer's Pasadise in Queensland is the Australian equivalent to old mining country in the middle of the barren California desert. "Right you are, Lane. I'll make certain he doesn't bother you anymore. He comes in here playing Mister Mysterious, we'll give him reason to regret it."

I never heard any more from the UFO Society.

It appears now this is a time for reflection. I feel somewhat uneasy about all this, because as a pilot, I *do not* make hard-and-fast decisions and then stick with those decisions no matter what may happen afterward.

In many cases that would be a most dangerous attitude to follow. The few exceptions would pertain to situations that require instant split-second actions, like dodging another aircraft on a collision course with your own, and you act *now* and get the hell out of the way, and you don't change what you're doing until the danger is well and gone.

But unless there is that kind of explosive emergency, you assess a situation as it develops and make a lot of little decisions as time passes, taking the best course of action at each opportune moment that you can.

However, as it turns out, I can be two different people in one body of flesh and bone. I'm hardly alone in this respect; the airlines flying business is chock full of people who can be Mr. Cool almost all the time, but in an emergency they become firebrands with catlike, instant reflexes, and they absolutely take command of the immediate situation. Moments later they're as calm as a cat sunning itself on a wooden fence. For myself, I operate under one set of rules when I'm in an aircraft cockpit; I'm precise, tight, quick, professional, always trying to do my absolute best with the greatest efficiency and safety. When I climb down from that cockpit, I don another hat and go by another set of rules, rather loosely organized, which always seems a guarantee that my personal life is screwed up.

In this instance it took a long time for me to realize that I turned my back on a possible source of information of the greatest interest to me when I avoided that stranger who called and then came to find me. I should have realized that the UFO Society in Australia was actually being extremely discreet and low-key, that they gave no one the first idea of who they were or why they wanted to talk with me. I should have cooperated with them, because they clearly were respectful of my privacy.

To this day I regret that I never did that and I never made any contact with them.

The only thing I did do was to enter the word *oops!* in the remarks column in my logbook pertaining to that incredible encounter that night.

Postscript to the foregoing: As things turned out, I did leave Australia within the next year. Not alone, as I suspected this might happen, but with a stunning Australian girl, Cherylle, who had just become my bride.

Then the past came back to visit me, but in a quiet and distant way. Another year went by, and I received news that a student pilot flying in roughly the same area in New South Wales had contacted Sydney Air Traffic Control. The pilot was hysterical, almost frantic with fear. He screamed into his radio that out of nowhere a bright light had appeared, rushed at his aircraft, taken up formation, and was close to blinding him with its intense light.

Air Traffic Control determined that the pilot did everything he could to get away from that light. No matter what he did, it not only matched with contemptuous ease his every maneuver but kept closing the distance between the light and his aircraft. Suddenly, in the middle of a sentence, all communications ceased.

The authorities immediately launched an intensive aerial search of the area within which that pilot might have flown. They checked the on-board fuel he had entered in his flight plan before he took off, and they searched every square foot of that area with dozens of planes and experienced search crews.

Three days later they called off the search. They had scoured the area so thoroughly they would have found a tricycle, let alone an airplane. Neither the pilot nor the airplane were ever seen or heard from.

It could have been me.

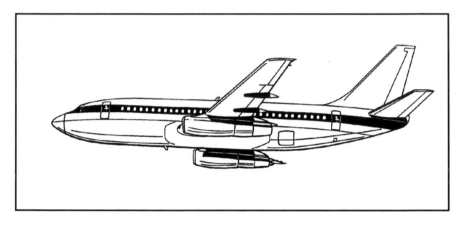

Boeing 737

Martin Caidin Archives

Chapter 18

≡ BELIEVING

Do you really believe the events portrayed in these pages?
I do.
I know personally several of the people who have honestly, candidly, given us these special moments in their lives. I have flown for decades with some of them. I know of their many years of training and experience, their long-proven skills as master aviators, test pilots, engineers, and airline captains. That's critical to consider when you judge the elements of belief.

I commend to you that *they that were there, they were involved*, they are superior witnesses and skilled veterans of their trade. They are also talking to us in the *first person* and their own direct, intimate, all-embracing personal involvement. Consider those truths.

Recall the opening pages of this book: that moment when naval aviation cadet Don Cochrane, flying a jet trainer, saw own aircraft and himself in formation with his aircraft. The word "impossible" is an immediate and understandable reaction. Yet Don Cochrane described to us honestly and *accurately* what happened that morning of October 10th in 1967.

Now, consider this question: Can Don Cochrane *prove* those events he described for us?

No.

Now let's place you, the reader, in a situation easily acceptable to you. Have you, in the month preceding your reading these words, seen an aircraft in flight? Any kind of aircraft? See it clearly, hear it, watch its progress against the clouds or through blue sky or, if at night, see its red and green position lights, possibly the white tail light, or the white and red flashing strobes? Let's accept that you saw an airplane in flight during this past month (or more).

You remember it clearly. *But can you prove it?* Absolutely *not.* Not even if your life depended on it. No matter how veteran an observer you are, no matter how great your reputation for integrity or honesty. You cannot *prove* what you saw.

Think on that a moment. Now, consider how pilots *and* nonpilots, when we play the role of passengers, place our lives entirely in the hands of strangers we have never met, whose names we don't know and may never know. As airline passengers we walk blithely into the cavernous hold of a huge jetliner and we accept *on faith* the skills, qualifications, and legality of the people up forward on the flight deck.

Did you ever demand to see your airline captain's documents certifying his position as a bona-fide and qualified pilot? Ever ask to check his medical papers? Check his logbook to confirm that he's kept up his proficiency for instrument flight? Or confirm that he's type-rated in the airliner in which you're going to strap yourself and your family and go hurtling through the skies, calm weather and storms, at speeds greater than the muzzle velocity of a .45 caliber Colt automatic?

I'll bet you a thousand to one you haven't done it. In fact, if people everywhere would take that bet with such ridiculous odds, I would still make a killing. People just don't do that sort of thing. We file aboard the airliners and we all put our lives on the line with perfect strangers *without asking anyone to prove a damn thing.* And we shell out good money for this privilege.

Let me carry this point a bit further to gain relevancy for this book. Consider, carefully, the professional standards and requirements for a man or woman to become the captain of a jetliner that weighs more than four hundred tons at takeoff and carries more than five hundred souls aboard. Consider the extensive medical checks by both the government and the airline staff. Keep in mind the stringent training tests, qualifications and constant upgrading and requalifications to remain at the controls of that jetliner. Consider the years of training and the decades of experience. Consider, as well, the medical and psychological probing, the constancy of watching and judging. These captains of the jetliners or military aircraft are among the most intensively guarded and rechecked people of any business in the world.

The faith in these people is so great that even those doctors who perform surgery, and beneath whose hands a person may live or die, will board that airliner with unquestioned confidence in the pilots.

What does all this mean? How do we translate it into everyday affairs *and* our own lives and the lives of our loved ones?

We believe our pilots, and, we believe *in* them. If our faith and confidence could be translated into energy we'd be able to levitate without need for fuel burning engines!

Now I wish you to consider this situation one step further. If this same crew in which we have such absolute life-risking faith, reports to us that they have observed an object in the sky that is circular, or that performs in a manner inconsistent with the manufactured aircraft we know, or that seems to be nothing with which we're familiar anywhere in this world, *almost automatically we no longer believe those pilots*. With a smug demeanor quickly we reject what they have observed, simply because it doesn't fit into *our* limits of knowledge or experience.

In just a single snap of our mental fingers all that trust and confidence and faith in these people, with whom we repeatedly entrust our lives, goes right into the nearest trash can.

Another element to consider. If this same crew reports something else, an experience we consider uncanny or strange, an apparition or a phantom, or something labeled a ghost, we're willing to bet that crew is hallucinating (*all* of them and at the same time, which is really a neat trick), or they're suffering from food poisoning, or that inexplicably they have all, suddenly, gone bananas.

Well, not *all* of us would judge them so harshly. Those of us who have spent lifetimes in flying would withhold judgment until we knew or understood more of what was seen or claimed.

But *most* of you, including those in the passenger seats, would reject any such sightings or reports. Now, consider those who immediately demean these same pilots. These naysayers, and that includes many who have read this book, will refuse what the pilots report. Yet, they willingly accept in their particular religion or theological belief the validity of saints or deities they cannot see, hear, speak to and hope for a response, of whom they have absolutely no *proof,* but will accept as unquestionably real.

The saints of our many religious haven't got so much as a single ounce more corporeal solidity than what we call a ghost, and certainly they don't show up on radar screens as do unexplained objects in the sky. Or that can be photographed.

But the majority of people will venerate and pray to their saints or gods with unshakable belief. Why? Because, mainly, that's how they (we) were raised, what we were taught, and what has been impressed upon us from our most tender years.

And few people find anything puzzling in this strangest of dichotomies.

The contents of this book have been studied by pilots who have spent most of their lives in widely divergent areas of flight and aviation. It's their profession and they're the best at it; they're men and women who fly everything from hang gliders and balloons to massive 400-ton jets and triple-supersonic fighters. Some of them have even walked on the moon (and it's difficult to recall that not too long ago it was much easier to believe in ghosts than to accept men walking, running, hopping, whistling and dancing and roostertailing their way across an airless planet!).

The people involved in the telling of this book include nonpilots: air-crew, engineers, mechanics, meteorologists, aerodynamicists, historians, scientists—the whole lot who make up the aviation community

Obviously, as you've seen, despite the "Ghosts" in our title, this book goes far beyond ghosts, whatever *they* are. But whatever these contribu-tors have offered us, they emphasize through their experiences that we don't *have* to understand something in order to accept it as real or affect-ing their lives.

Look, try this one on for size. I defy *anyone*, scientist or philosopher, to tell us *what is gravity*. To a very great extent we know what gravity *does*. We can and we do measure its effect and its force. Some scientists consider gravity the weakest force known to man, but at the same time it's the cosmic glue that keeps the universe from flying apart like an explod-ing alarm clock. *But we don't what it is.* Is gravity a wave? Is it quanta, a particle? Recently, gravity waves are gaining favor (not proof; *favor*) with physicists. But just as many physicists hoot at their fellows and insist gravity is made up of quanta they call gravitons. What's a graviton? Um, well, uh, it's a particle of gravity.

Can anyone prove this? No. Does it matter? Apparently not in terms of keeping celestial bodies, from tiny asteroids to massive galaxies, in their orbits.

The point is that we don't have to understand gravity to accept its reality, or to use it in our daily lives. It's *here,* with or without our proof.

That's the crux of all this. That's the point of what the people in this book have told you.

They are not trying to *prove* anything.

They're telling it like it is. Belief is up to you. And your belief or disbelief won't change a thing.

Now, one of the things an author is never supposed to do is take off—lower the boom—on anticipated critics and reviewers. But sometimes the author, or compiler, judges that step as necessary. This is one of those times.

We understand there's an audience "out there" that won't believe what you've read in these pages. For that matter, there's *always* a group that won't believe in something they can't weigh or measure or wrap in cellophane. Included in these naysayers are the same people who *"never* trust anyone" but will swallow their distrust when they troop aboard airliners with nary an ounce of preventive safety beyond buying their ticket.

So let's get this "rational only" crowd out of the way.

I don't know what is a ghost. Some people say they know. I don't. Earlier in these pages I put my name to "inexplicable events" in that neither I nor the others involved with me could explain how—in "normal terms"—they happened. Implicitly and absolutely I believe what the others have told us in this book.

Keep in mind the *professional qualifications* of many of the contributors to these pages. And keep in mind that if you did not trust, totally, their skills and reliability, why would you *ever* strap yourself into an airliner in such blind faith?

One of the groups I'm certain we'll encounter with gnashing of teeth and cries of "Nonsense! It can't be true!" is CSICOP, the Committee for the Scientific Investigation of Claims of the Paranormal. It seems only fair to my readers that I offer them some explanation of who and what is CSICOP, so they'll better understand the reasons for CSICOP outrage.

CSICOP and its wide cross-section of members, from magicians to professional debunkers to scientists, is one of those national groups that shouts "Integrity!" from the rooftops, but really devotes much of its time and energy to begging money from the public to further their own beliefs and pay the tab for their activities. It's really that simple.

Am I unfair to list them as money-beggars? Let me (perish the thought) not be unfair to CSICOP. Let me not be even a touch misleading about my description of this group. *They beg money; period.* They send out mail beseeching contributions. They'll take all the long green you'll send to them. Since the vast majority of Americans are judged and described by CSICOP as scientifically illiterate, CSICOP proves its own convictions by appealing to those very people they condemn to send them money!

Let us be specific:

"Dear Friend," began one letter I received, dated January 16th, 1989 (plus others of the same ilk). "Your financial support is *urgently* needed to help stem the flow of irrationalism currently sweeping America. CSI-COP...earnestly request(s) your contribution to our current fund drive... Anyone who has been monitoring trends in public opinion cannot help but wonder what strange days are ahead for the United States."

CSICOP doesn't think much of Americans. CSICOP has repeatedly quoted the Public Opinion Laboratory at Northern Illinois University in its statement that "The national level of scientific literacy is only 5%."

I suppose the "scientific literates" are standing in line to demand credit for such smashing successes as the Hubble Telescope, the worst case of astronomical myopia with a bill of nearly two billion dollars.

CSICOP thinks little of American youth and again it grabs at another quote, this time from the Gallup Youth Survey (quoted in the same letter from CSICOP pleading for money):

74% of teenagers believe in angels
58% believe in astrology
50% believe in ESP
29% believe in witchcraft

After warning us that such lack of rational thinking places grave risks on the future of our country, CSICOP offers its solution to these ghastly beliefs by sounding its *real* message—

"...We critically need your financial support.

"It costs a good deal of money to publish and deliver the Skeptical Inquirer...

"It costs money to maintain our library...

"It costs money to maintain a network and information service...

"And it costs money to sponsor our annual conferences..."

(I'll just bet it does.)

Then CSICOP gets down to what it really wants from you, the American citizen (italics mine):

"We count on your contribution.

"Any amount will help.

"...fill out the enclosed card and return it *with your check* in the envelope provided."

Right. Go ahead, sucker.

But before you do, consider the hard and unshakable and accurate findings of the kind of people who preceded CSICOP and now help to fill its ranks.

Consider that N-rays "discovered" in 1903 by the French scientist, R. Blondlot, were touted for years as radiated from metals and human beings. Never from such a mundane substance as wood. About one year after Blondlot *confirmed* the incredible N-rays, *hundreds of other scientists also confirmed the N-rays.* They touted their scientific proof.

Experiment piled atop experiment "proved" that if you shrouded a brick in black paper it was certain to absorb N-rays from the sun. If you banged loudly on a drum or tambourine the racket decreased N-ray output.

It sounds pretty stupid, doesn't it? But scientists raved about the N-rays until common sense mounted its own assault with a very basic question: *What the hell are you talking about?* In the long run it was decided finally that the N in N-rays stood for *nothing.* But it took years to rid us of this nonsense.

Earlier in this century more than five hundred scientific papers, describing experiments that absolutely *proved* their findings, described incredible "mitogenetic rays" hurled about by plant and animal cells. Scientific journals bulged with fascinating reports of "mitogenetic ray tests with onions and sheets of glass." Alas, the mitogenetic effect turned out to be scientific rubbish and it was finally committed to the trash heap. Yet, men of science, pure of mind and clear of thinking, for some forty years after the mitogenetic rays turned out to be imagination rather than fact kept right on publishing "mitogenetic ray experiment results" in highly respected scientific journals.

We needn't go that back in this century for what might be considered the "paranormal conclusions" of scientists whose science was finally dumped as errant nonsense. As late as 1958 an experimental fusion reactor, dramatically called Zeta, was given an awesome reception by British scientists. One scientist representing a research group announced on television that "this discovery is greater than the Russian Sputnik." Other scientists reporting controlled fusion from Zeta brought forth headlines claiming limitless fuel for millions of years.

Alas. *Sputnik* at least *was* in orbit. But Zeta was a monstrous flop. No fuel, no rationale. Just hyped nonsense. Scientifically pure nonsense.

Here are a few other zonkers to keep in mind—

"Inventions have long-since reached their limit—and I see no hope for further developments." That clunker from the world-famed engineer Julius Frontinus, who offered his pearl of wisdom in Rome—*in 10 AD!*

"I thank God there are no free schools, nor printing and I hope we shall not have them these hundred years; for learning has brought disobedience and heresy and sects into the world, and printing has divulged them and libels against the best government." Governor William Berkeley speaking on Education in 1670.

Then, a bit closer to home:

"...The demonstration that no possible combination of known substances, known forms of machinery and known forms of force, can be united in a practical machine by which man shall fly long distances through the air, seems to the writer as complete as it is possible for the demonstration of any physical fact to be."

That winner is a quote from the famed scientist Simon Newcomb, in *Sidelights on Astronomy*, page 345, published in New York *in 1906—three years after the Wright Brothers had already made hundreds of flights.*

Drop back in history just a bit and let's look at medicine. *"Small-pox is a visitation from God, the cowpox is produced by presumptuous man; the former was what Heaven ordained, the latter is, perhaps, a daring violation of our holy religion."* That's a joint statement of English *doctors* in 1796, quoted by R.R. Butler in his 1947 work, *Scientific Discovery*, English Universities Press.

Then, in the late fall of 1945—

"There has been a great deal said about a 3,000 mile-high-angle rocket. In my opinion such a thing is impossible and will be impossible for many years...I don't think anybody in the world knows how to do such a thing and I feel confident it will not be done for a very long period of time

to come." That's from the testimony of Dr. Vannevar Bush to the U.S. Senate, Special Committee on Atomic Energy (pp. 179–180). Dr. Bush, by the way, was the special science advisor to President Franklin D. Roosevelt during World War II.

Raising our sights a bit higher, we have this gem from the Aristotelian professors who stood as the contemporaries of Galileo: *"Jupiter's moons are invisible to the naked eye, and therefore can have no influence on the Earth, and therefore would be useless, and therefore do not exist."*

Right.

When Bruno Garabaldi proposed that it was the Earth that revolved around the sun, rather than the opposite as the Church insisted, the Church solved the dispute by scientifically burning Garabaldi alive at the stake. The system worked. Garabaldi never again made such an absurd claim.

Much, much later, Professor A.W. Bickerton, a highly respected British scientist, stated in 1926 that *"this foolish idea of shooting at the moon is an example of the absurd length to which vicious specialization will carry scientists. To escape the earth's gravitation a projectile needs a velocity of 7 miles per second. The thermal energy at this speed is 15,180 calories. Hence the proposition appears to be basically impossible."*

Right again. Now, just a few more for a wrap up:

As late as 1935 Dr. Robert Millikan said it would take at least 250 years to develop atomic power.

And three years later, in 1938, Dr. Edward Teller said we *might* be able to achieve atomic power by the year 2,000…

Seven years later, in 1945, General Groves, who managed the Manhattan Project that produced our atomic bombs in World War II, said it would take the Russians at least fifty years to build such a bomb.

And in 1949, only four years later, when the Russians *did* build the atomic bomb and explode it, President Harry Truman said he didn't believe it, and the whole thing was just a fake.

The foregoing leads one to lend great credence to certain theories postulated by the editors of *Omni* magazine and several of their write-in readers. These theories, fascinating as well as enchanting, answer one mystery that has confounded observers for years; namely, why no one ever sees a baby pigeon in city parks.

That proves spontaneous pigeon generation, of course.

It also explains why "days are short in the winter and long in the summer [because] cold contracts and heat expands."

Finally, one reader offered *Omni* the incredibly perceptive Theory of Gastrointestinal Learning. Fred Wickham of California explained the "scientists have already shown that flatworms, having been taught mazes, can be fed to other flatworms, which actually acquire the knowledge of the original maze through ingestion. This explains how cannibals learned the missionary position."

Right on.

To order additional copies of this book,
please send full amount plus $4.00 for
postage and handling for the first book and
50¢ for each additional book.

Send orders to:

Galde Press, Inc.
PO Box 460
Lakeville, Minnesota 55044-0460

Credit card orders call 1–800–777–3454
Phone (952) 891–5991 • Fax (952) 891–6091
Visit our website at http://www.galdepress.com

Write for our free catalog.